DESIGNING CITIES

Leonhard Schenk

DESIGNING CITIES

Basics – Principles – Projects

With contributions by Oliver Fritz, Rolo Fütterer and Markus Neppl

Birkhäuser
Basel

PICTOGRAM-KEY

- Project
- Competition
- Author(s)
- Website
- Award
- Year
- Category
- Theme
- Tags

Prof. Dipl.-Ing. **Leonhard Schenk,** Architect

Leonhard Schenk, Prof. Dipl.-Ing., born 1965, directs the urban design program at HTWG Konstanz. He is an architect in private practice, a municipal
architect, and urban planner who is a member of the Association of German Architects (Bund Deutscher Architekten, BDA), the German Work Fe-
deration (Deutscher Werkbund, DWB), the Association of Town, Regional
and State Planning (Vereinigung für Stadt-, Regional- und Landesplanung,
SRL) and the German Academy for Urban and Regional Planning (Deutschen Akademie für Städtebau und Landesplanung, DASL).

As owner of the firm LS Architektur Städtebau in Stuttgart, he deals with
urban planning from both the client's viewpoint – as a consultant to mu-
nicipalities, corporations and governmental institutions as well as NGOs
– and the architect's point of view – through draft plans, master planning,
and competition entries. One such competition led to his co-founding of
the firm LEHEN drei Architektur Stadtplanung, where he remained a partner until 2008. It was during that time that he won the German Urban Design Award and the European Urban and Regional Planning Award, both
conferred for the "French Quarter" project in Tübingen.

The perspective taken in this book is represented by the question "How
is a city designed?" – which Leonhard Schenk regularly explores with his
students. This viewpoint has given rise to this compendium of abstrac-
ting and thus universal design methods and tools, both old and new, that
Schenk analyzes, discusses, and evaluates for their applicability by refer-
ring to successful designs, frequently exemplified by winning competition
entries. The author draws upon numerous publications, above all from
those on urban design and housing in Germany and the Netherlands, and
a wealth of experience – from his own participation in competitions but
especially from his extensive activities as a consultant and as a member
of juries for urban design projects.

"Even the most loving engagement with the theoretical problems of art must never hinder the creator from working intuitively. [...] Art theory exists to elucidate creative activity, not to arouse it."[1]

— **Fritz Schumacher,** 1926

THE above quote from *Das bauliche Gestalten (The design of buildings)* describes the possibilities and limitations of this book. We can approach the creative process from many different angles and analyze methods and processes – yet a fundamental aspect of designing, namely that which Schumacher calls intuition, will remain closed to rational examination.

This book is intended to elucidate the design principles of urban design and make them understandable. It is not meant to be a book of recipes for how to produce good urban designs. Nevertheless, with this book I hope to be able to give aspiring as well as established architects and urban planners new impulses for one's own design practice.

My sincere thanks go to the master students in my two seminars. Without the discussions we held and the seminal thoughts that arose in the process, this book would not have been possible in its present form. Steffen Maier has done much to improve the graphic representations of the historical examples and three colleagues have provided written contributions: Prof. Rolo Fütterer and Prof. Markus Neppl each depict how prizewinning designs can be implemented successfully, and Prof. Oliver Fritz describes new, computer-based design instruments for urban design. Here, too, many thanks!

Special thanks go to my family for their patience; my editor, Annette Gref; my colleagues Martin Feketics and Prof. Dr.-Ing. Dittmar Machule, who were helpful in providing me with valuable references; the many offices that kindly placed their know-how – namely plans, sketches, and model photos – at my disposal; and the Lebendige Stadt Foundation for their financial support.

Constance/Stuttgart, Fall 2012
Leonhard Schenk

1 Fritz Schumacher, *Das bauliche Gestalten* (Basel/Berlin/Boston: Birkhäuser, 1991; orig. publ. 1926), p. 53.

1 Introduction

Urban Planning – Urban Design – Design Principles

__ SINCE 2009, for the first time in our history, more people live in cities than in rural areas. Whereas there are approximately 3.5 billion city dwellers at present, the United Nations forecasts that up to 6.3 billion people will be living in urban areas in 2050.[1] Even if the number of so-called megacities – cities with 10 million or more inhabitants – increases, more than half of city dwellers will continue to live in smaller urban centers with fewer than half a million inhabitants each. Presumably only a tiny fraction of this increased urbanization will occur in a planned manner. But for this portion alone, urban planning and urban design – the design-oriented facet of urban planning concerned with built form and space – will be faced with tasks of an unimagined scope.

[1] Here and below, see http://esa.un.org/unpd/wup/pdf/WUP2009_Highlights_Final_R1.pdf (accessed December 20, 2012), p. 1.

URBAN PLANNING is the "endeavor to give order to spatial coexistence while meeting human needs – on the level of the city or the community."[2] This endeavor em-
braces the social, economic, and environmental aspects, the balance between
public and private concerns, and also aspects of urban design like development,
conservation, and continuation of the urban form, the townscape, and the landscape.[3] Whereas urban planning focuses more on the general planning process
and how it is embedded in society, urban design is concerned with the specifics
of a designed, built spatial organization: Thus urban design has the objective of
establishing physical identity and creating memorable places.

Every era had and has its own notion of physical identity and its expression in
the form of built urban structures. Especially with the founding cities of the ancient
world yet continuing to the Asian new towns of our day, the fundamental social and
artistic orders behind city concepts are clearly legible. The power of the church,
feudalism, or civil society was manifested in the medieval city. The Baroque city
celebrated the claim to power of the sovereign ruler; the city of the nineteenth century celebrated the newly emerged middle-class self-image; and the modern city
of the twentieth century celebrated the achievements of industrialization, economic growth, and mobility.

FREIBURG IM BREISGAU, 1120 (D)

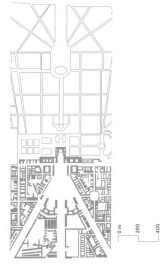

VERSAILLES, Louis Le Vau/André Le Nôtre et al., 1668 (F)

---

2 Gerd Albers, *Stadtplanung: Eine praxisorientierte Einführung* (Darmstadt: Wissenschaftliche Buchgesellschaft, 1988), p. 4.
3 See BauGB – Baugesetzbuch (Federal Building Code), §1 (5), last amended on July 22, 2011.

Whereas the classic Chinese city reflects the divine cosmic order, cities like Timgad that were founded by the Romans reflect the pragmatic basic structure of a Roman military camp, the Castrum Romanum. Interestingly, both of these urban models have an orthogonally divided square as their basic form, but the significance of the individual parts is completely different. The ideal form of the square is exemplified by the Renaissance city of Freudenstadt in the Black Forest as well as by Masdar City, the ecocity currently under construction in the United Arab Emirates.

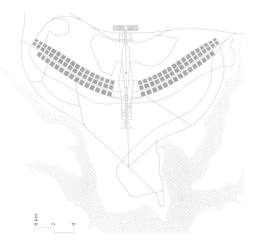

BRASÍLIA, Lúcio Costa/Oscar Niemeyer, 1956 (BR)

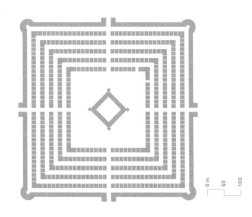

FREUDENSTADT, Heinrich Schickhardt, 1599 (D)

MASDAR CITY, Foster + Partners, 2007 (UAE)

Since none of the examples is directly related to any of the others, it becomes clear that urban design has fundamental principles of design and order that can be applied irrespective of the social model, era, zeitgeist, or fashion trends. Even concepts that are regarded as particularly innovative, like that of Masdar City, routinely make use of previously known design methods. The fundamental artistic and compositional principles are largely timeless even though the substance behind them is not. The shift in meaning takes place in the details, as the changing significance of the middle shows: the center of the Chinese city is the site occupied by the imperial palace, but in the ancient Greek city that position is taken by the public agora; in the Roman city, it is the forum; the medieval town has its market; Ledoux's design for the ideal city of Chaux at the Royal Saltworks in Arc-et-Senans places the factory director's house there; in L'Enfant's plan for the US capital of Washington, D.C., it is the United States Capitol; Le Corbusier's Ville contemporaine envisages a transportation hub, where air taxis land on a plaza-like roof; and in Masdar City, by Foster + Partners, it is the future science city's hotel and conference center.

The urbanistic principles of design and order presented in this book are the outcome of a more than 5,000-year-long history of the city. Whereas some principles, like the orthogonal grid, are very old, others came into existence roughly 140 years ago, for example the nongeometric, picturesque settlement patterns that were consciously applied in North American suburbs as of 1870 as well as European garden cities beginning in 1900. The situation is similar with urban building blocks, the various components comprising the city. The various urban building blocks that are available to us in contemporary urban design have evolved over a very long period of time – some over thousands of years and others, like the Zeile, only in the last hundred years.

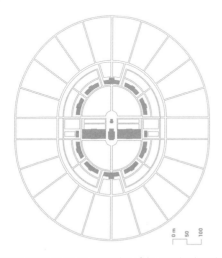

IDEAL CITY OF CHAUX, expansion of the Royal Saltworks in Arc-et-Senans, Claude-Nicolas Ledoux, 1790 (F)

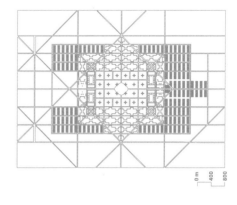

VILLE CONTEMPORAINE, Le Corbusier, 1922 (F)

For urban design as for architecture, the entire canon of contemporary and traditional forms is available today for our use. Two points should be emphasized:

• Not everything that is possible also makes sense. The main focus of each and every design ought to be, as described by Gerd Albers, the "endeavor to give order to spatial coexistence while meeting human needs."[4] Urban design can only succeed if residents can identify with their urban environment.

• Urban designs are always developed from an aerial perspective, but the city is perceived from the pedestrian's viewpoint. Only when the user is also able to experience the urban design qualities that arise from the interplay of order and surprise – and of harmony and excitement – has the designer achieved the goal.

The most important principles are explained in the following chapters with the aid of selected historical examples as well as projects and award-winning entries to urban design competitions from Germany and elsewhere over the past ten to fifteen years. In each case, attention should be focused on the questions of how the project was designed and what methods and instruments were available to the designer.

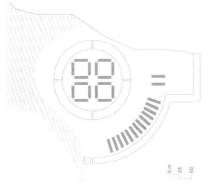

TRELLEBORG VIKING CAMP, 980 (DK)

LINGANG NEW CITY, gmp Architekten von Gerkan, Marg and Partners, 2003 (PRC)

SEASIDE, Andrés Duany/Elisabeth Plater-Zyberk, et al., 1979 (US)

4 Albers, *Stadtplanung*, p. 4.

2 Qualitative Traits

MOST of the urban design schemes presented here were created in recent years as entries to competitions. It never ceases to amaze how broad the range of submissions can be in a competitive process – despite the fact that the competition program usually sets forth unambiguously formulated requirements for the competitors to follow. The intention in the following is to examine which traits and properties make one entry stand out from the others.

AN urban design must satisfactorily address such differing aspects as context, functionality, economic efficiency, sustainability, and design. Some of these only allow a limited margin for interpretation and can be reviewed according to a list of criteria. Functionality, for instance, is one such objective property. For an urban design to be functional, it needs a suitable concept for vehicular and pedestrian access and a sensible distribution of uses, it must protect and conserve the natural conditions (trees, biotopes, water protection zones), and much more.

Many designs that resolve the functional issues in a reasonable way nevertheless lack an "exceptional" design, a coherent idea, or a memorable Gestalt – a unified whole. At first glance, matters of design seem to be as subjective as personal preferences: Whereas one person may enjoy living in the countryside, in the midst of nature, another may prefer the varied and eventful life of the city. In the context of designing, these preferences can also be identified as positions or attitudes of the author that are reflected in the design. If a competition jury holds the same position and the functional aspects are correct, their scrutiny is then focused on the quality of the design.

Experience shows that a design is successful when two factors combine in perfect harmony: on the one hand are the expectations of the client and the jury, and on the other are the functionality and design of the scheme itself and the attitude it represents.

Most people can intuitively recognize whether or not a handmade object or an industrial product like a car is well designed. This ability can perhaps also be applied to architecture and, to a lesser extent, urban design. The traits of a good design are not easy to identify, however, and it raises the question as to whether – in addition to subjective criteria – there are also criteria that are objective and transferable.

Answers are provided by perceptual and Gestalt psychology. The Austrian philosopher Christian von Ehrenfels was one of the first to examine the question of good design. In his 1890 essay "On 'Gestalt Qualities,'" he points out that while a melody consists of individual sounds, it is nevertheless more than their sum total. It is also possible to create other melodies with the same notes, whereas the original melody, transposed into another key, might also contain other notes. The release of the whole from the original parts – and the abstraction that goes along with it – is, according to Ehrenfels, an important aspect for Gestalt quality – or, in the words of Aristotle: the whole is greater than the sum of its parts. With regard to art history, Ehrenfels states in his essay: "What we call a feeling for style in a given province of art almost certainly consists principally in nothing other than the capacity to grasp and to compare Gestalt qualities of the relevant category." [1]

---

1 Christian von Ehrenfels, "Über Gestaltqualitäten," *Vierteljahrsschrift für wissenschaftliche Philosophie* 14 (1890): 249–92. Translated by Barry Smith as "On 'Gestalt Qualities,'" in *Foundations of Gestalt Theory*, ed. Barry Smith (Munich and Vienna: Philosophia Verlag, 1988), p. 106. Essay avail. online: ontology.buffalo.edu/smith/book/FoGT/Ehrenfels_Gestalt.pdf

If the newly emerged wholeness (Ganzheit) distinguishes itself through a Gestalt quality, one immediately questions how it can be measured. In a few lines about his teachings that he dictated shortly before his death, Ehrenfels observes: "Every determinate body has some kind of Gestalt. He who compares the Gestalt of a clod of earth or of a heap of stones with the Gestalten of say a swallow will however at once have to admit that the tulip, or the swallow, has realized the particular genus Gestalt to a greater degree than have the clod or the heap."[2] He identifies quintessence as: "Higher Gestalten are those in which the product of the unity of the whole and the multiciplicity [sic] of the parts is greater."[3]

Succeeding Ehrenfels, the cognitive psychologist and Gestalt theory specialist Wolfgang Metzger investigated the human perception of sight in a series of experiments. Thus he formulated the Gesetze des Sehens (laws of seeing), which is also the name of the book he first published in 1936. In it, Metzger examines the structure of the Sehwelt—the "visual world"[4] —and thus the way in which people perceive their environment.

2 Christian von Ehrenfels, "Über Gestaltqualitäten (1932)," first published in *Philosophia* (Belgrade) 2 (1937): 139–41. Translated by Barry Smith and Mildred Focht as "On Gestalt Qualities (1932)," in *Foundations of Gestalt Theory*, ed. Barry Smith (Munich and Vienna: Philosophia Verlag, 1988), p. 121. Essay avail. online: ontology.buffalo.edu/smith/book/FoGT/Ehrenfels_Gestalt_1932.pdf
3 Ibid., p. 123.
4 Wolfgang Metzger, *Gesetze des Sehens*, 1936. Translated by Lothar Spillmann, et al. as *Laws of Seeing* (Cambridge, MA: MIT Press, 2006), p. viii.

2.1 VISUAL PRINCIPLES

THE following visual principles – which are dealt with to some extent in one of the last chapters as regards the legibility of city layouts in site plans or bird's-eye views and their perception from the pedestrian's perspective within the city or in the representations of urban design plans – should be mentioned here in exemplary fashion:

The Principle of Figure and Ground

Human perception differentiates what is seen as either figure or ground. "Of all shapes projected into the eye, we can usually only really see those that give the impression of figures, of things, of solid bodies."[5] In contrast, we appear to be largely blind to the background and the intermediate space between figures.[6] What are perceived as figures tend to be darker areas on a lighter background – like the letters in a book. Except that symmetrical areas move in front of asymmetrical areas such that, when seen on a darker background, the light symmetrical areas represent the figure.

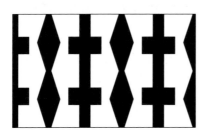 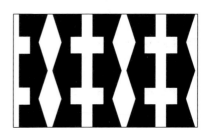

Fundamentally, convex areas (curved outward) of a figure are perceived as more tangible than concave areas (curved inward). Metzger calls this the "Law of the Interior."[7]

5 Ibid., p. 4.
6 Ibid.
7 Wolfgang Metzger, *Gesetze des Sehens*, 3rd rev. ed. (Frankfurt: Kramer, 1975), p. 41. Only available in German.

In urban design, figure-ground plans (poche plans) are a clear application of the figure-ground principle. Black buildings on a white background allow precise recognition of the composition of built forms. By reversing the situation, however, to have white buildings on a black background, the contiguous spaces between the buildings – the urban space – come to the fore.

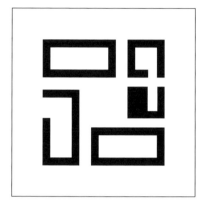 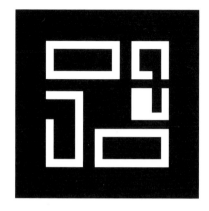

The Law of Closure

Lines that enclose an area are more readily perceived as a figure than those which are not closed, provided that the enclosed area and the background are of the same color. "If an area that is not entirely surrounded by outlines is nevertheless seen as a figure, the open places are completed with [invisible] outlines"[8] – provided that we have knowledge of the actual figure. Thus, for example, the shapes of the buildings can be implied solely by virtue of lightly delineated shadows cast by buildings in the site plan.

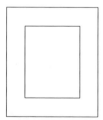 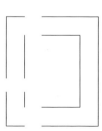 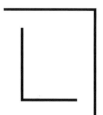

8 Ibid., p. 38.

The Law of Good Continuation

Lines and curves always follow the easiest path, a smooth course.[9] When two lines intersect, the human eye does not assume that the lines abruptly change course at this point. Instead, two continuous lines are recognized – even if they are partly interrupted at the point of intersection. In urban design, this can be experienced firsthand in the alignment of building facades or cornice lines, for example.

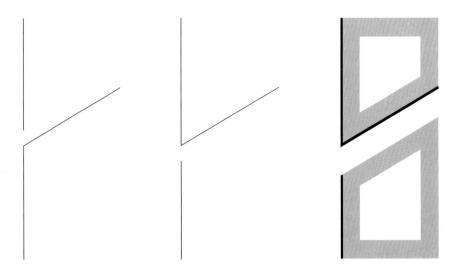

The Law of Proximity

Elements that are in close proximity are more readily perceived as a group than those that are further away from one another—"neighbors fuse into groups."[10] Example: When several buildings are close together, they are perceived as a group even if there are no other similarities in design.

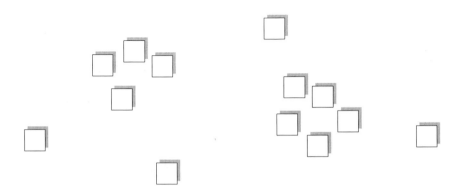

9 Ibid., p. 32.
10 Ibid., p. 30.

The Law of Similarity

Elements that resemble one another in form are more readily experienced as belonging together than unlike elements are. In addition, similar elements result in more uniform groups than dissimilar ones.[11]

The Law of Symmetry

Symmetrical figures or arrangements attract the viewer's attention to themselves more than do unsymmetrical ones.[12] This effect appears to be stronger with vertical axes of symmetry than with horizontal ones.

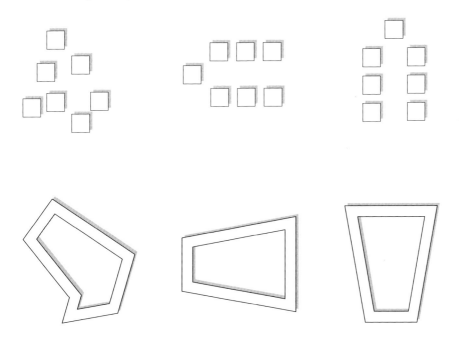

11 Ibid., p. 88.
12 Ibid., p. 10 ff.

The Law of Good Gestalt (or of Prägnanz)

According to this principle, "that which naturally 'belongs together'" is "that which 'fits' together," and "that which together results in a well-organized, unitary structure."[13] Human sensory organs are capable of recognizing regularities and hence order. Therefore Metzger speaks of "the love of order of our senses."[14] Thus by placing a triangle on top of a square of the same color, we do not see an irregular polygon, but a triangle lying on a square (or vice versa). It does not matter if the form is easy for us to assess, but that it seems "harmonious, from one stroke."[15]

 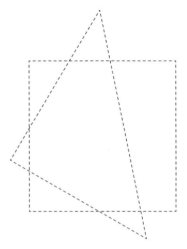

13 Ibid., p. 22.
14 Ibid., p. 19.
15 Ibid., p. 26.

In the competition between various good figures, the simpler one is generally superior.

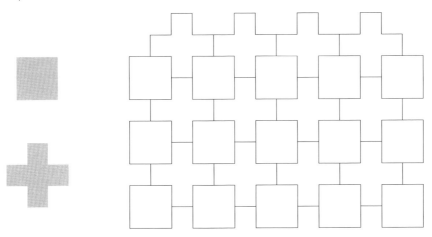

Metzger notes that Prägnanz (a conciseness that is rich in meaning) indeed also has to do with negative entropy, in the sense of an absence of chaos, and with redundancy. If one contemplates these statements further, then an excess of Prägnanz can ultimately lead to monotony.

<u>2.2</u> GESTALT LAWS AND URBAN DESIGN

IN his design primer *Grundlagen der Gestaltung zu Bau und Stadtbau*, published in 1985, Rudolf Wienands succeeded in transferring the insights of Ehrenfels, Metzger, and others to architecture and urban design. Wienands deplores therein the Gestaltverlust (loss of form) in architecture and urban design and makes the principles of wholeness (Übersummenprinzip), figure-ground, and Prägnanz into central themes of his design theory.

Wholeness and Gestalt

Wienands defines wholeness and Gestalt as follows: "Gestalten [forms, figures] are entities whose parts are determined by the whole and in which all the parts support and determine one another; entities whose essential properties cannot be captured through the summation of the characteristics of their parts."[16]

Figure-Ground Principle

Wienands draws attention to the background – the intermediate space – which he sees as being equivalent in design terms to buildings in urban design: "The easier it is to also see the background between the buildings as an equal and intentional object of contemplation – meaning the more the intervening spaces display the same figurative qualities as the building masses themselves – the more the buildings and intervening spaces form an insoluble unity or (city- or district-) Gestalt." [17]

Prägnanz

Borrowing from Metzger, Wienands suggests that Prägnanz has the following properties: "Every perception of gestalt/form is subject to the tendency to find, in the appearance of maximum regularity, symmetry, unity, simplicity, balance, and scarcity."[18] The Gestalt quality depends largely on its boundaries: "The more distinct, strict, and closed the border, the boundary, the more prägnant the figure or Gestalt."[19]

Boundaries can be external borders, like the outline of the city, or internal borders, as with public squares.

By implication, the formation of clear boundaries and of concise shapes and forms becomes more difficult as the parts are scattered more freely. With the vast majority of large-scale housing estates from the 1960s and 70s, this is perceived as a deficit – and not as the improvement in quality of life promised by their planners.

---

16 Rudolf Wienands, *Grundlagen der Gestaltung zu Bau und Stadtbau* (Basel/Boston/Stuttgart: Birkhäuser, 1985), p. 17.
17 Ibid., p. 32.
18 Ibid., p. 47.
19 Ibid.

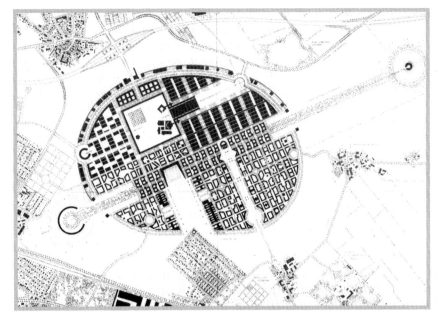

Prägnanz comes from Gestalt-like external and internal boundaries.

Detail of plaza area

⊙ — **Conversion of Airport Grounds, Munich-Riem** (D)

✎ — Andreas Brandt, Rudolf Böttcher, Berlin

⊚ — merit award

📅 — 1991

🗀 — urban redevelopment — airport conversion — new district and trade fair grounds

◆ — **Ganzheit/Prägnanz** (external and internal boundaries)

◗ — geometric principle; divisional approach; orthogonal grid; layout of development sites: axis, symmetry, hierarchy, datum; place making through modeling

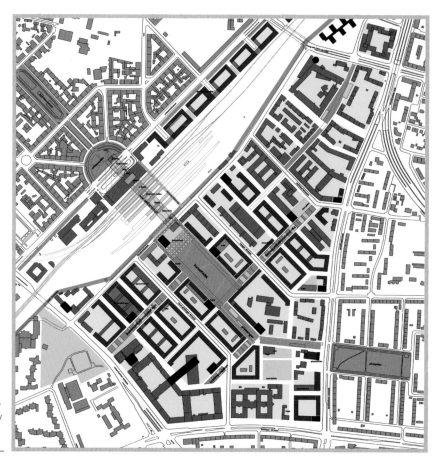

Like both of the historical squares, the newly designed square is also distinguished by a concise form rich in meaning.

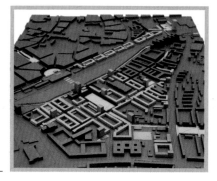

Model

⊙ — **Rund um den Ostbahnhof,** (Around the east train station), Munich (D)

✏ — 03 Architekten GmbH, Munich

▢ — www.03arch.de

▣ — 1st prize

▦ — 2002

▤ — urban redevelopment — new urban district

◈ — **Prägnanz** (internal boundaries)

◣ — geometric principle; additive approach; orthogonal grid; urban building blocks: closed city block, high-rise tower, hybrid; layout of development sites: axis; place making through assembly; green space delimited by buildings

Are these three principles sufficient for urban designers to create memorable places and living environments? Doesn't an excess of unity and conciseness become boring? Isn't a concise design too simple and predictable? Doesn't Gestalt need a certain amount of disorder for it to be exciting?

Contrast Principle

Wienands introduces the notion of contrast and refers to the human idiosyncrasy of simultaneously striving to meet opposing needs, like commitment and freedom, order and chaos, tradition and innovation.[20] And indeed: it is the introduction of diagonals into an orthogonal city layout, the interruption of a grid that is too rigid, the removal of parts of the building fabric – for public squares, for instance – and the exciting rhythm of built and unbuilt areas, restricted and expansive spatial settings, high and low buildings that make a design unique and full of meaning.

20 Ibid., p. 30.

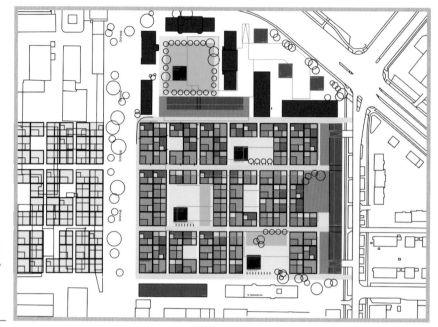

The design is particularly memorable for its exciting contrast of built and unbuilt areas, restrictive and expansive spatial settings, and high and low buildings.

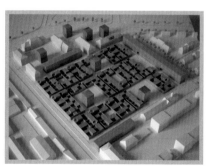

Model

🎯 — **Werkbundsiedlung Wiesenfeld,** Munich (D)

✏️ — Meck Architekten with Burger Landschaftsarchitekten, Munich

🖥 — www.meck-architekten.de

🏅 — Prizewinner (housing)

📅 — 2006

🗂 — urban redevelopment – military conversion – new residential district

🗂 — **contrast**

🏷 — geometric principle; additive approach; orthogonal grid; urban building blocks: high-rise tower, carpet development, freestanding building; place making through exclusion/ omission; representation: presentation model

ANOTHER APPROACH TO QUALITATIVE TRAITS

Positive Properties and Attributes

At the end of competitions it is customary to issue a jury report that documents in writing the shortlisted projects, those awarded honorable mentions, and the winning entries. The following overview assigns the positive descriptions from such jury minutes to the categories of Wholeness, Diversity of Parts, Conciseness, and Contrast.

Wholeness (Ganzheit)	Diversity (of the parts)	Conciseness (Prägnanz)	Contrast	Other Features
balanced	varied	legible	dynamic	appropriate
uniform	detailed	attractive	striking	need-oriented
harmonious	differentiated	balanced	complementary	efficient
homogenous	structured	justified	rich in contrast	logical
compact	playful	independent	exciting	functional
cultivated	multifaceted	unambiguous	full of excitement	high-quality
to scale		memorable		feasible
restrained		skillful		robust
serene		generous		stable
sensitive		individual		deep
sensible		clear		economical
meticulous		consistent		contemporary
calm		conceptual		fragmentary
		powerful		
		concise		
		precise		
		straightforward		
		confident		
		compelling		
		unmistakable		
		well-proportioned		

Several properties can be assigned to the category of wholeness as well as the category of Prägnanz, which is not surprising since wholeness can be seen as a trait of Prägnanz.[21] Properties described as "need-oriented," "functional," "economical," "efficient," and "feasible" are, by contrast, clearly associated with the functionality of a design.

---

21 See Metzger, 1975, p. 218 ff.

At this point, some key terms that have not yet appeared in the context of discussion should be explained in more detail:

Depth

The depth of an urban design can be understood as signifying the degree to which the design idea penetrates all of its levels: the macrocosm and the microcosm of the design are both constructed according to the same or related design principles. Example: The city or the new district is made up of a certain grouping of different districts; the district organizes the building lots according to the same principle, and the buildings on the building lots are likewise organized according to this principle.

Fragmentary Quality

What is meant by the fragmentary quality of an urban design is that a portion of the built fabric might already have a high spatial quality and Prägnanz of its own – such as a completed first phase of construction that, for whatever reason, is not followed by others to complete the original design. Since the implementation of an urban design often takes place over a very long time frame, it is possible that guiding principles will change or that the initial goals are not pursued due to political or economic developments.

Robustness

Due to the long periods of time needed for implementation, a design must also be sufficiently robust and flexible; this way it can be adapted to the changing needs for other building types, uses, etc., without abandoning the basic urban design idea and its qualities.

Since the responsibilities for the urban design concept and its architectural implementation are seldom in the same hands, robustness can also mean that the design is able to withstand different architectural languages and, above all, architectural qualities. In his lectures and critiques at the University of Stuttgart, Prof. Klaus Humpert was fond of saying that urban design should be made "architect-safe."

The building lots are organized on the development site according to the same principle as the urban building blocks on the building lot: grouping around a shared square.

2.4 PROPORTIONS

SINCE ancient times, people have given thought to when – and when not – a Gestalt, a building, a sculpture, a form, or an image appears especially well proportioned, beautiful, and harmonious. Publications on the theory of proportions – about "how unequal proportions of individual parts relate to the whole body"[22] – abound, and here we shall only refer briefly to exemplary systems of order:

The Mathematical Order

Pythagorean mathematicians attempted to understand the world as a mathematical order, declaring mathematics to be the "principle of all being." The discovery of music's dependence on numerical proportions, also known as harmonic proportions, made a fundamental contribution to this perception. Thus the vibrating strings of an instrument are tuned in intervals when their lengths are in simple, precisely defined proportions to one another: the octave as 1:2, the third as 4:5, the fourth as 3:4, the fifth as 2:3, etc.[23] A complex knowledge of geometry and studies on the proportions of the human body reinforced the belief of the ancient Greeks that the universe must be constructed according to mathematical rules and that harmony could be expressed in numerical proportions.

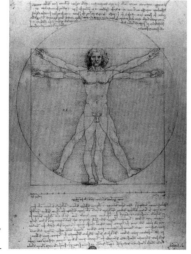

The Vitruvian Man
proportion diagram
of the human figure
according to Vitruvius,
Leonardo da Vinci,
Gallerie dell'Accademia,
Venice

The Scale of the Human Body

The Roman architect Vitruvius places the principles of the proportions of the human figure in a direct relationship with the tectonic order. Depending on their order, the columns have a ratio of diameter to overall height of 1:6 to 1:10. The column diameter, when multiplied, specifies the spacing of the columns. And Vitruvius divides the human body into parts: the foot amounts to 1/6, the face 1/10, and the chest breadth with outstretched arms is 1/4 of the total height.[24] According to Vitruvius, even the basic forms of square and circle can be derived from the human body.

22 Roland Knauer, *Entwerfen und Darstellen: Die Zeichnung als Mittel des architektonischen Entwurfs*, 2nd ed. (Berlin: Ernst & Sohn, 2002), p. 31.
23 Paul von Naredi-Rainer, *Architektur und Harmonie: Zahl, Maß und Proportion in der abendländischen Baukunst*, 5th ed. (Cologne: DuMont, 1995), p. 13.
24 See Knauer, *Entwerfen und Darstellen*, p. 34.

The best-known visualization of this thesis is the Vitruvian Man, a drawing by Leonardo da Vinci in which the human body is shown standing with outstretched arms and also with splayed arms and legs in relation to a square and a circle.

The Golden Section
Hardly any rule of proportion has continuously remained as current as the golden section, also known as the golden mean, which describes a division or aspect ratio of 1:~1.618 (minor to major). This ratio has been regarded since antiquity as the epitome of aesthetics and harmony.[25] The golden section is still an important rule of composition in photography and art. The proportions are often simplified to the ratios 3:5 or 5:8.

The golden section is fascinating in many ways:
• It can be derived from human proportions as well as from geometry and algebra. In algebra, the golden section is represented by the formula a:b = (a+b):a ab. Then the lengths of both lines A and B are exactly in the proportion of the golden section and a:b is equivalent to approximately 1.618.

Geometric construction of the golden section (l.) and relationship between square, circle, and triangle (r.)

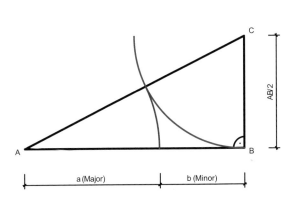

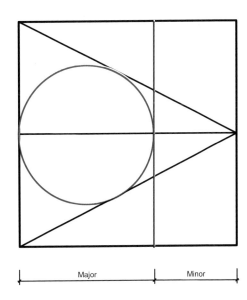

25 See http://en.wikipedia.org/wiki/Golden_ratio (accessed on November 24, 2012).

The golden section is also found very often in the human body – for example, the navel divides the upper body from the lower body (from tip to toe) roughly in the golden mean, the upper and lower body can be divided in the same way, and even the width of the first upper incisor is related to the width of the adjacent second one like major to minor.[26]

• The golden section appears to be one of the most important principles of architectural design. It can be identified in buildings of all periods, although the measurements are seldom mathematically precise. The golden section was probably often used unconsciously.[27] The most prominent example from antiquity is the Parthenon temple on the Acropolis in Athens, erected in the fifth century BC. In the modern era, Le Corbusier availed himself of the golden section for developing the Modular, his theory of proportions based on human scale.

• Repeatedly conducted empirical studies verify that a rectangle with an aspect ratio of the golden section (also known as the golden rectangle) is perceived by most observers as being the most pleasing of a number of differently proportioned rectangles.

• Using the term *arrangement* (Lat. ordinatio), Vitruvius refers to a consistent proportioning of the parts and the whole: the proportions derive from "the members of the work itself and, starting from these individual parts of members, constructing the whole work to correspond."[28] This requirement is fulfilled by the golden section: A golden rectangle can always be divided into a square and another but smaller golden rectangle. It can be divided in this way infinitely, and thus it can be used for consistent proportioning (of the parts in relation to the whole).

A golden rectangle can always be divided into a square and another but smaller golden rectangle, and this can proceed infinitely.

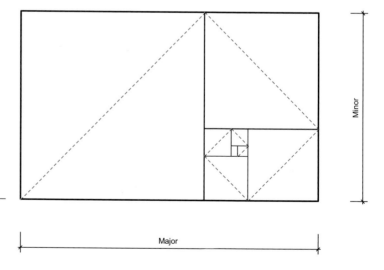

Minor

Major

26 See http://www.golden-section.eu/kapitel5.html (accessed on November 11, 2011; German only).
27 See Naredi-Rainer, *Architektur und Harmonie*, p. 196 f.
28 Vitruvius, *The Ten Books on Architecture*, translated by M. H. Morgan (New York: Dover Publications, 1960), p. 13.

PROPORTIONS IN URBAN DESIGN

URBAN design also generally follows established rules of proportion, for example when establishing the dimensions of districts and building lots, streets, squares, and open spaces, in plan as well as in section, or even in defining the proportions of streets or buildings in terms of width, depth, and height.

Nonetheless, the use of harmonious proportions in design is not a recipe for success. Leonardo da Vinci even warns against a blind application of the rules: "These rules are of use only in correcting the figures ... if you try to apply these rules in composition you will never make an end, and will produce confusion in your works."[29]

29 Jean Paul Richter, ed., *The Notebooks of Leonardo Da Vinci: Compiled and Edited from the Original Manuscripts*, vol. 1 (New York: Dover Publications, 1970), p. 18.

3 General Organizing Principles

URBAN design schemes are fundamentally based on two organizing principles: geometric and nongeometric.

3.1 THE NONGEOMETRIC PRINCIPLE

Biomorphic/Organic

Many nongeometric urban structures seem biomorphic – think of picturesque, curved, medieval city layouts. They seem as if they have evolved over the centuries and have been shaped by the forces of nature. For some of these cities, such as the towns founded by the Dukes of Zähringen in the twelfth and thirteenth centuries – Freiburg im Breisgau, Rottweil, and Villingen, in Germany, as well as Bern, in Switzerland – we know that they were planned according to a standardized scheme.

It is suspected that uniform planning rules were also used in the founding of other cities in the Middle Ages.[1] Irrespective of this, an evolved, vibrant, dynamic, or fluid appearance is also identified colloquially as "organic."[2] In this regard, it defines the antithesis of a mathematical, additive system like that which is found, for example, in a rational, rectangular street grid. From the nineteenth century until about World War I, the planners of dwellings and settlements deliberately employed a picturesque and organic urban design to create exclusive suburbs for the upper classes or, as in the case of the garden city movement, to establish an alternative model to the compact, dense, and hostile industrialized city. By contrast, organic forms in urban design were by and large alien to Modernism. It was not until Postmodernism's rejection of Modernism that the attraction of this design principle was rediscovered.

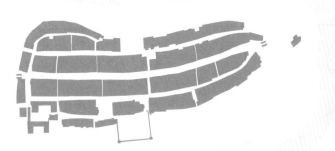

BERN, 1191 (CH)

---

1   See Klaus Humpert and Martin Schenk, *Entdeckung der mittelalterlichen Stadtplanung: Das Ende vom Mythos der gewachsenen Stadt* (Stuttgart: Konrad Theiss, 2001), p. 378 ff.
2   Organic, as used here, is not to be confused with the "organic urban design" (*organische Stadtbaukunst*) that Hans Reichow presented in his book *Von der Großstadt zur Stadtlandschaft* (1948). His model is the organic city, defined as an urban landscape determined by natural landscapes and organized into neighborhoods, in contrast to the compact, historical city.

From its center at the highest point, the settlement extends down to the sea like the arms of a starfish.

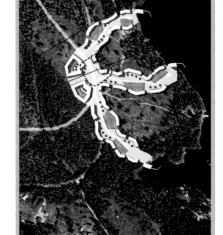

Illustrative site plan

 — **Europan 8,** Kalakukko, Kupio (FIN)

 — CITYFÖRSTER architecture + urbanism, Berlin/Hannover/London/ Oslo/Rotterdam/Salerno

 — www.cityfoerster.net

 — 1st prize category

 — 2006

 — urban expansion – new residential district

 — **biomorphic/organic principle**

 — urban building blocks: closed city block, row; cul-de-sac network; place making through modeling; widened street space

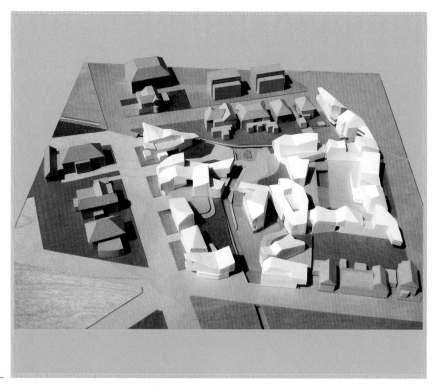

It seems as if the buildings were formed by nature.

Site plan

 — **Europan 7,** Hengelo O-kwadraat, Hengelo (NL)

— architectuurstudio Bötger-Oudshoorn, Den Haag

— www.botgeroudshoorn.nl

— 2nd prize

— 2004

— inner-city development – new residential district

— **biomorphic/organic principle**

— dissolved city block, row, Zeile, point

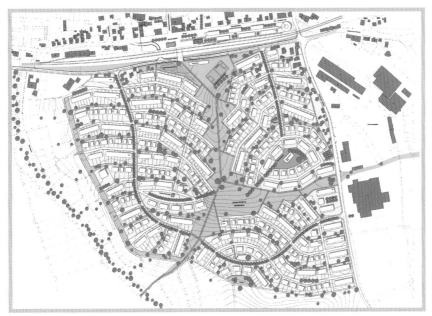

The built fabric consistently follows the undulating natural topography.

Working model

⌖ — **Mühlpfad/Herrengrund,** Schwaigern (D)

✎ — Prof. Günter Telian with P. Valovic, Karlsruhe

🖥 — www.competitionline.com/de/bueros/13178

🏅 — 4th prize

📅 — 2004

🗂 — city extension – new residential district

◆ — **biomorphic/organic principle**

🔖 — additive approach; urban building blocks: row, point; cul-de-sac network; widened street space; district-level green and open space

Scenic residential areas
in front of a dense
urban district.

Illustrative site plan

 – **New Town Dujiangyan** (PRC)

– florian krieger – architektur und städtebau, Darmstadt, with Irene Burkhardt Landschaftsarchitekten Stadtplaner, Munich

– www.florian-krieger.de

– 2008

– urban expansion – reconstruction project following earthquake

– **biomorphic/organic principle** (subarea)

– additive approach; urban building blocks: city block, point; layout of development
sites: grouping; loop street network; curved street space; waterfront living

☄ — **Kartal Pendik Master Plan,** Istanbul (TR)

✍ — Zaha Hadid Architects, London

🖥 — www.zaha-hadid.com

🏅 — 1st prize

📅 — 2006

🗂 — urban redevelopment – new sub-center

📑 — **biomorphic/organic principle**

🔖 — stretched grid, urban building blocks: dissolved city block, high-rise tower; curved street space; representation: Illustrative site plan

The captivating form is suggestive of anatomical cross sections.

Some residential neighborhoods are rigorously structured geometrically, others appear to have evolved organically.

Living in a village-like atmosphere.

 — **Beckershof,** Henstedt-Ulzburg (D)

 — Schellenberg + Bäumler Architekten, Dresden

⬛ — www.schellenberg-baeumler.de

⬛ — 1st prize

⬛ — 2004

⬛ — urban expansion − new district

⬛ — **biomorphic/organic principle** (subarea)

⬛ — additive approach; urban building blocks: row, point; layout of development sites: repetition/rhythm, grouping; cul-de-sac network, loop street network; bent and widened street space

Free, Artistic Compositions and Collages

A second group of nongeometric organizing principles comprises free or artistic compositions and narrative collages. The free, loose arrangement of building groups in a park landscape, detached from traffic routes (and which can reach the scale of chains of high-rise buildings, as in Märkisches Viertel in Berlin), is a product of postwar Modernism.[3] Narrative collages were developed later, in the deconstructivist architecture of the 1990s. Put simply, in deconstructivist urban design – analogous to the architecture of this style – the elements of the urban structure are disassembled – deconstructed – and recoded, meaning they are reassembled with a new meaning. Examples are the urban design schemes of this era by Daniel Libeskind and Zaha Hadid.

Whereas many of these designs appear severe and provocative, more recent master plans – especially those by Hadid – exhibit a soft and fluid but no less dynamic, biomorphic formal vocabulary. In this group, too, terms like *free, artistic,* or *collaged* are merely descriptive aids, because these designs are indeed planned and not merely random or arbitrary. The design criteria, however, are individual and not transferable, and in some cases, they are barely comprehensible without explanation from their authors. While Libeskind refers to things and events beyond the realm of architecture and urban design – a good architectural example is the Jewish Museum in Berlin – Hadid describes her goal as achieving a new spatial understanding: "The most important thing is motion, the flux of things, a non-Euclidean geometry in which nothing repeats itself: a new order of space."[4]

---

3 See Dietmar Reinborn, *Städtebau im 19. und 20. Jahrhundert* (Stuttgart: Kohlhammer, 1996), p. 244 ff.
4 http://www.mak.at/en/program/event/132fluid_terrains147 (accessed December 20, 2012).

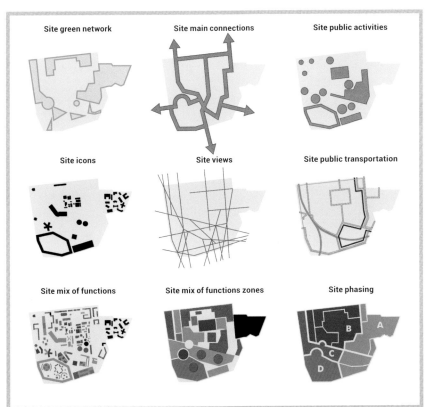

Site green network

Site main connections

Site public activities

Site icons

Site views

Site public transportation

Site mix of functions

Site mix of functions zones

Site phasing

Functional diagrams

The collage of varied urban building blocks does not offer a finished design, but demonstrates instead a wide variety of development possibilities.

— **Europan 9, Urban cocktail,** Warsaw (PL)

— BudCud with Michal Palej, Artur Michalak, Patrycja Okuljar-Sowa, Krakow

— www.budcud.org

— 1st prize

— 2008

— urban redevelopment — inner-city development — new urban district for culture, living, and work

— **free artistic composition/collage**

— Diagram, model

47

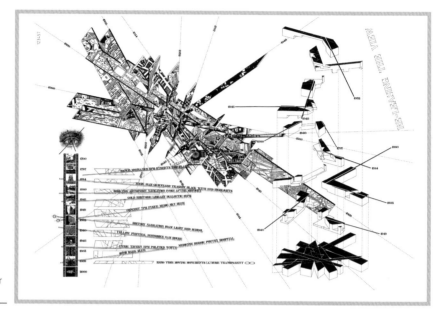

The design is derived from "the symbolic fragments of the memory of Potsdamer Platz."

Site plan

☉ — **Potsdamer Platz/Leipziger Platz,** Berlin (D)

✎ — Studio Daniel Libeskind, New York

🖳 — www.daniel-libeskind.com

📅 — 1991

🗂 — urban repair — reconstruction/rein- terpretation of districts and squares

◆ — **free artistic composition/collage**

🏷 — urban design as grand form; urban building blocks: Zeile/high-rise slab, point/high-rise tower, hybrid

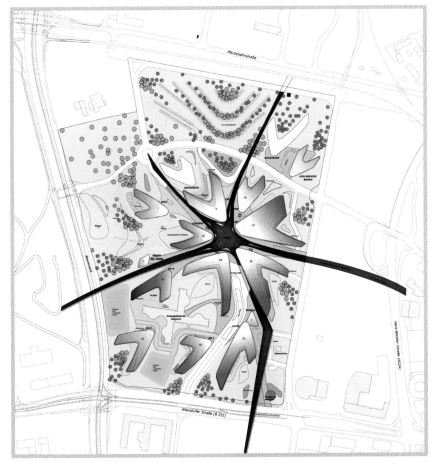

Author's statement:
"Axes span spiral-like in all directions creating a centrifugal field that forms the outline of the buildings and the surrounding landscape."

 — **ThyssenKrupp Quarter,** Essen (D)

 — Zaha Hadid Architects, London, with ST raum a. Landschaftsarchitekten Berlin/Munich/Stuttgart

🖥 — www.zaha-hadid.com

🏆 — 3rd prize

📅 — 2006

🗂 — urban renewal – continued development of industrial areas – new corporate group headquarters

◈ — **free artistic composition/collage**

◣ — Prägnanz, additive approach; layout of development sites: hierarchy, grouping

Visualization

49

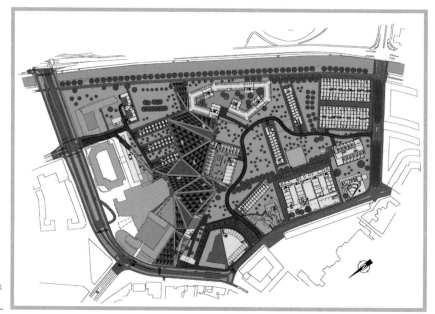

Compact but diversely built lots are freely interspersed in the park landscape.

Model

🎯 — **Chassé Terrein Master Plan,** Breda (NL)

✏️ — OMA, Rotterdam/Beijing/Hong Kong/New York, with West 8 Urban Design & Landscape Architecture, Rotterdam/New York

🖥 — www.oma.eu

🏆 — 1st prize

📅 — 1996

🗂 — urban redevelopment – military conversion – new urban district

🏷 — **free artistic composition/collage**

🔖 — urban building blocks: dissolved city block, courtyard, Zeile, high-rise tower, spatial
___ structure; flowing green space

THE GEOMETRIC PRINCIPLE

The Orthogonal Grid
The orthogonal grid, also known as the gridiron checkerboard, is to this day still the most commonly applied organizing principle in urban design. "It is universal both geographically and chronologically."[5] And has been used by diverse cultures throughout history. As a standard scheme, the orthogonal grid can be used on nearly every terrain; with its help, the division of land is also easily and efficiently accomplished. Within the grid pattern, centers and hierarchies can be formed and building structures can be flexibly replaced. Geographic features can be dealt with through omissions, deformations, tilted shifts, and/or curves. Old paths, like New York's Broadway, can be superimposed by a street grid, and diagonals, like those in Barcelona or Washington, D.C., can be incised into the grid without having to abandon the logic of the system. Building lots that are arranged in an orthogonal grid can, depending on the design, accommodate many different building typologies. Early examples of orthogonal settlement patterns are already found in ancient Egypt, such as a workers' settlement with row houses in Tell el-Amarna from the fourteenth century BC – or later, entire cities in China that are based on orthogonal grids.

From here, a wide arc spans to the present day. Gridded urban development is found in entirely different social and cultural contexts throughout the history of the city – from Greek and Roman colonial cities, newly formed medieval towns, ideal city concepts from the Renaissance, planned cities of the modern era, and city expansions from the nineteenth century, all the way to current urban projects like Luxembourg's Belval, on the site of a former steelworks (from 2001 onward), or the Qingdao Science and Technology City, in China (from 2011 onward).

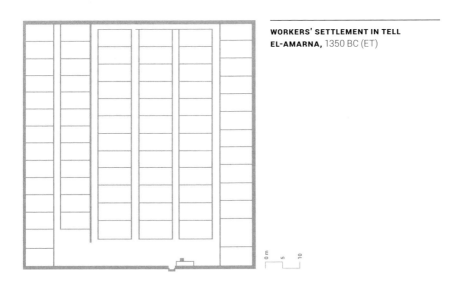

WORKERS' SETTLEMENT IN TELL EL-AMARNA, 1350 BC (ET)

0 m 5 10

---

5 Spiro Kostof, *The City Shaped: Urban Patterns and Meanings Through History* (Boston: Bulfinch, 1991), p. 95.

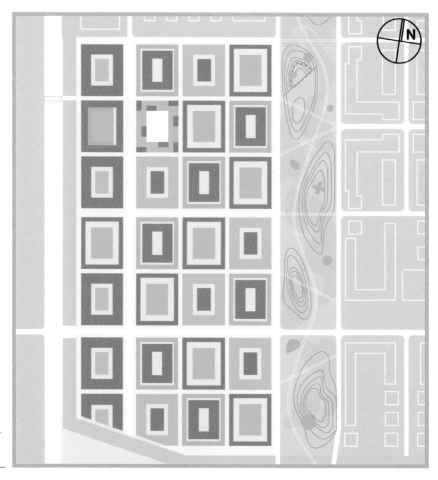

Various combinations of buildings and greenery are offered within the orthogonal grid.

Detail of model

⊙ — **Europan 7, Suburban Frames,** Neu-Ulm (D)

✎ — florian krieger — architektur und städtebau, Darmstadt

▣ — www.florian-krieger.de

◉ — 1st prize

▦ — 2004

▱ — urban redevelopment — military conversion — new residential district

◈ — **geometric principle**

⬕ — robustness; additive approach; orthogonal grid; urban building blocks: closed city block, point, freestanding building; complete road network

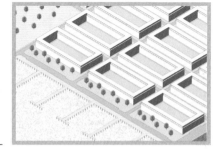

♻ – **Vatnsmyri International Urban Planning Competition,** Reykjavik (IS)

✏ – Graeme Massie Architects, Edinburgh

🖥 – www.graememassie.com

🏆 – 1st prize

📅 – 2008

🗂 – urban renewal – airport conversion – new district

📑 – **geometric principle**

🏷 – additive approach and superimposition; superimposed orthogonal grid; urban building blocks: closed city block; complete road network; place making through exclusion/omission and assembly

The diagonals disrupt the rigorous geometry of the grid without having to abandon the logic of the system.

Axonometric of waterfront city blocks

⊕ — **Goethe University - Westend Campus,** Frankfurt a. M. (D)

✎ — Rolf-Harald Erz for SIAT GmbH, Munich; with Dieter Heigl, Munich; and EGL GmbH, Landshut

⊡ — www.erz-architekten.de

✪ — 2nd prize

▦ — 2003

🗂 — urban redevelopment – military conversion – new college campus

◈ — **geometric principle**

🏷 — Prägnanz; divisional approach; orthogonal grid; urban building blocks: closed city block, spatial structure, layout of development sites: datum; place making through exclusion/omission; green space delimited by buildings

Varying grid sizes and contents create diversified urban spaces.

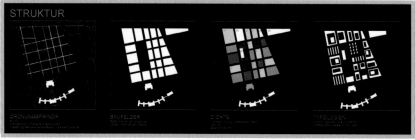

Design diagrams

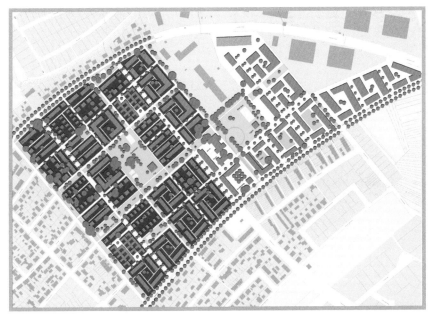

The orthogonal grid is a suitable universal organizing principle in urban as well as suburban contexts.

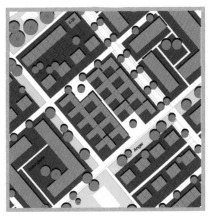

Detail with varied urban building blocks

 — **Barracks site conversion,** Karlsruhe-Knielingen (D)

— Jutta Rump, Roetgen

— www.competitionline.com/de/bueros/10372

— 2nd prize

— 2003

— urban redevelopment – military conversion – new residential district and industrial park

— **geometric principle**

— additive approach; orthogonal grid; urban building blocks: opened city block, row, point, spatial structure; place making through exclusion/omission and assembly, community/adjacent green and open space

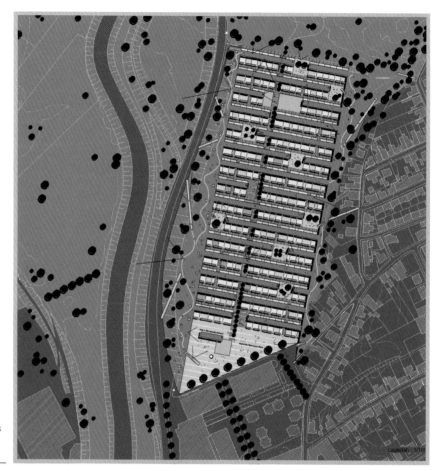

Small omitted squares loosen up the otherwise rigorous grid.

Model

🎯 — **Mobile Regional Airport (MOB),** Greven (D)

📝 — LK | Architekten, Köln

🖥 — www.lkarchitekten.de

🏆 — 1st prize

📅 — 1999

🗂 — urban redevelopment – military conversion – new residential district

📑 — **geometric principle**

🏷 — additive approach; urban building blocks: Zeile; place making through
___ exclusion/omission

Additional Geometric Principles

Thanks to its great flexibility and functionality, the orthogonal grid is the most successful organization principle in urban design. But at the same time, there have been numerous experiments with nonorthogonal geometries that, due to geometric constraints, have led less often to success.

Circular Shapes

In 1552 the author Antonio Francesco Doni conceived of a circular model city with radial streets leading to a round temple at the center.[6] This model was not, however, adopted in urban design: following the geometric order, the city blocks in the individual circular segments would have increasingly become narrower and closer together as one moved toward the center.

By contrast, this problem was avoided in the city layout of Karlsruhe, the planned city founded in 1715 as a seat of absolutist power based on the model presented by Versailles: The royal residence, which occupies the circular center of the fan-shaped, radial city layout, stretches across an oversized court of honor that serves as a forecourt to the city, so that the city blocks facing it are already endowed with sensible proportions and dimensions. The opposite problem arose, however, because as one gets further from the royal residence, the segments of the circle become deeper – and hence the city blocks become larger. Aided by a tangential street known as Kriegsstraße, which was originally built for military purposes around 1799 as a bypass road outside the city gates, later city expansions were able to resolve the radial geometry by connecting nearly orthogonally to the tangent.

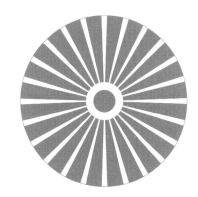

IDEAL CITY "GRAN CITTÀ ," Antonio Francesco Doni, 1552

KARLSRUHE, ideal concept from 1715 with classicistic and late-nineteenth-century expansion (D)

---

6 See Virgilio Vercelloni, *Europäische Stadtutopien: Ein historischer Atlas* (Munich: Diederichs, 1994), plate 59.

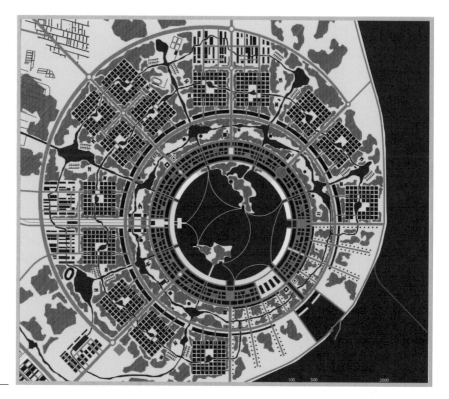

The design skillfully avoids the geometric constraints of the circular shape.

Model

- **Lingang New City,** Shanghai (PRC)
- gmp Architekten von Gerkan, Marg and Partners, Hamburg
- www.gmp-architekten.de
- 1st prize
- 2003
- new city
- **circular shapes**
- Prägnanz; geometric principle; representation: presentation model

Designed and under construction since 2003, Lingang New City, one of several new towns built to accommodate Shanghai's population overspill, is also based on a radial system. At the center of the circular layout, the architects von Gerkan, Marg and Partners have placed a lake with a diameter of more than two kilometers, which is encircled by a densely built inner-city ring that is roughly 400 meters deep. Due to the large distance between the ring and the center of the circle, the individual building lots are only slightly trapezoidal in shape. The adjoining second ring is a park landscape that is bounded by an outer highway. This highway, as well as the radial roads that head outward from the inner ring, provide access to square residential districts that measure roughly 750 × 750 meters each and are positioned around the circular figure like satellites. The districts are then subdivided by an orthogonal street grid, demonstrating another means of resolving the constraints of a circular geometry.[7]

Hexagonal, Star-Shaped, and Honeycomb Patterns

Early in the history of the United States, there were attempts to breach the orthogonal "national grid" that regulated the land division of town and country.[8] In Detroit around 1807, for example, experiments were made with a hexagonal grid that also included streets running to the center in a radial system, which yielded city blocks of greatly different sizes and shapes. Fragments of the design, which was already abandoned by 1820, are still recognizable today in the center of the city.

Other nonhierarchical hexagonal structures – such as those in which the hexagons are interlocked in a star shape through equilateral triangles inserted between them, thus yielding an excess of triangular residual areas, or even hexagonal city blocks modeled after honeycombs – have also not proved successful as an overarching organizing principle in urban design. Thus as early as 1890 in his book *Der Städtebau*, the urban planner Josef Stübben examined a design from the United States and characterized the districts, which were designed according to the latter principle and lacked thoroughfares, as "foolishness."[9]

DETROIT, Plan of downtown Detroit, Augustus B. Woodward, 1807 (US)

---

7   Comparing the design to the constructed reality as seen in satellite images, it is conspicuous that some of the square residential districts are built upon with diagonal rows of buildings. In Chinese urban design, the north-south alignment of housing is almost mandatory.

8   See Gerhard Fehl, "Stadt im 'National Grid': Zu einigen historischen Grundlagen US-amerikanischer Stadtproduktion," in *Going West? Stadtplanung in den USA – gestern und heute*, ed. Ursula von Petz (Dortmund: Institut für Raumplanung, 2004), p. 46.

9   Josef Stübben, *Der Städtebau* (Stuttgart: A. Kröner, 1907), p. 62.

4 The Relationship of the Parts to the Whole

___ MOST urban designs can be described as an assembly of equal, similar, or varying parts to form a whole. What always matters is the relationship of the parts to the whole and vice versa.

In his design primer *Grundlagen der Gestaltung zu Bau und Stadtbau*, Rudolf Wienands identifies three fundamental approaches that are possible when designing: additive, divisional, and superimposing.[1] More than one of these principles is usually discernable in a design, although one of them generally dominates.

1 Rudolf Wienands, *Grundlagen der Gestaltung zu Bau und Stadtbau* (Basel: Birkhäuser, 1985), p. 135 ff

4.1 ADDITIVE APPROACH

WITH the additive approach, the parts are precisely defined in advance; the result is the sum of the assembled parts. Depending on the scale, objective, level of detail, and design intent, the parts can be entire urban districts, individual building fields, or − at the scale of a building field − urban building blocks. The overall figure remains open for change, augmentation, and extension − or it is restricted, for example due to topographic conditions.

An early historical example for orthogonal additive assembly is the layout of the Greek colonial city of Miletus, in present-day Turkey. For the reconstruction of the war-damaged city in the fourth century BC the "Hippodamic system" − named after Hippodamos of Miletus − was employed. The peninsula where Miletus is situated has many bays and an irregular shape. The agora, the political, religious, and cultural center, is located crosswise at the widest point in the middle of the peninsula. Above and below, equally sized residential building fields join together in a grid pattern. The shape of the peninsula limits the maximum extent of the residential districts, confronting the internal homogeneity with a more or less ragged outer edge.

Additive growth is also demonstrated by the US city of Savannah, which was founded in 1733 as a seaport by the English nobleman, general, and governor of the British colony of Georgia, James Oglethorpe. Small neighborhood units, each comprising elongated building lots and space left free in the middle for a square or park, were added together. Whereas only four of these neighborhood units had been laid out in 1734 and they were only partly built upon with the simplest of wood houses, around the year 1800 fifteen such groupings had been joined together, established according to a uniform layout and varying only slightly in their widths. It is remarkable that well into the nineteenth century, the pattern of the original basic module continued to be employed for extensions and was only then replaced by a basic block pattern. Altogether twenty-three of these districts and squares can still be found in the city layout today.

Additive assembly must not necessarily be confined to a grid. The parts can also be joined together in a free manner unrelated to a grid, as is the case in many rural settlement patterns, for instance.

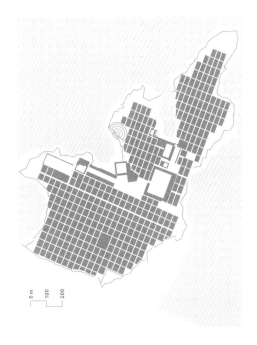

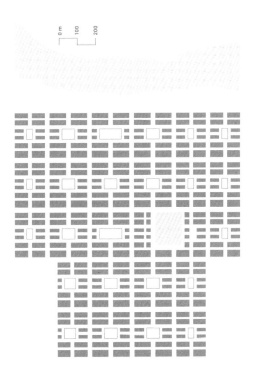

MILETUS, Hippodamos of Miletus, 479 BC (TR)

SAVANNAH, James Oglethorpe, 1733 (US)

THE RELATIONSHIP OF THE PARTS TO THE WHOLE

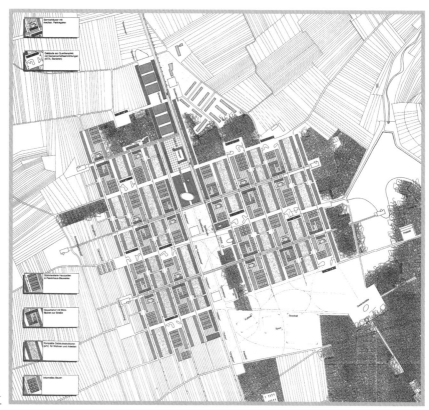

The overall figure re-
mains open for change,
addition, and extension.

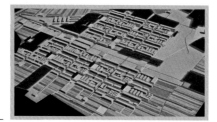

Model

⊙ – **Layenhof/Münchwald District,**
Mainz (D)

✎ – Ackermann+Raff with Alexander
Lange, Stuttgart/Tübingen

▭ – www.ackermann-raff.de

◉ – 1st prize

▦ – 1996

▱ – military conversion – new district

◈ – **additive approach**

◈ – orthogonal grid, regular grid; layout
of development sites: axis, symmetry, hierarchy, datum, repetition/
rhythm, grouping; place making
through assembly; linear street space

- **Messestadt Riem,** Housing, Munich (D)
- ASTOC Architects and Planners, Cologne, with lohrer.hochrein landschaftsarchitekten, Munich
- www.astoc.de
- 1st prize
- 2008
- urban redevelopment – airport conversion – new district
- **additive approach**
- irregular orthogonal grid; urban building blocks: dissolved city block; layout of development sites: datum, grouping; place making through assembly; adjacent green and open space

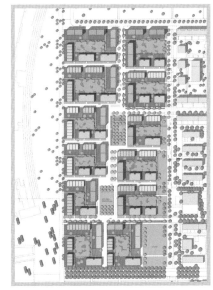

Assembly of similar blocks of buildings of different sizes

Perspective

Additive approach
using rows of varying
city blocks

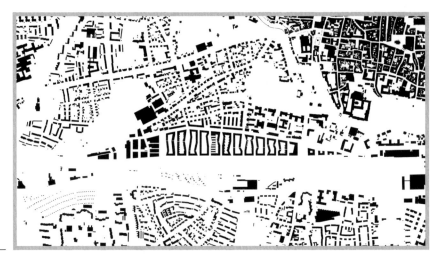

Figure-ground plan
(poche plan)

  ⟲ — **Innerer Westen,** Regensburg (D)
  ✐ — 03 Architekten with Keller Damm Roser Landschaftsarchitekten Stadtplaner, Munich
  🖳 — www.03arch.de
  🏅 — 3rd prize
  📅 — 2011
  🗁 — urban redevelopment – railway conversion – new residential district
  ❤ — **additive approach**
  🏷 — urban building blocks: closed city block; layout of development sites: sequence/
  ___ repetition; widened street space

DIVISIONAL APPROACH

WITH the divisional approach, or simply division, the overall form is defined at the outset. The parts result from division of the whole according to certain rules that are defined or grounded in the cultural context, depending on the objective. The Chinese ideal city and the Roman colonial city are both based on the form of a square, even though each developed entirely independently. The Chinese imperial city was a reflection of the cosmos. According to Chinese cosmology, the earth was a cube and the earth's surface was square. At the center of the empire was the capital, which was aligned to the four cardinal directions. In the center of the city (Chengzhou, Peking) was the palace; the north-south axis was an image of the meridian[2] and reserved solely for the ruler. The residential districts and their associated markets were to the left and right of the main axis.

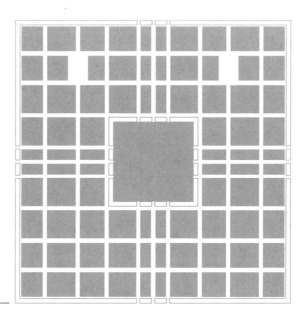

CHENGZHOU, 1000 BC (PRC)

---

2 See Spiro Kostof, *The City Shaped: Urban Patterns and Meanings Through History* (Boston: Bulfinch, 1991), p. 174 f.

The Roman colonial city, by contrast, developed from the castrum, a standardized military encampment. Two main axes, the north-south axis (cardo) and the east-west axis (decumanus) divided the camp and city into four quadrants. At the intersection in the center of the military camp was the headquarters building (principia) and its counterpart in the city was the forum, which, like the Greek agora, served as the cultural, religious, economic, and political center. All other streets ran parallel to the main axes and divided the city into orthogonal residential areas (insulae).

In the history of urban development, there are countless further examples for the divisional approach, including the ideal city concepts of the Renaissance and the Baroque – essentially wherever the form of the city ought to serve formal representational functions or, as with fortified towns, where there were functional and military justifications.

The possibilities for optimizing physical characteristics, appearance, and design qualities prove to be advantageous with the divisional approach; the extendability and capability for modification, however, suffer because the bond of the parts to the whole implies that new parts cannot be added or removed at will. A solution is offered by the additive approach or by grouping districts that are individually formed by the divisional approach.

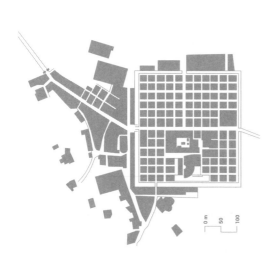

TIMGAD, 100 AD (DZ)

MANNHEIM, 1720 (D)

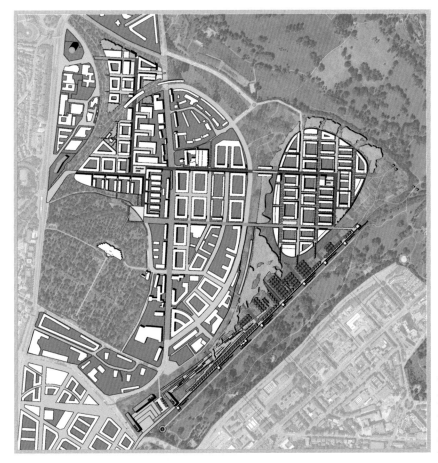

With the divisional approach, there is a fixed overall form and the elements are created through division of the whole.

 — **Rosenstein District,** Stuttgart (D)

 — Prof. Dr. Helmut Bott, Darmstadt, with Dr. Michael Hecker, Cologne, and Dr. Frank Roser landscapearchitect, Stuttgart

Photomontage

— www.hmw-architekten.de

— 2nd prize

— 2005

— urban redevelopment – railway conversion – new district

— **divisional approach**

— Prägnanz; orthogonal grid; urban building blocks: closed, dissolved city block, row, Zeile; place making through assembly

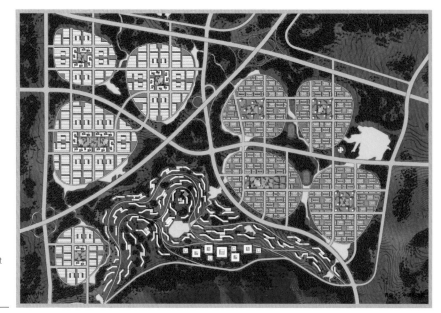

The design remains
flexible by grouping
together development
sites that are them-
selves formed by a
divisional approach.

Perspective

☉ — **EcologyPark,** Qingdao (PRC)

✐ — gmp Architekten von Gerkan, Marg and Partners, Hamburg

▣ — www.gmp-architekten.de

♀ — 1st prize

▦ — 2011

▭ — urban expansion – new sustainable district

◈ — **divisional approach**

◆ — Prägnanz; orthogonal grid; urban building blocks: city block, inner-city urban block,
bent Zeile, high-rise tower, hybrid; layout of development sites: hierarchy, repetition,
grouping; place making through assembly

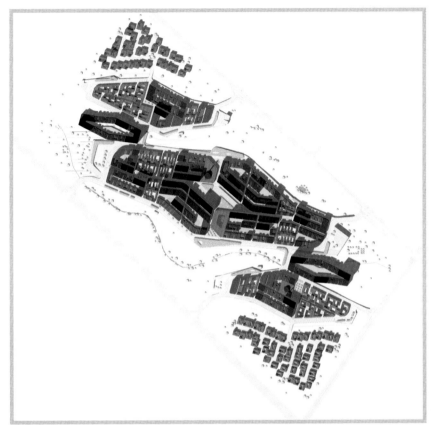

The rules for division vary depending on the precinct.

Perspective

⚙️ — **Master Plan for Paramount Xeritown,** Dubai (UAE)

📝 — SMAQ – architecture urbanism research, Berlin; Sabine Müller and Andreas Quednau with Joachim Schultz, with X-Architects, Dubai; Johannes Grothaus Landschaftsarchitekten, Potsdam; reflexion, Zurich, and Buro Happold, London

🖥️ — www.smaq.net

📅 — 2008

🗂️ — urban expansion – new sustainable urban districts

📑 — **divisional approach**

🔖 — Prägnanz; urban building blocks: city block, row, spatial structure, high-rise; layout of development sites: grouping; place making through assembly and modeling

4.3 SUPERIMPOSITION

WITH superimposition, the city layout is created by overlaying two or more systems of order. While the additive approach carries with it the risk of monotony, the divisional approach can also have negative effects, such as geometric constraints that impair the proper functioning of the parts. Superimposition, by contrast, creates ambiguity and enriches the spatial experience. A historical example for this is the 1792 city plan for Washington, D.C., by Pierre Charles L'Enfant, in which a grid pattern of city blocks is superimposed by diagonals that relate to the Capitol Building or the White House and also connect districts to one another.

The 1859 city plan for the extension of Barcelona that was laid out by Ildefons Cerdà also features a similar superimposition of diagonal streets over a uniform orthogonal system. In both designs, the diagonals serve as superordinate formal boulevards.

For the logic of the design to be legible, superimposition requires a planning site of sufficient size. This design principle not only pertains to whole cities but can also be applied at the district or neighborhood level. The contemporary design for the conversion of the Röttiger-Kaserne in Hamburg by MVRDV works with the superimposition of greenery and the building fabric: A small-scale orthogonal grid of lots for building individual single-family houses is superimposed over the existing buildings and trees in such a way that the grid, as soon as it encounters something worthy of retaining, flows around these elements.

WASHINGTON, Pierre
Charles L'Enfant, 1792
(USA)

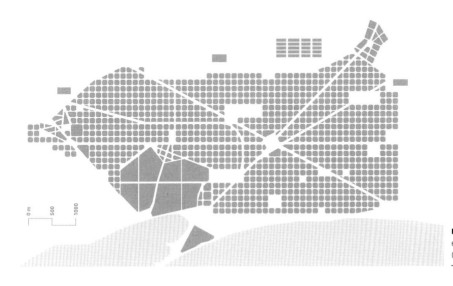

BARCELONA, city
extension, Ildefons
Cerdà, 1859 (E)

THE RELATIONSHIP OF THE PARTS TO THE WHOLE

A finely spaced orthogonal grid is superimposed over the existing buildings and trees.

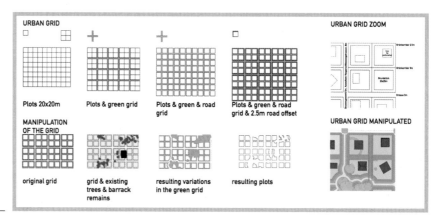

Diagrams explain the design process.

— **Architektur Olympiade Hamburg 2006, Röttiger Barracks,** Hamburg (D)

— MVRDV, Rotterdam

— www.mvrdv.nl

— gold medal for urban design

— 2006

— urban redevelopment — military conversion — new residential district

— **superimposition**

— incomplete orthogonal grid; urban building blocks: point; incomplete road network; representation: diagrams

A thoroughfare and green corridors are overlaid on the settlement pattern.

Perspective of pedestrian zone

⊙ — **Masdar Development,** Abu Dhabi (UAE)

✎ — Foster + Partners, London, with Cyril Sweett Limited, W.S.P Transsolar, ETA, Gustafson Porter, E.T.A., Energy, Ernst and Young, Flack + Kurtz, Systematica, Transsolar

🖵 — www.fosterandpartners.com

📅 — 2007

🗀 — urban expansion – new emission-free district

◈ — **superimposition**

🏷 — Ganzheit; Prägnanz; divisional approach; urban building blocks: city block, courtyard, row, Zeile, spatial structure; incomplete road network; district-level green and open space; representation: perspective

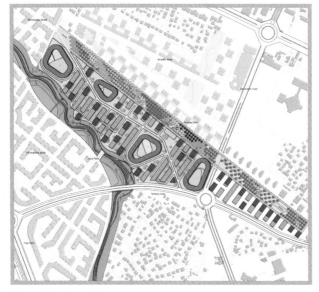

The overlap of several settlement patterns creates an eventful townscape.

Diagrams explain the design process.

⊘ — **Park City,** Tirana (AL)

✎ — CITYFÖRSTER architecture + urbanism, Berlin/Hannover/London/Oslo/Rotterdam/Salerno, with Ulrike Centmayer Landschaftsarchitektin, Rotterdam

▣ — www.cityfoerster.net

♔ — 1st prize

▦ — 2008

▭ — urban redevelopment — airport conversion — new urban district

◆ — **superimposition**

◈ — contrast; urban building blocks: closed city block, row, Zeile/high-rise slab, hybrid; cul-de-sac network; circulation loop network; representation: diagrams

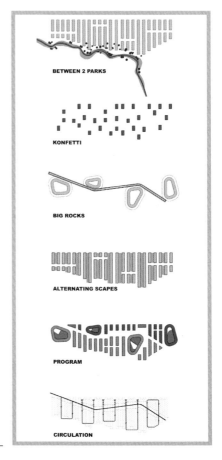

4.4 **URBAN DESIGN AS A SINGLE ENTITY (GRAND FORM)**

IN addition to the aforementioned approaches of assembly, division, or superimposition, an urban design can also be established as a single entity in which the individual parts coalesce into an overall form. The figure can be geometric, organic/biomorphic, or free-form, and the parts can be organized in a seamlessly additive way or, if starting from a single form, in a seamlessly divisional way.

Such objects cannot of course be extended arbitrarily over every planning site. Such a design is usually restricted to an urban district the size of several building fields. When the urban figure and the architecture constitute a unified artistic whole, however, its implementation by a third party is rarely feasible: the architect then assumes the role of the urban planner or vice versa.

The Viennese Wohnhöfe (courtyard housing estates) that were built in the 1920s as part of a social housing program are residential examples. The largest of these complexes is Sandleitenhof, which comprises multiple irregular perimeter blocks and has more than 1,500 apartments. Somewhat fewer residents live in the best known of these housing estates, Karl-Marx-Hof, an ensemble with two enormous courtyards separated by a monumental forecourt and composed of L-shaped corner buildings, rows, and Zeile. Both of these complexes are based on the idea of housing a community of working-class families. While they appear closed from the outside, they each constitute a kind of city in the city. Because courtyards stand for the idea of community, the shared inner courtyards are consequently used for gaining access to the apartments.

Current examples of grand forms in urban design are the schemes for the Werkbundsiedlung Wiesenfeld in Munich by Allmann Sattler Wappner Architekten and the Nymphenburger Höfe, a new development on the former site of a brewery in Munich, by Steidle Architekten. While the grand form in the first design reflects a community of diverse and individualized apartment buildings, considerable traffic noise coming from all sides is what led in the second example to the arrangement of a sequence of introverted courtyards.

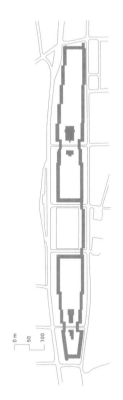

SANDLEITENHOF IN VIENNA, Emil Hoppe, et al., 1924 (A)

KARL-MARX-HOF IN VIENNA, Karl Ehn, 1927 (A)

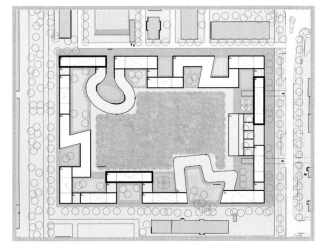

The large-scale form represents a community of diverse, individualized residential buildings.

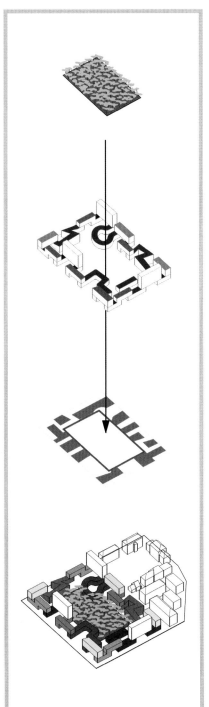

Design concept

🎯 — **Werkbundsiedlung Wiesenfeld,** Munich (D)

📝 — Allmann Sattler Wappner Architekten GmbH, Munich, with Valentien + Valentien & Partner Landschaftsarchitekten und Stadtplaner, Weßling

🖥 — www.allmannsattlerwappner.de

🏆 — Prizewinner (urban design)

📅 — 2006

🗂 — urban redevelopment – military conversion – new residential district

📚 — **large-scale/grand form**

🏷 — urban building blocks: dissolved city block, courtyard, meanders, hybrid; place making through modeling; community green and open space, integrated green space; trees in a
___ tight grid

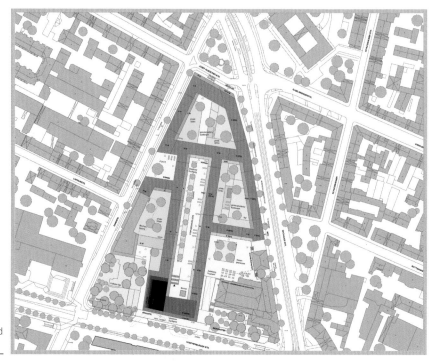

The design exhibits a sequence of introverted courtyards.

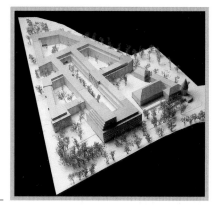

Model

⚙ — **Nymphenburger Höfe,** Munich (D)

✏ — Steidle + Partner Architekten with realgrün Landschaftsarchitekten, Munich

💻 — www.steidle-architekten.de

🏆 — 1st prize

📅 — 2003

🗂 — urban redevelopment – commercial conversion – new inner-city district

🔷 — **large-scale/grand form**

🏷 — urban building blocks: closed city block, courtyard, hybrid; place making through modeling; community green and open space

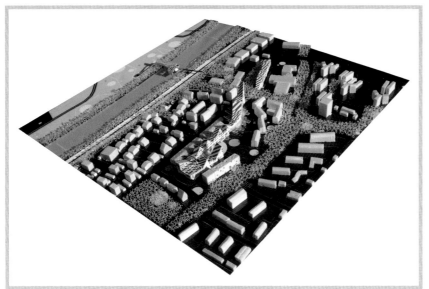

The undulating roofscape expresses the diversity of the uses accommodated within the buildings.

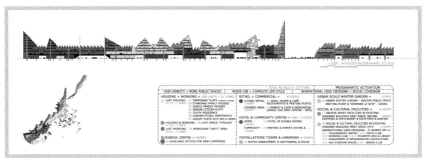

Use diagram

⌖ — **Europan 10, Eine urbane Schnittstelle neu denken (Rethinking an urban interface),** Forchheim (D)

✎ — gutiérrez-delafuente arquitectos, Madrid

▣ — www.gutierrez-delafuente.com

✦ — merit award

▦ — 2010

▣ — urban redevelopment – industrial conversion – new residential district

◈ — **large-scale/grand form**

◆ — urban building blocks: row, Zeile, meanders, hybrid; place making through modeling;
___ representation: section, model

5 "Grid" Design Principle

— IN the long history of the city, grid patterns have proven successful as a universally valid organizing principle. One advantage is that, inherent to their system, grids can yield efficient transport networks in which all uses are connected to the overall structure almost automatically and are linked to one another with a minimum of changes in direction. Subsequent expansions also present no problems.

5.1 **THE REGULAR GRID**

THE ideal regular grid is square or rectangular. Most realms of urban life can be easily and functionally arranged in an orthogonal structure. In addition, settlement areas can be rationally divided in the orthogonal system without creating unwanted residual areas.[1] The disadvantage of a regular grid is that along with the numerous repetitions, monotonous characteristics also increase. But relief can be provided by establishing a hierarchy of subareas and streets, grouping building lots within larger grid cells, superimposing additional layers, and/or inserting squares and open spaces.

The variation of urban building blocks and the insertion of open spaces can prevent monotony in a regular grid.

---

1 See Gerhard Curdes, *Stadtstruktur und Stadtgestaltung* (Stuttgart/Berlin/Cologne: Kohlhammer, 1997), p. 45.

✐ — jan foerster teamwerk-architekten with ergebnisgrün, Büro für Landschaftsarchitektur, Munich

▣ — www.teamwerk-architekten.de

◉ — 1st prize

▦ — 2008

▱ — metropolitan area development concept

◈ — **regular grid**

◈ — orthogonal grid; layout of urban building blocks: repetition/sequence/rhythm;
complete road network; place making through exclusion/omission; district-level/
___ community/adjacent green and open space

Functional diagrams

5.2 THE IRREGULAR GRID

IRREGULARLY subdivided grid patterns have attributes that can be interpreted both positively and negatively. To the degree that irregularities increase, the building lots differ more strongly in respect to size and form. Porosity can be constrained by irregularities, but on the other hand, they can also make the urban realm more pleasantly diversified. It is common to find irregular grids that are divided at more regular intervals along one direction and are irregular in the perpendicular direction. These are used when one direction should be given preference, for instance in order to ensure the smooth flow of traffic or to keep open visual connections – and conversely, in order to slow the flow of traffic or to spatially terminate street spaces rather than allowing them to simply fade away.

The grid is divided regularly in one direction and irregularly in the other direction.

Detail of model

🎯 — **Europan 6, 3x2 Elements for the Urban Landscape,** Mönchengladbach (D)

✍ — florian krieger – architektur und städtebau, with Ariana Sarabia, Urs Löffelhardt, Benjamin Künzel, Darmstadt

🖥 — www.florian-krieger.de

🏆 — 1st prize

📅 — 2002

📁 — urban redevelopment – military conversion – new residential district

📑 — **irregular grid**

🔖 — contrast; robustness; additive approach; urban building blocks: row, Zeile/high-rise
___ slab; place making through exclusion/omission; rows of trees, tight grid of trees

87

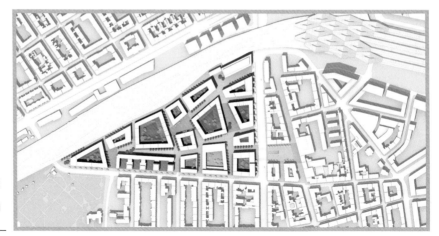

The irregularly formed grid yields large and small building lots and varied urban spaces.

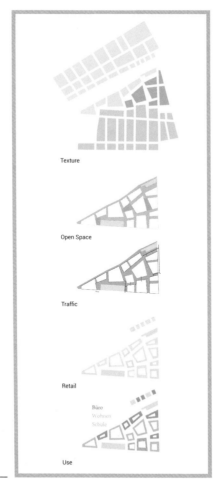

Texture

Open Space

Traffic

Retail

Büro
Wohnen
Schule

Use

Functional diagrams

– **Development Site D, ÖBB-Immobilien,** Vienna (A)

– Wessendorf Architektur Städtebau with Atelier Loidl, Berlin

– www.studio-wessendorf.de
www.atelier-loidl.de

– 1st prize

– 2010

– urban redevelopment – railway conversion – new urban district

– **irregular grid**

– additive approach; urban building blocks: closed city block, inner-city urban block, hybrid; layout of development sites: grouping; place making through assembly; bent and widened street space

⦿ — **Freiham Nord, Housing and District Center,** Munich (D)

✎ — florian krieger – architektur und städtebau, Darmstadt, with lohrberg stadtlandschaftsarchitektur, Stuttgart

▣ — www.florian-krieger.de

✪ — 2nd prize

🗓 — 2011

🗂 — urban expansion – new residential district and district center

◈ — **irregular grid**

➤ — additive approach; urban building blocks: opened city block, row, point, high-rise tower; layout of development sites: repetition/variation/rhythm; combined access network;
___ place making through assembly

The irregular grid pattern's variations create differentiated green spaces and neighborhood identities.

Bird's-eye perspective

"GRID" DESIGN PRINCIPLE

5.3 THE TILTED GRID

DEPENDING on the topography, the orientation, or the need to tie into existing urban structures or circulation patterns, it can be helpful to interrupt uniformly laid-out grids and shift portions of the grid by tilting them against one another. The resulting points of discontinuity and residual areas can be treated as special situations, emphasized, or intentionally ignored and simply filled, for example, with special uses, unique building forms, or green and open spaces.

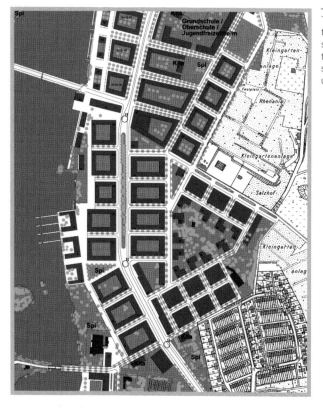

The points of discontinuity that result from shifts in the angle of the grid are used as special situations in the urban fabric.

⚙ — **Master Plan for Wasserstadt Berlin-Oberhavel,** Berlin (D)

✎ — Arbeitsgemeinschaft Kollhoff, Timmermann, Langhof, Nottmeyer, Zillich, Berlin

🖥 — www.kollhoff.de

📅 — 1996

🗂 — urban redevelopment – commercial conversion – new urban districts

◆ — **tilted grid**

◈ — additive approach; urban building blocks: closed city block, dissolved city block, point; place making through assembly; linear street space, bent street space; waterfront living

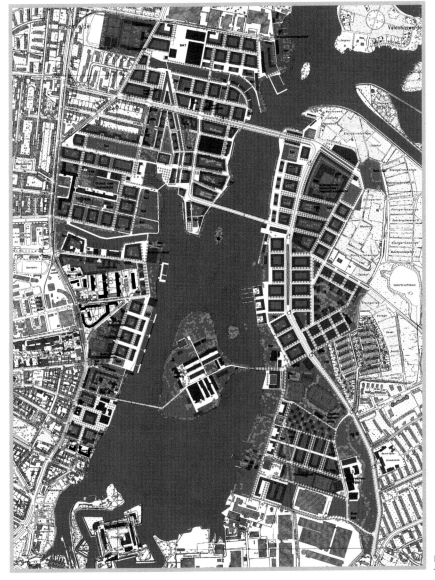

Illustrative site plan

"GRID" DESIGN PRINCIPLE

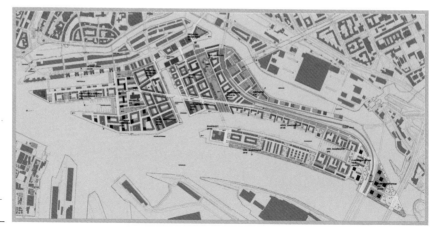

The layout of the piers was decisive for orienting the grid patterns.

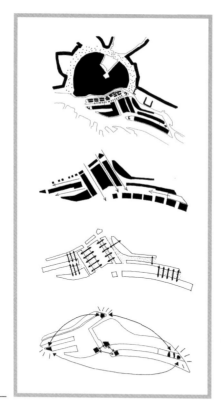

Design diagrams

⊙ — **HafenCity,** Hamburg (D)

▨ — ASTOC Architects and Planners, Cologne, with KCAP Architects&Planners, Rotterdam/Zurich/Shanghai

▣ — www.astoc.de, www.kcap.eu

▣ — 1st prize

▦ — 1999

▭ — urban redevelopment – harbor conversion – new district

◈ — **tilted grid**

◆ — additive approach and superimposition; urban building blocks: closed, dissolved city block, inner-city urban block, row, point, hybrid; layout of development sites: axis, datum, sequence/repetition/rhythm, grouping;

— waterfront living

The gaps in the grid are used for a community park.

Detail

 — **Auf der Freiheit,** Schleswig (D)

 — studioinges Architektur und Städtebau, Berlin

— www.studioinges.de

— merit award

— 2006

— urban redevelopment – military conversion – new residential district

 — **tilted grid**

— additive approach; layout of urban building blocks on building lot: hierarchy, repetition/sequence/rhythm, grouping; integrated green space delimited by buildings; representation: Illustrative site plan

93

5.4 THE DEFORMED GRID

GRIDS must not necessarily be laid out orthogonally. Stretched or curved grids also belong to the urban design repertoire. Some reasons for the deformation can be the topographic conditions, the integration of superordinate green corridors, or even the specific shape of the available site to be built upon. Curved streets, moreover, are a proven means for avoiding monotony. Views along a curved street do not lead to a void or to a distant horizon, but are instead always guided by the facades of the buildings along the road.

Deformations of the grid result in exciting street spaces.

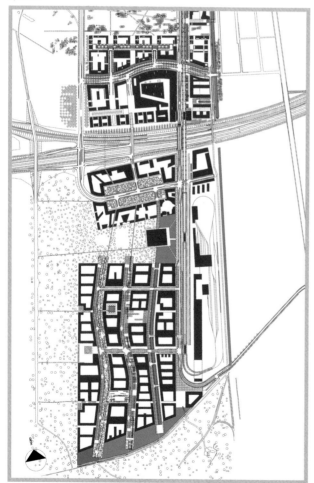

Perspective of public space with canal

⊙ — **Ørestad Master Plan,** Copenhagen (DK)

✎ — ARKKI ApS. (KHR arkitekter, Copenhagen, with APRT, Helsinki)

🖥 — www.khr.dk

🏆 — 1st prize

📅 — 1995

🗂 — urban expansion – new district

🗎 — **stretched grid**

🗨 — urban building blocks: city block, courtyard, hybrid; place making through assembly; curved street space

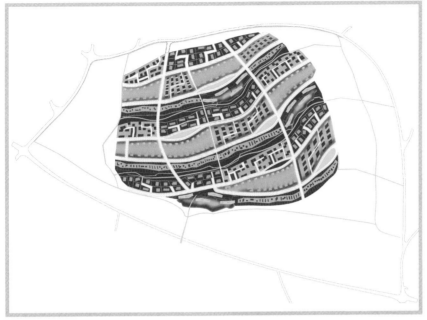

The deformed grid surrounds the verdant residential landscape with soft edges and provides space for widening the streets in places.

Detail of model

⊙ — **Herzo Base Residential District,**
Herzogenaurach (D)

✎ — netzwerkarchitekten, Darmstadt

▣ — www.netzwerkarchitekten.de

◉ — 2nd prize

▦ — 2002

▭ — urban redevelopment — military conversion — new residential district

◈ — **stretched grid**

◗ — urban building blocks: row, Zeile, point, spatial structure; curved/bent street space, widened street space; community and adjacent green and open space; integrated green space

5.5 __ THE TRANSFORMED GRID

TRANSFORMATION (from Latin preposition *trans*, "across" + *forma*, "form") denotes a change in appearance, form, or structure. In a transformed grid, the uniform grid pattern is altered toward the edges or the center. The transformation process can occur in perceptible increments or it can be fluid and barely perceptible. Thus an unbroken and complete grid can become an incomplete grid, such as a cul-de-sac network, or a rational, geometric system can yield an organic settlement pattern that appears to have evolved over time. The streets generated by the grid pattern are either incorporated or can be connected with one another (for example, by means of peripheral roads) and, in such a way, brought to a conclusion.

The overall structure of the development site follows an orthogonal system, which is further subdivided with an irregular grid pattern.

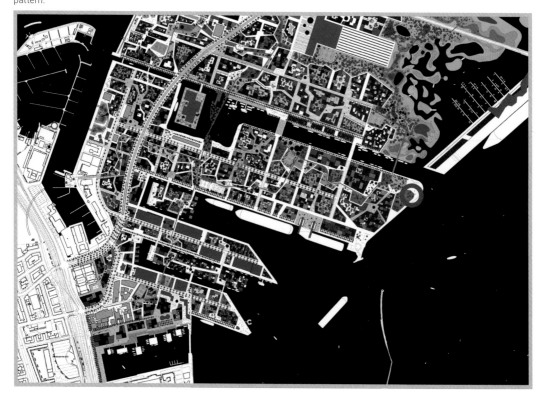

- ⌖ — **Copenhagen Northern Harbor: The sustainable city of the future,** Copenhagen (DK)
- ✐ — POLYFORM ARKITEKTER APS, Copenhagen, with Cenergia Energy Consultants, COWI, Deloitte, Oluf Jørgensen a/s
- ▣ — www.polyformarkitekter.dk
- ⚙ — 1st prize category
- ▦ — 2008
- ▭ — urban redevelopment/urban expansion − harbor conversion − new district
- ⬙ — **transformed grid**
- ⬚ — additive approach/superimposition; irregular grid; place making through modeling; linear, curved/bent, widened, amorphous street space; representation: Illustrative
- ___ site plan, diagrams

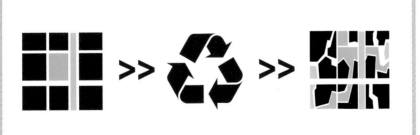

Perspective (a.)

Design idea (b.)

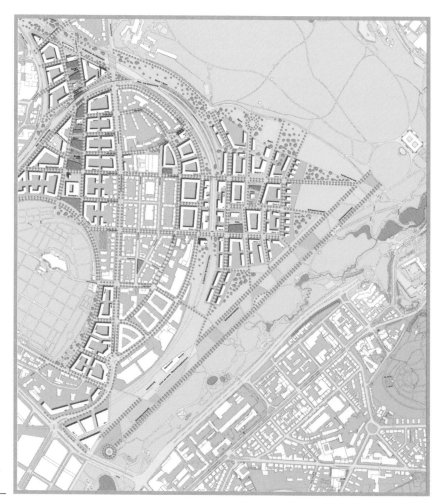

The grid derived from the existing fabric dissipates into the park.

- **Rosenstein District,** Stuttgart (D)
- KSV Krüger Schuberth Vandreike, Berlin
- www.ksv-network.de
- merit award
- 2005
- urban redevelopment – railway conversion – new district
- **transformed grid**
- urban building blocks: closed, dissolved city block, row, point; place making through exclusion/omission; linear, bent street space; integrated green space

The geometric grid is transformed incrementally into an organic settlement pattern.

Bird's-eye perspective

5.6 THE SUPERIMPOSED GRID

THE superimposed grid develops through the additive layering, or superimposition,[2] of systems of order. Usually one system of order remains dominant while the added system of order creates supplementary qualities. The superimposition of too many systems, however, leads to chaos, in which the possibilities for users to orient themselves within the city layout are disturbed, perhaps even resulting in complete disorientation. Here the old adage applies: Less is more.

Green corridors and green areas are superimposed on the orthogonal grid.

⊙ — **A101 Urban Block Competition, 100% BLOCK CITY,** Moscow (RUS)

✎ — KCAP Architects&Planners, Rotterdam/Zurich/Shanghai, with NEXT Architects, Amsterdam

⬚ — www.kcap.eu

⊙ — 2nd Phase

🗓 — 2010

🗁 — new city — new district

◈ — **superimposed grid**

◆ — superimposition; irregular orthogonal grid; urban building blocks: closed, dissolved city block, hybrid; integrated green space; rows of trees, tight grid of trees, freely grouped trees

Visualization

2 See also 4.3 Superimposition

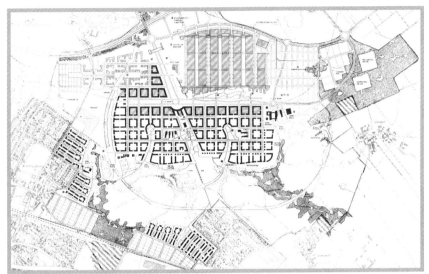

Green areas delimited
by buildings extend
deep into the rigorous
square grid.

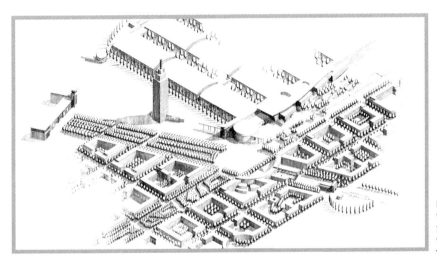

Perspective showing
the juncture between
the urban district and the
trade fair grounds

📷 – **Conversion of Airport Grounds, Munich-Riem,** Munich (D)

✏️ – Frauenfeld Architekten, Frankfurt a. M. with Baer + Müller Landschaftsarchitekten,
Dortmund

🖥️ – www.frauenfeld-architekten.de

🏆 – 1st prize

📅 – 1991

🗂️ – urban redevelopment – airport conversion – new district and trade fair grounds

📑 – **superimposed grid**

🏷️ – Prägnanz; superimposition; incomplete grid; urban building blocks: closed, dissolved
city block; place making through modeling; representation: perspective

6 Urban Building Blocks

A city is based on a spatial structure that is experienced primarily through built elements. These offer the city's inhabitants different impressions: rural, suburban, or urban situations, open or compact settlement patterns, low or high building densities, and outdoor spaces that can be differentiated into public-, shared-, or private-use areas. The urban building typologies, so-called urban building blocks, play a significant role here. Urban building blocks are the raw materials of urban design. Just as sequences of notes are used time and again to create new musical compositions, urban building blocks can also be assembled together into new building groups, districts, or entire cities; or they can be used to repair existing urban structures.

The various urban building blocks available to the makers of contemporary urban design have developed over a very long period of time – some over thousands of years, others only in the last century. Building structures can usually be clearly attributed to a certain urban building block type, but compound forms and hybrids possessing a combination of properties are occasionally found. Given the palpable diversity of a city, there are surprisingly few basic forms of urban building blocks. Knowledge of their ways of working, their dimensioning, and their cultural significance, as well as their advantages and disadvantages and their potential applications for urban design are part of the basic knowledge of both architects and urban planners.

6.1 CLASSIFICATION OF URBAN BUILDING BLOCKS

URBAN building blocks can be differentiated into three categories: standard, large, and small building blocks.[1]

Standard Building Blocks
Standard building blocks are the urban building blocks that comprise the predominant part of cities, urban fields, urban districts, or housing developments and substantially determine the settlement morphology, the form, and the appearance of the built fabric. These standard built elements include, for example, the city block, row, Zeile, and point.[2]

Large Building Blocks
Large building blocks are elements that are clearly distinguishable from the standard building blocks due to their size, function, or uniqueness. These urban building blocks usually play a prominent role in the cityscape and can have positive or negative effects on how people identify with their city. Large building blocks can be larger versions of standard building blocks, such as city halls, administration complexes, schools, and institutions of higher education, but they can also be places of assembly, such as event halls, arenas, sports stadiums, movie theaters, churches, train stations, shopping arcades, and malls, as well as production and storage facilities. Vertical elements, such as church steeples, minarets, high-rise buildings, radio and television towers, and finally historical and modern elements of infrastructure, such as city fortifications, bridges, gasholders, raised highways, railways, and power plants, are also considered large building blocks. In specialized areas of the city, large built elements can also be seen as standard building blocks, in vertically concentrated city centers, apartment tower complexes, or commercial districts, for example.

---

1 Thomas Herrmann and Klaus Humpert, "Typologie der Stadtbausteine," in *Lehrbausteine Städtebau*, 2nd ed., ed. Johann Jessen (Stuttgart: Städtebau-Institut, 2003), p. 234.
2 Ibid., p. 249 ff. An overview of urban structures, housing developments, and districts – illustrated with plans and aerial photos – is also found there.

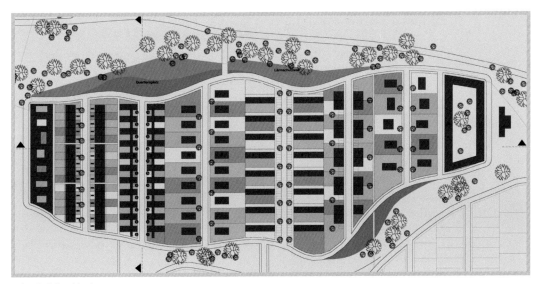

Urban building blocks on display: the design shows the most important standard building blocks, like spatial structure, row, point, Zeile, and city block.

Illustrative site plan

Herzo Base Residential District, Herzogenaurach (D)

— ENS Architekten BDA, mit Regina Poly, Berlin

— www.eckertnegwersuselbeek.de

— 1st prize

— 2002

— urban redevelopment – military conversion – new residential district

urban building blocks

— robustness; superimposition; layout of building lots: sequence/repetition; adjacent green and open space; rows of trees, freely grouped trees

Small Building Blocks

Small building blocks include minor structures like garages and garden sheds, kiosks, "commemorative and beautification structures" like monuments, sculptures, and fountains, small infrastructural elements like wells, transformer stations, and bus shelters, and also temporary structures such as market stalls or advertising stands.[3]

Special Building Blocks

Contextually related special building blocks comprise a category not mentioned at the beginning. Built elements that deviate from the predominant structure of the building fabric can be referred to as special building blocks. This is the case when a deviating urban building block, possibly with a special use, is placed as a counterpoint within an otherwise homogeneous building fabric,[4] for example, an apartment tower in a neighborhood of single-family homes or a large housing complex for the elderly in a residential area. Special building blocks can be either standard building blocks or large building blocks.

3 Ibid., p. 242
4 See also Contrast Principle, p. 72 ff.

STANDARD BUILDING BLOCKS

Block Development

The block of buildings is one of the oldest building forms in the city.[5] As early as the first millennium BC, Chinese cities already had regularized building blocks of single-story courtyard houses surrounded by a planned, orthogonal street grid. Similar blocks of buildings can also be found in another cultural context, in the residential districts of the ancient Greek cities that were planned in a strict orthogonal grid according to the Hippodamic system. Excavations in the Roman cities of Pompeii and Herculaneum have revealed magnificent atrium houses grouped into blocks of 800–1,000 square meters. Along the public frontage, many of these houses had an outer layer of commercial spaces that not only provided additional income for the homeowner but enlivened the public realm and simultaneously also shielded the privacy inside the house. Less luxurious in contrast were the Roman insulae, block-sized, three- to seven-story apartment buildings that had a central courtyard along the lines of the atrium houses, but which was less about projecting a stately image and more about securing natural light and ventilation. The ground floor was used commercially and directly above that were the more comfortable living quarters. As the floors ascended, the apartments became cheaper and simpler.

Whereas the blocks of buildings in medieval towns were characterized by rows of craftsmen's houses on narrow, deep lots, the city block still in use today originated during the Baroque period. These multistoried perimeter block buildings are built around a large, more or less built-up courtyard.

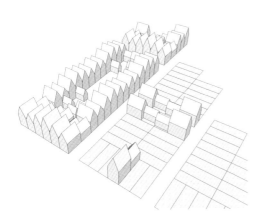

The blocks of the medieval town consisted of gabled rows of craftsmen's houses on narrow, deep lots (from Gruber)

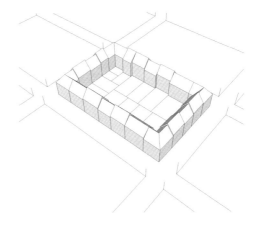

The Baroque city block has eaves parallel to the street, is multistoried, and forms a perimeter around a courtyard (from Gruber)

---

5 Extensive plan materials from all epochs can be found in Leonardo Benevolo, *History of the City*, trans. Geoffrey Culverwell (London: Scolar Press, 1980).

The city block came into disrepute at end of the nineteenth century as, in the course of explosive urban growth in Europe, substandard tenements were routinely built as speculative housing with a series of narrow rear courtyards. The size of the courtyards, which was only coordinated with the turning radius of fire-fighting equipment, proved to be scarcely suitable for adequate natural lighting and ventilation. Some courtyards were also used for industrial manufacturing businesses – with devastating consequences for the health of the residents. Against this backdrop, the Berlin artist and satirist Heinrich Zille said at the time that you could kill a man with an apartment as easily as with an ax.

The city block celebrated the start of its still-ongoing comeback after the 1973 energy crisis and the nearly simultaneous beginning of Postmodernism, in which the void and facelessness of modern cities was denounced. Resorting to traditional building forms ought to counteract these failings.

The Closed Perimeter Block

The city block with continuous perimeter block development, or simply the perimeter block, is an important element in contemporary urban design: it clearly defines the public realm as well as the private open space within the block, which is understood today primarily as recreational space near to the home. Access is gained directly from outside via the public space, thus allowing the open space within to remain undisturbed. Because of its continuous street front and occupied corners, the perimeter block helps to define the urban space. It is suitable for commercial purposes or for purely residential use and can also accommodate different mixed forms of living and working. Perimeter block development can be created as a single element or by assembling individual lots. The northeast corner is problematic because the limited exposure to direct sunlight makes it rather inappropriate for residential purposes.

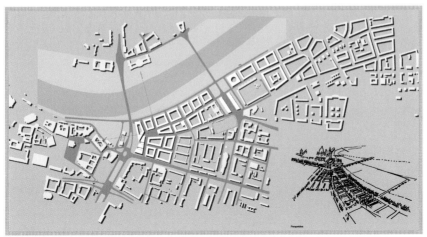

For reconstruction of the fragmented urban pattern, the authors propose using closed city blocks as standard components.

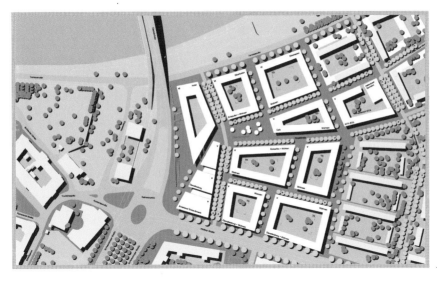

Detail of district center

🎨 — **Am Terrassenufer - Urban Redevelopment Ideas for the Pirnaische Vorstadt,** Dresden (D)

📝 — Prof. Günter Telian, Karlsruhe

🖥 — www.competitionline.com/de/bueros/13178

🏅 — 3rd prize

📅 — 2001

🗂 — urban renewal – new district center and residential districts

🔷 — **closed city block**

🔖 — additive approach; layout of building lots: hierarchy, datum, sequence/repetition; ___ place making through assembly; curved street space

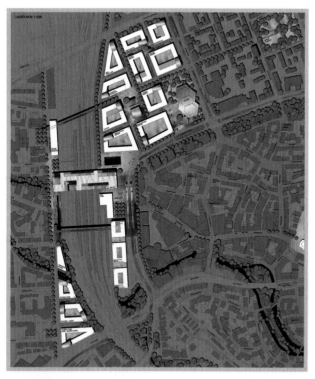

⬡ — **City-Bahnhof,** Ulm (D)

✎ — HÄHNIG|GEMMEKE Freie Architekten BDA, Tübingen

🖥 — www.haehnig-gemmeke.de

🏵 — Prizewinner

📅 — 2011

🗂 — urban redevelopment — railway conversion — new train station and renewal of an adjoining urban district

◆ — **closed city block**

🏷 — Prägnanz; geometric principle; additive approach; orthogonal grid; layout of building lots: grouping; place making through assembly; representation: illustrative site plan, presentation model

The closed blocks clearly define and separate public and private open spaces.

Model

The Inner-City Urban Block

The dense, inner-city urban block presents a special case. The ground floor area is sometimes entirely reserved for commercial purposes, the internal courtyard is minimal in size due to the high site utilization, and residential use that reflects today's standards is only possible on the top floors.

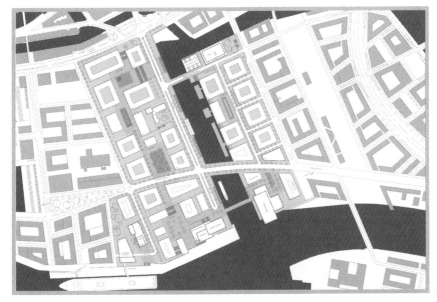

In the compact inner-city urban block, residential use is only possible on the uppermost floors.

Digital model

🎯 — **Magdeburger Hafen/Übersee-quartier, HafenCity,** Hamburg (D)

✏️ — David Chipperfield Architects, Berlin, with Wirtz International Landscape Architects, Schoten

🖥️ — www.davidchipperfield.com

🏆 — 4th prize

📅 — 2003

📁 — urban redevelopment – harbor conversion – new urban district

◈ — **closed city block/inner-city urban block**

🔖 — additive approach and superimposition; orthogonal grid; layout of building lots: grouping; place making through assembly; waterfront development

The Opened-Up City Block

In this variant, the block's continuous perimeter is decomposed into townhouses, individual houses, and/or apartment buildings, although spatially the block still remains clearly legible. Gaps enable views into the inner portion of the block and, conversely, from there out to the public realm. The opened-up city block meets the call for better ventilation and natural lighting, and freer corner conditions make it possible to avoid the difficulties of the problematic northeast corner. Compared to the courtyard of a closed perimeter block, however, the block's interior is more susceptible to disturbances such as traffic noise. A variant of opened-up city blocks are U-shaped structures. The orientation is determined by the context, for example closed to the street space and open to the landscape, the water, a greenbelt, etc.

The dissolved city block fosters ventilation and natural lighting.

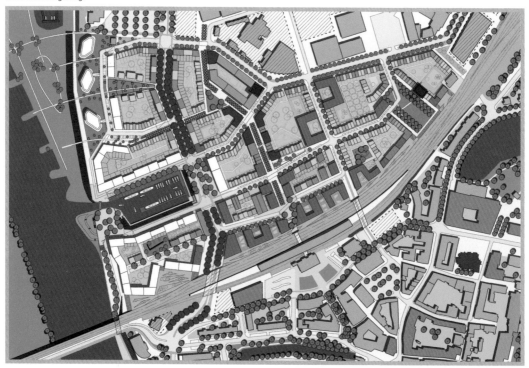

⊙° — **Noorderhaven,** Zutphen (NL)

✎ — KCAP Architects&Planners, Rotterdam/Zürich/Shanghai

🖥 — www.kcap.eu

📅 — 2007

🗂 — urban redevelopment – harbor conversion – new urban district

◈ — **dissolved city block**

🏷 — biomorphic/organic principle; additive approach; place making through assembly and modeling; bent and widened street space; community/adjacent green and open space

Bird's-eye perspective

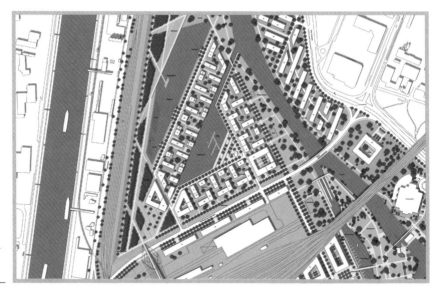

The buildings away from the water also offer visual connections to the Neckar.

Waterfront living

 — **Master Plan for Neckarvorstadt,** Heilbronn (D)

— Steidle Architekten with t17 Landschaftsarchitekten, Munich

— www.steidle-architekten.de

— 1st prize

— 2009

— urban redevelopment — railway/commercial conversion — new district

— **dissolved city block**

— geometric principle; additive approach; layout of building lots: hierarchy, datum; district-level/community/adjacent green and open space; integrated green space;

— waterfront living

- ⊘ — **Residential district in the European Quarter,** Frankfurt a. M. (D)
- ✎ — rohdecan architekten with Till Rehwaldt, Dresden
- ▣ — www.rohdecan.de
- ◉ — 3rd prize
- ▦ — 2002
- ◱ — urban redevelopment – railway conversion – new urban district
- ◈ — **dissolved city block**
- ◆ — Prägnanz; contrast; robustness; geometric principle; additive approach; orthogonal
  grid, layout of building lots: axis, (partial) symmetry, hierarchy, datum, sequencing/
  repetition

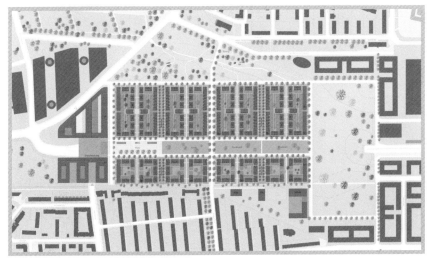

The spatially defining effect of the city blocks is not diminished by the intentional gaps.

Model

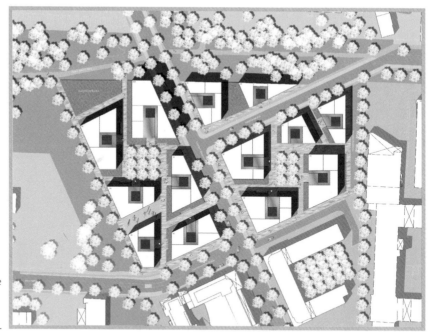

The city blocks dissolve into sculptural points, yet the outer building lines remain.

Perspective of neighborhood square

🎯 — **Pelikan Viertel,** Hannover (D)

📝 — pfp architekten, Hamburg

🖥 — www.pfp-architekten.de

🔍 — 2nd stage participant

📅 — 2009

🗂 — urban redevelopment — commercial conversion — new urban district

📑 — **dissolved city block**

🏷 — divisional approach; layout of development sites: grouping; place making through assembly; representation: illustrative site plan, perspective

The Courtyard Building

The courtyard building is, figuratively speaking, a city block turned inside out. Access is gained via the block's interior, the courtyard, which thereby obtains a shared or public character. Ideally the gardens and private outdoor spaces are located on the side of the building facing away from the courtyard. These outdoor spaces should not lie directly along the street, which can be avoided by cleverly positioning other building forms. In the Viennese courtyard housing from the period between the world wars (see page 77 f.), private open spaces were deliberately omitted with the intention of strengthening the feeling of community in the workers' housing.

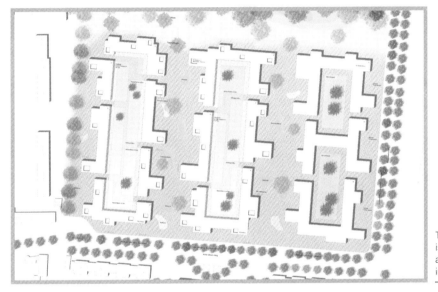

The courtyard building is, figuratively speaking, a city block turned inside out.

🎯 — **Rennplatz-Nord Development Zone,** Regensburg (D)

✏ — 03 Architekten with Keller Damm Roser Landschaftsarchitekten Stadtplaner GmbH, Munich

🖥 — www.03arch.de

🏆 — 3rd prize

📅 — 2010

🗂 — urban redevelopment – new residential districts

◆ — **courtyard**

🔖 — Prägnanz (internal boundaries); additive approach; community green and open space; individual trees; representation: figure-ground plan

Figure-ground plan (poche plan)

The compact courtyard housing blocks are islands within the park landscape.

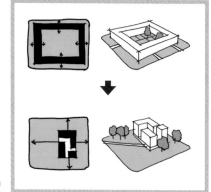

Diagram of design idea

— **Gutleutmatten District,** Freiburg im Breisgau (D)

— ASTOC Architects and Planners with urbane gestalt, Johannes Böttger Landschaftsarchitekten, Cologne

— www.astoc.de

— 1st prize

— 2010

— urban expansion – new urban district

— **Courtyard**

— geometric principle; additive approach; layout of development sites: repetition/rhythm; cul-de-sac network; district-level green and open space, flowing green space;

— representation: diagrams

The access zone is likewise a residential courtyard with small private gardens.

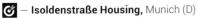

🌐 — **Isoldenstraße Housing,** Munich (D)

✏️ — LÉON WOHLHAGE WERNIK with J. Menzer, H. J. Lankes and ST raum a. Landschaftsarchitekten, Berlin

🖥️ — www.leonwohlhagewernik.de

⚙️ — 1st prize

📅 — 2003

🗂️ — urban redevelopment – commercial conversion – new residential district

🗂️ — **courtyard**

🖐️ — additive approach; layout of development sites: sequence/repetition/rhythm; district-level/community/adjacent green and open space

Visualization of residential courtyard and green corridor

119

Directional Development Rows and Zeilen

The Row

The row, like the block, is among the oldest building forms. Excavations in Egyptian Tell el-Amarna attest to a workers' settlement with a system of row houses dating back to the fourteenth century BC. In Europe, the row has its origin in single-street villages, where the farmsteads were on both sides of the village road and strips of farmland extended out from the rear of the buildings. Medieval cities are characterized by rows of residential houses that join to form blocks of continuous buildings. The eighteenth century saw row houses assembled to create imposing large-scale forms, such as the Royal Crescent in the English spa town of Bath, built in 1767 by John Wood, the Younger.

Rows can be formed with freestanding, semidetached, or attached houses – whether single- or multifamily units – of the same or different heights. As with a block, access is gained via a straight or curved street running parallel to the building, and with certain building types, also from a paved front zone with parking or a small front yard that establishes a setback. The private open space is usually behind the house, so that the row also clearly separates the public sphere from the private. Especially if built in a solid, closed manner, the row appears as a space-defining element in the urban space. In principle, it can be continued endlessly; to interconnect building lots sensibly, however, it is necessary to limit the length.

Since single-family row house types should naturally have individual private gardens, the orientation of the rows is crucial. While townhouses with yards facing south or west can be marketed and sold easily, yards facing east are not in great demand except in very popular dense urban areas.

Inner-city row houses are also called townhouses. These can be integrated into a parcelized perimeter block without any problems. Especially if additional uses (retail, parking, etc.) are accommodated at the ground level, orientation plays a lesser role than with the suburban type. Apartments can be laid out as through-units on the first upper floor and to both sides on the floors above.

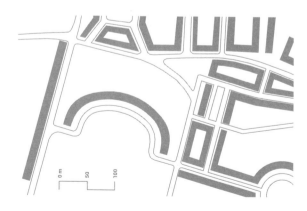

ROYAL CRESCENT IN BATH, John Wood, the Younger, 1767 (GB)

- **Western Fringe Development and Restructuring,** Cologne-Roggendorf/Thenhoven (D)
- Dr. Michael Hecker, Architekt+Stadtplaner with urbane gestalt, Johannes Böttger Landschaftsarchitekten, Cologne
- www.hmw-architekten.de
- 1st prize
- 2011
- urban redevelopment – railway conversion – new residential districts
- **row**
- contrast; additive approach; layout of development sites: sequence/repetition/rhythm; bent and widened street space

The design idea is inspired by the existing village's linear settlement pattern, which is characteristic for the area.

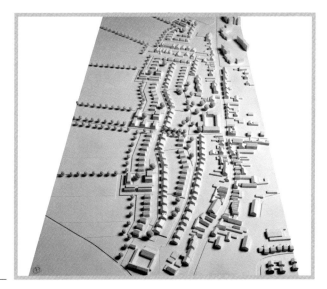

Model

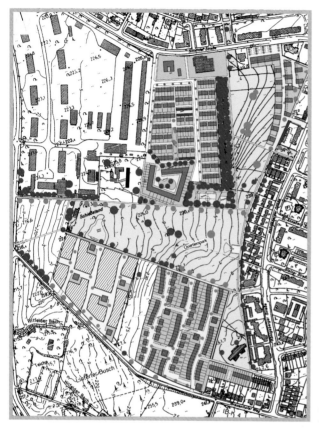

 — **Grauenhofer Weg,** Aachen-Forst (D)

— Baufrösche Architekten und Stadtplaner with Planungsgemeinschaft
Landschaft + Freiraum, Kassel

— www.baufroesche.de

— 1st prize

— 1999

— urban expansion – new residential
districts

— row

— additive approach; irregular grid;
additional components: Zeile (north
section), open city block; place
making through exclusion/omission;
— linear/curved, widened street space

Rows, as opposed to
Zeilen, define space
– as a comparison of
these two residential
areas demonstrates.
Unlike with rows, the
gardens associated
with the Zeile are
optimally oriented to
the south.

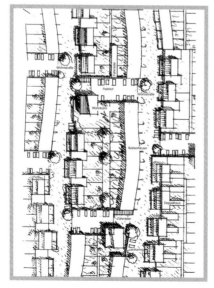

Detailing of the private
and public open spaces

The Zeile

As a modern alternative to the block and the row, the latter was refined and developed further into what is known in German as the Zeile. By uncoupling the row from the access road to create the Zeile, the orientation could be optimized according to the Modernist slogan "light, air, and sun for all" and motor vehicles were separated from pedestrian traffic.

With regard to housing forms, Zeilen – just like blocks and ordinary rows – are adaptable and can be composed of townhouses, maisonettes, and single-level apartments (either with stairwells or external access galleries). The building shapes are also greatly varied, ranging from linear or bent housing blocks of two or more stories to high-rise slabs.

Historical examples of Neues Bauen (New Building) from the late 1920s are the Siedlung Dammerstock in Karlsruhe by Walter Gropius and the Siedlung Westhausen in Frankfurt by Ernst May, which was constructed somewhat later. Inherent to both housing developments is the rigid repetition of identically oriented units of row houses and apartment buildings that are aligned perpendicular to the streets. Whereas Dammerstock is still fairly traditional in that the buildings flank both sides of a shared path, Westhausen has a serial pattern in which each building has its own footpath at the rear.

SIEDLUNG DAMMERSTOCK IN KARLSRUHE, Walter Gropius, 1928 (D)

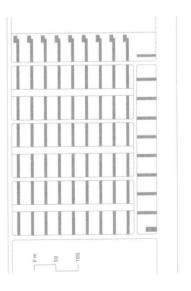

SIEDLUNG WESTHAUSEN IN FRANKFURT A. M., Ernst May, 1929 (D)

Few other urban building blocks are as controversial as the Zeile. Critics accuse it of negating urban space because the buildings are positioned freely in space or because only the first and last buildings in each row are positioned along the street space. Residential use can also suffer from the weak differentiation between public and private open space, because the usual serial arrangement of buildings means that the access path for one building runs in front of the open space of the adjacent one. Proponents emphasize that in development with Zeilen, all apartments are optimally oriented and car-free neighborhoods can be established.

The Zeile still has a firm place in the repertoire of urban designers, though the dogmatism and radicalism of the Modern era have largely disappeared. Zeilen are now used for both office buildings and housing, sometimes in combination with other urban building blocks, like punctiform buildings.

This small, car-free housing complex consists of a short Zeile of duplexes and townhouses, which are set perpendicular to the communal space.

West elevation with assembly hall (r.)

⟲ — **Das bezahlbare eigene Haus (The affordable single-family house),** Bamberg (D)

✏ — Melchior, Eckey, Rommel, Stuttgart

▭ — www.marcus-rommel-architekten.de

◉ — 1st prize

▦ — 1997

▱ — inner-city development – car-free neighborhood

◈ — **Zeile**

◆ — additive approach; layout of development sites: datum, repetition/rhythm, grouping; layout of urban building blocks on building lot: datum, sequence; place making

___ through assembly

With the simple combination of a Zeile and points, some of which are also connected together, the designers succeed in creating a great diversity of public and private open spaces.

View of the central green corridor

☌ — **Gartenstadt Falkenberg,** Berlin (D)

✏ — Architekten BDA Quick Bäckmann Quick & Partner, Berlin

🖥 — www.qbq-architekten.de

☊ — 1st prize

📅 — 1992

🗂 — urban expansion — extension of Bruno Taut's Garden City Falkenberg from 1913

◈ — **Zeile**

◈ — additive approach; additional components: row, point, combination of Zeile and point; cul-de-sac network, place making through exclusion/omission; integrated green space, representation: Illustrative site plan; perspective

Punctiform Buildings

Points

As a building form, points have their origin in rural settlement patterns. Farmsteads, usually comprising two or three freestanding buildings, are grouped rather haphazardly in clustered villages, whereas in single-street (linear) villages, by contrast, they are lined up along the street.

The prototype for contemporary punctiform residential buildings is the upper-class villa. Derived from it is the freestanding single-family house, which is also often used in its more economical form of a duplex (semidetached) house. So-called urban villas are commonly built as apartment buildings. This is a compact and distinctive, three- to five-story building type that has two or three units per floor and also can be used commercially. The advantages of a punctiform building are the possibility for a unique address, a limited number of dwelling units, and very good exposure to daylight for all the apartments.

Points are flexible urban building blocks: They can be added together or placed in rows, and moreover, they can be positioned independently from the street.

With punctiform buildings, their dimensions are an important indicator of economic efficiency because the amount of circulation space must be in due proportion to the usable floor area. Urban villas, for example, can only be economically built with a minimum size of 15 × 15 meters. Vertical points like high-rise buildings need a much larger footprint.

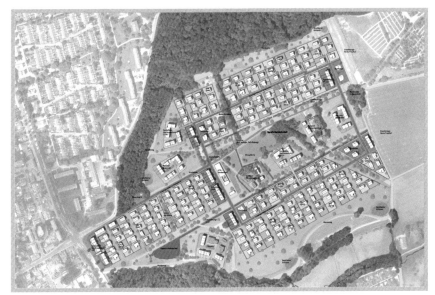

The predominant
settlement pattern
comprises points –
detached single-family
and duplex houses
arranged in rows or
groups.

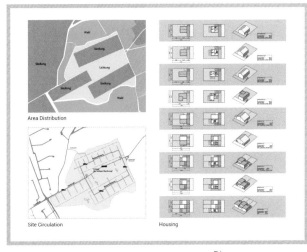

Diagrams

 — **Knollstraße Residential Development,** Osnabrück (D)

— ASTOC Architects and Planners, Cologne, with Lützow 7, Berlin

— www.astoc.de

— 1st prize

— 2006

— settlement extension – new residential district

— **point**

— additive approach; layout of development sites: datum, grouping; layout of urban building blocks on building lot: repetition/sequence, grouping; circulation loop

Vertical Points/High-Rise Towers

High-rise towers constitute a special case within the group of points. A high-rise is a building of at least approximately eight floors. High-rise towers can accommodate residential, commercial, or mixed uses. Due to the large number of dwellings they contain, high-rise residential buildings are viewed as an anonymous housing form that is less suitable for families but well-suited for singles and young couples, for service-oriented luxury living, or for pieds-à-terre and hotels.

Whereas the residential high-rise still represents more of an exception in Europe despite numerous unbuilt projects in the 1950s through the 1970s, it has meanwhile become a standard building block in the megacities of Asia, in part due to the steep angle of the sun near the equator. In most other regions, the residential high-rise generally has more of a solitary character, if only because of the spacing needed between them.

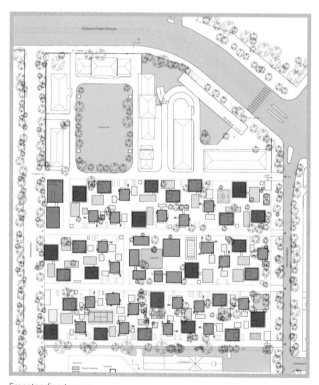

Freestanding towers of different heights are positioned in a flowing and flexible open space.

Model

⌖ — **Werkbundsiedlung Wiesenfeld,** Munich (D)

✐ — Kazunari Sakamoto with Ove Arup, Tokyo

🖥 — www.arch.titech.ac.jp/sakamoto_lab

🏆 — Prizewinner (urban design), 1st prize after 2nd stage

📅 — 2006

🗂 — urban redevelopment – military conversion – new residential district

◈ — **point, high-rise tower**

⬚ — additive approach; orthogonal grid; flowing green space

Spatial Structures

In contrast to the standard blocklike, linear, or punctiform building blocks, spatial structures occupy more area and space. Spatial structures include clusters, carpet developments with corner bungalows or atrium houses, and a repeatedly bent Zeilen such as molecular structures and meanders.

Carpet Development

Carpet development refers to an arrangement of buildings that resembles a woven, textile structure. Carpet patterns have their origin in the Mediterranean region, where narrow streets and alleys provide necessary shade and introverted housing types are often climatically and culturally based. But also in more temperate regions, courtyard houses enjoy great popularity: they offer protected privacy combined with generous living space on one or two stories, as well as high building density with relatively low building heights. Access is usually gained via a system of pedestrian pathways and, if desired, shared open spaces can be carved out from the built fabric when being designed. Problematic is the lack of a unique address, especially for buildings in the second or third row, and parking, which can be partially accommodated within the building but must be supplemented by parking lots. Exemplary settlements with courtyard houses are the Garden City Puchenau (Upper Austria) from the 1960s or the Tamariskengasse housing development in Vienna, completed in 1992 by Roland Rainer.

The layout of the buildings resembles a woven textile pattern.

 – **Am Bergfeld Residential District,** Poing/Munich (D)

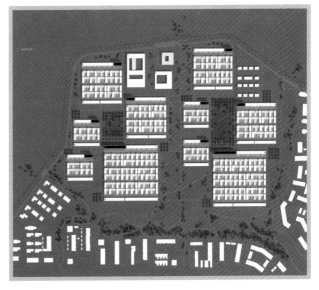

– keiner balda architekten, Fürstenfeldbruck, with Johann Berger, Freising

– www.keiner-balda.de

– 4th prize

– 2007

– urban expansion – new residential districts

– **spatial structure/carpet development**

– Prägnanz; contrast; geometric principle, additive approach; additional components: row, Zeile/high-rise slab, point; place making through assembly, tight grid of trees

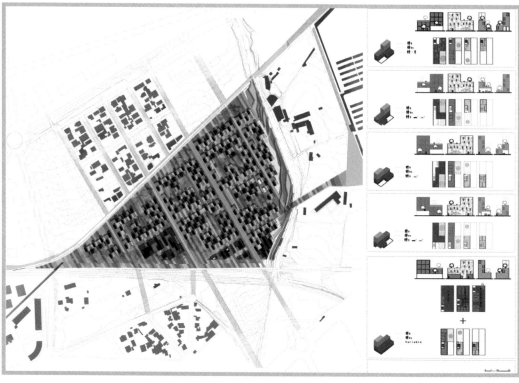

The traditional courtyard house is transformed into an apartment building.

Perspective

🎯 — **Europan 10, PIXELES URBANOS (URBAN PIXELS),** Reus (ES)

✏️ — Florian Ingmar Bartholome, Ludwig Jahn, José Ulloa Davet, Barcelona

🖥️ — http://europaconcorsi.com/projects/119706-Pixeles-Urbanos-

🏅 — honorable mention

📅 — 2010

🗂️ — urban expansion – new residential district

📑 — **spatial structure/carpet development**

🔖 — additive approach; orthogonal grid;
____ integrated green space

Clusters

A cluster in urban design refers to an accumulation of buildings grouped together very closely. Historical residential clusters include the pueblos, the terraced settlements of the Pueblo Indians in the border area between the US and Mexico.

Modern planned clusters were built primarily in the 1960s and into the 1970s. Due to many disadvantages, new projects of this sort are rarely encountered today. One of the best-known examples is the Habitat 67 housing development, which was designed by the architect Moshe Safdie for the 1967 Universal Exhibition in Montreal. It comprises 148 cubic dwelling units stacked like mounds up to ten stories high.[6] The quality of living is, on the one hand, very high due to the numerous resulting roof terraces and diverse opportunities for outward views, but on the other hand, each of the individual apartments or house units does not have a clear address and the access paths within the complex are confusing and often too long; moreover, beneath the terracing there are heavily shaded areas and numerous unattractive soffits. Last but not least, the energy efficiency of clustered structures is significantly handicapped by an unfavorable surface-area-to-volume (SA/V) ratio inherent in the system.

---

[6] For further info on Moshe Safdie's Habitat 67, see http://www.habitat67.com.

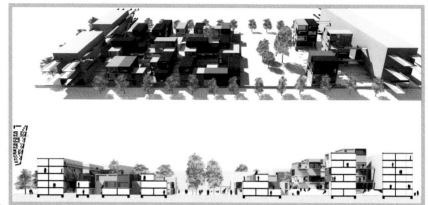

In urban design, *cluster* refers to an accumulation of buildings grouped together very closely.

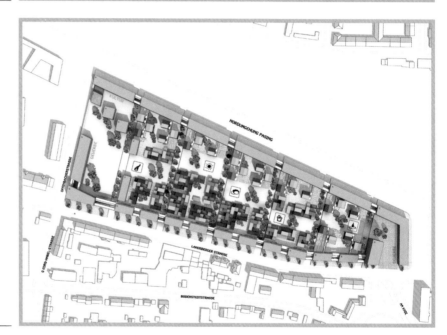

Illustrative site plan

— **Former Freight Yard,** Munich-Pasing (D)

— Daniel Ott and Robin Schraml, Berlin

— www.robinschraml.com

— 2010

— urban redevelopment – railway conversion – new urban district

— **spatial structure/clusters**

— additive approach; additional components: row, point, combination of row and point; layout of development sites: datum, repetition/rhythm, grouping; place making through exclusion/omission; representation: section

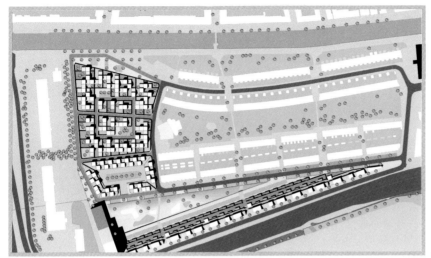

Like with an Indian pueblo, the upper terrace apartments are accessed across the roofs of the apartments below.

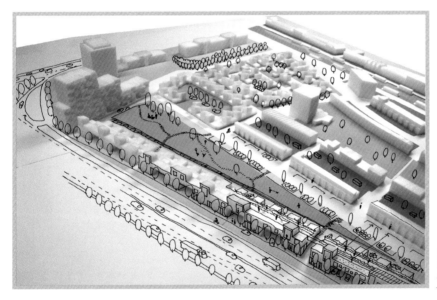

Rendering made by sketching over a photo of the working model

⚙ — **Intense Laagbouw De Meeuwen,** Groningen (NL)

✎ — DeZwarteHond, Groningen/Rotterdam

🖥 — www.dezwartehond.nl

📅 — 2009

🗂 — urban redevelopment − inner-city development − new residential district and office building

◈ — **spatial structure/clusters**

🔖 — additive approach; additional components: carpet development, high-rise; place making through exclusion/omission; representation: working model

Molecular Structures and Meanders

In postwar modernity, pure Zeilen arrangements were soon criticized as too monot-onous and boring. Beginning in 1960 and until the energy crisis in 1973, the model of the "green and spacious city" that had prevailed from 1950 to 1960 was replaced by the guiding principle of "urbanity through density." As a chief cause for the lack of urbanity, the protagonists identified insufficient residential density. For ideologi-cal reasons, the planners were not inclined to resort to traditional building forms like the city block. As a solution, they instead proposed a bent or meandering Zeilen placed freely in space, independent of the street. Examples can be found as strings of high-rise buildings and molecular-like, branched housing in Märkisches Viertel in Berlin or in the vast Bijlmermeer housing estate in the Netherlands, a Zeile that consists of a honeycomb pattern of eleven-story buildings that wind through the green space.

Today there is no dispute that – along with diversity, density, and a functional mix – architecturally defined public space plays a crucial role in the development of urbanism. Meander patterns can help here if the meander purposefully defines different areas. Thus a meander can be used to establish buildings running along streets as well as public squares, semipublic courtyards, and private rear garden areas.

**MÄRKISCHES VIERTEL IN
BERLIN,** Werner Düttmann
et al., 1963 (D)

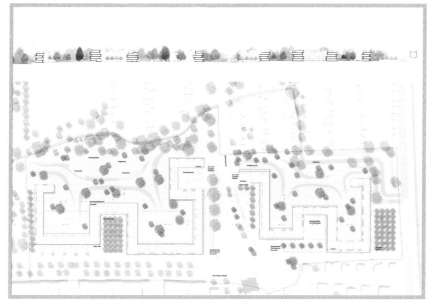

Meander patterns can emerge from buildings that follow the streets, and they can also encompass public squares, semipublic courtyards, and rear green areas.

Figure-ground plan (poche plan)

🎯 — **Gutleutmatten District,** Freiburg im Breisgau (D)

✏️ — 03 Architekten, Munich, with Lex Kerfers Landschaftsarchitekten, Bockhorn

🖥️ — www.03arch.de

🏆 — honorable mention

📅 — 2010

🗂️ — inner-city development – new residential district

🗂️ — **spatial structure/meanders**

🔖 — large-scale/grand form, place making through modeling; intermittent, widened street space; integrated green space, casually grouped trees,

___ representation: figure-ground plan

The meandering plan shape combines city block and courtyard.

Model

⚙ — **Isoldenstraße Housing,** Munich (D)

✍ — Georg Scheel Wetzel Architekten, Berlin, with Dr. Bernhard Korte, Grevenbroich

🖥 — www.georgscheelwetzel.com

🏆 — 3rd prize

📅 — 2003

🗂 — urban redevelopment – commercial conversion – new residential district

◆ — **spatial structure/meanders**

🏷 — additive approach; layout of building lots: sequence/rhythm; integrated green space

Solitary Buildings

A solitary building, a term derived from the Latin word *solitarius* (isolated, alone), is used in architecture and urban design to refer to a freestanding, compact, and spatially dominant building that stands out clearly from the surrounding area. Historical examples are temples, castles, churches, and town halls.

A solitary building radiates in several directions and acts as an urban landmark.[7] Thus the building's proportions and the design of its facade have special importance. In addition to the traditional large building blocks mentioned above, and depending on the urban context, standard building blocks can also develop a solitary character: dense blocks as sculptural elements, vertical points in the form of residential or administrative towers, or Zeilen in the form of high-rise slab buildings.

Freestanding buildings occupy the beginning and the end of the elongated green space.

☑ — **Siemens Site Isar-Süd,** Munich (D)

☑ — JSWD Architekten with Lill + Sparla, Cologne

☐ — www.jswd-architekten.de

☐ — 1st prize

☐ — 2002

☐ — urban redevelopment – continued development of a commercial site – new urban district

◆ — **freestanding building**

◆ — additive approach; orthogonal grid; additional components: closed, dissolved city block, row; layout building lot: grouping; green space delimited by buildings

Bird's-eye perspective

7 Kevin Lynch, *The Image of the City* (Cambridge, MA: MIT Press, 1960), p. 96 ff.

Hybrids

Hybrids are an exceptional case within the group of standard building blocks. One speaks of hybrids when the characteristics of an urban building block is combined with those of at least one other to form a new building complex. The merger usually occurs horizontally, vertically, or through transformation of the building form.

Examples of Horizontally Combined Hybrids

Combination of block and Zeile into a comblike, toothed structure: the street provides access to the spine from the exterior, as with a perimeter block, and the internal teeth are reached via the courtyards as with Zeilen. The reverse principle is also possible, in which case the teeth point toward the street and access is gained via forecourts between them.

Meander patterns[8] can also be understood as hybrids of block, courtyard, row, and/or Zeile types.

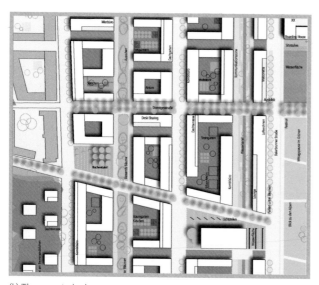

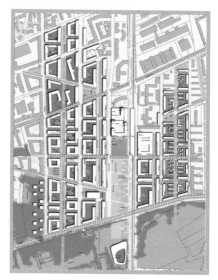

(l.) The repeated urban building block is a combination of city block and courtyard that opens like a square to the public realm.

(r.) Illustrative site plan

- ⟳ — **Siemens Site Isar-Süd,** Munich (D)
- ▨ — pp a|s pesch partner architekten stadtplaner, Herdecke/Stuttgart
- ▣ — www.pesch-partner.de
- ◉ — 2nd prize
- ▦ — 2002
- ▭ — urban redevelopment — continued development of a commercial site — new urban district
- ◈ — **hybrid of city block and courtyard**
- ◆ — additive approach and superimposition; additional components: closed, dissolved city block, Zeile, point, freestanding building; place making through assembly; green
- —— space delimited by buildings

8 See also Molecular Structures and Meanders , p. 134 ff.

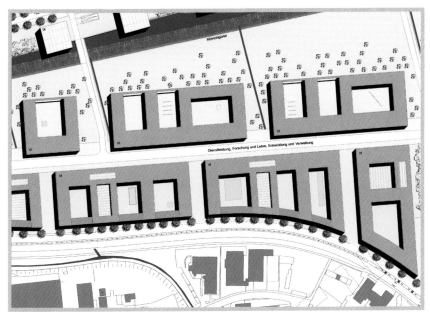

The toothed, multiwing structures are closed off in various ways, as a glazed bridge, transparent protection against noise, or a visual enclosure.

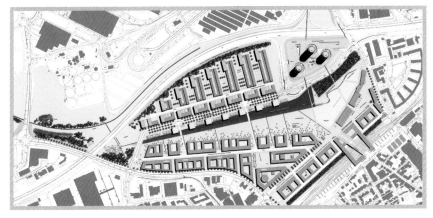

Illustrative site plan

⊙ — **Former Airport Grounds,** Böblingen/Sindelfingen (D)

✎ — ap'plan mory osterwalder vielmo architekten und ingenieurgesellschaft mbh with Kienle Planungsgesellschaft Freiraum und Städtebau mbH, Stuttgart

▣ — www.applan.de

⚙ — 1st prize

▦ — 2000

▭ — urban redevelopment – airport conversion – new district and industrial park

◈ — **hybrid toothed structures**

◆ — contrast; additive approach; additional components: large building block, closed, dissolved city block, freestanding building; place making through assembly; waterfront development

The hybrid of city block and point mediates between the main arterial road and the freestanding buildings.

View of the point-like element that anchors the perimeter block

⊙ — **Funkkaserne Nord Barracks Redevelopment,** Munich (D)

✏ — LÉON WOHLHAGE WERNIK with Atelier Loidl, Berlin

▣ — www.leonwohlhagewernik.de

◉ — 1st prize

🗓 — 2012

🗀 — urban redevelopment – military conversion – new residential district

◈ — **hybrid of city block and point**

◆ — additive approach; layout of development sites: axis, sequence/repetition/rhythm;
— representation: perspective

Examples of Vertically Combined Hybrids

Combinations of a city block with a high-rise: the high-rise building evolves from the perimeter block or is placed on top of the perimeter block.

Combination of a city block with points or Zeilen: the first stories of closed perimeter block development are fully or mostly dedicated to commercial use. Atop this are Zeilen in the form of townhouses or points in the form of multifamily urban villas or single-family homes.

The combination of high-rise tower and city block sets architectural accents and delimits the urban space toward the railroad.

Detail of model

⚙ — **Mannheim 21 Redevelopment Area,** Mannheim (D)

✎ — ASTOC Architects and Planners, Cologne, with WES Partner Landschaftsarchitekten, Hamburg

🖥 — www.astoc.de

◎ — 1st prize

📅 — 2002

📂 — urban redevelopment – railway conversion – new urban district

◆ — **hybrid of city block and high-rise tower**

🏷 — additive approach; additional components: dissolved city block, inner-city urban block; green space delimited by buildings

Examples of Transformation

A combination of Zeile and block types emerges, for instance, through the transformation of Zeilen that is either bent in plan or has wider ends to form an entry court or garden courtyard – possibly in combination with other projections and recesses in the building.

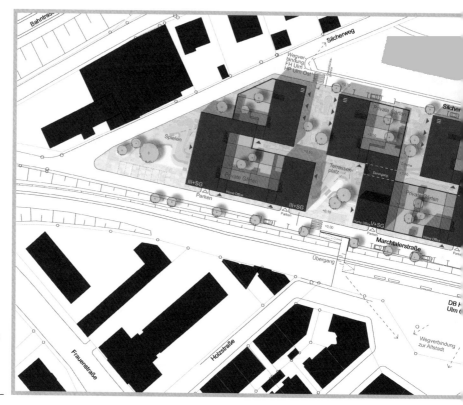

Small change – big impact: by joining Zeilen but also shifting them in relation to one another, differentiated urban spaces are formed.

 — **Marchtaler Straße,** Ulm (D)

— studioinges Architektur und Städtebau with H. J. Lankes, Berlin

— www.studioinges.de

— 1st prize

— 2005

— urban redevelopment – commercial conversion – new residential district

— **transformed Zeile**

— additive approach; place making through assembly; community/adjacent green and open space

Perspective and
dwelling unit stacking
diagram

The transverse units at the ends of the rows in a Zeile act as space-defining terminations.

Detail of model

- **Residential district in the European Quarter,** Frankfurt am Main (D)
- b17 Architekten BDA , Munich
- www.kuehleis-architekten.de, www.delaossa.de
- merit award
- 2002
- urban redevelopment – railway conversion – new urban district
- **transformed Zeile**
- additive approach; additional components: urban building blocks: row; place making through assembly; integrated green space

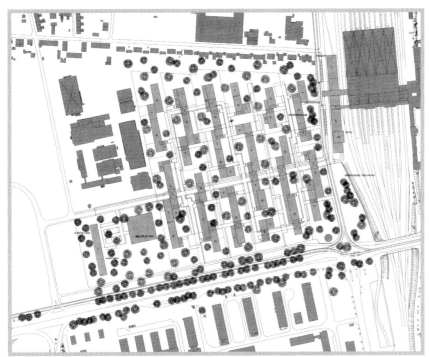

The varied projections and recesses create differentiated intermediate spaces.

View in one of the intermediate spaces

- **Westufer Hauptbahnhof ,** Darmstadt (D)
- Atelier COOPERATION Architekten & Ingenieure, Frankfurt am Main
- www.atelier-cooperation.de
- merit award
- 1996
- urban redevelopment – commercial conversion – new residential district
- **transformed Zeile**
- additive approach; cul-de-sac network, loop street network; flowing green space

7 The Layout of Development Sites, Building Lots, and Urban Building Blocks

— INSTEAD of beginning by assembling the smallest parts – the buildings – with urban design it is more sensible to start at a level higher with the building lots, and for larger schemes, with districts and development sites.[1] This facilitates the design process and also plays an important role in the overall life cycle of a city. After all, the city layout is significantly more persistent than the buildings on the individual lots.

1 Helmut Bott, "Stadtraum und Gebäudetypologie im Entwurf," in *Lehrbausteine Städtebau: Basiswissen für Entwurf und Planung*, 6th ed., ed. Johannes Jessen and Franz Pesch (Stuttgart: Städtebau-Inst., 2010), p. 150 ff.

7.1 PRINCIPLES FOR COMBINING DEVELOPMENT SITES INTO LARGER URBAN DISTRICTS AND BUILDING LOTS INTO DEVELOPMENT SITES

Building Lot

A building lot is buildable land on which "a contiguous and functionally coherent, self-contained building group and development unit can be conceived."[2]

Development Site

A development site brings together a group of two or more building lots that are related in terms of design or function. A self-contained development site can also be referred to as a (building) district or neighborhood.

The arrangement, location, shape, and size of the building lots or development sites is determined by the context, the topography, the opportunities for establishing links to the existing fabric or the landscape, the selected building types, and by the design goals. The buildings are then situated on the building lots according to the respective constraints.

With the general organizing principles and the assembly types, important design strategies have already been dealt with in depth with regard to the overall design. Beyond these, there are other, more specific organizing principles that the urban designer can draw upon. These principles are helpful at all scales of urban composition. To begin with, they shall be presented as the means for combining development sites into a larger urban district and – one level below – for combining building lots into a development site, district, or neighborhood. Then these principles will be applied to the arrangement of urban building blocks on building lots.

Axis

An axis is a straight line extending between two points, along which buildings, public squares, parks, districts, or building lots can be arranged. For logical reasons, the starting point (A) and endpoint (B) should be assigned functions of overriding importance so that the axis extends along a self-evident path between A and B.

In many concepts for ideal cities, monumental streets lined with buildings are defined with symmetrically assembled elements and components. In practice, however, the arrangement is less rigorous. As a general rule, the arrangement of elements along the entire length should be balanced as a whole. Additionally, the spatial presence of an axis will increase in proportion with how distinctly its boundaries are defined and its start and end points are marked.[3]

2 Ibid., p. 150.
3 Francis D. K. Ching, *Architecture: Form, Space, & Order* (New York: Wiley, 1979), p. 334 ff.

The new urban districts
are lined up along the
axial rapid transit line.

Green corridors
extend out to the open
landscape.

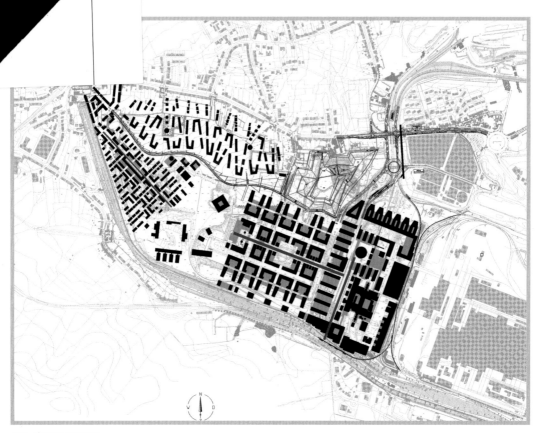

Axes give structure to three urban districts: the western residential district, the Hochofen-terrasse, with its link to the new train station, and the Square Mile, the central residential and business district.

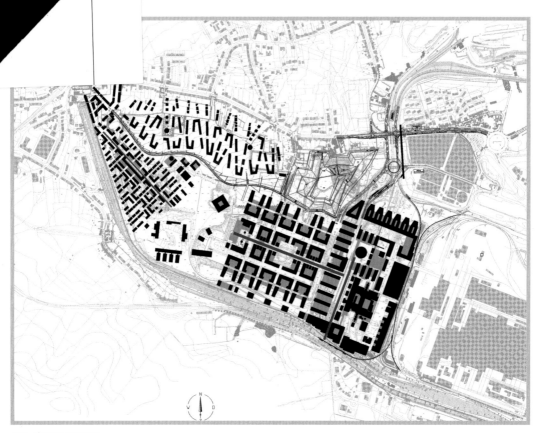 — **Belval-Ouest,** Esch-sur-Alzette (L)

— Jo Coenen Architects & Urbanists, Rolo Fütterer, Maastricht, with Buro Lubbers, 's-Hertogenbosch

— www.jocoenen.com, www.mars-group.eu

— 1st prize

— 2002

— urban redevelopment – industrial conversion – new district

— **layout of building lots: axis, symmetry**

— Prägnanz; contrast; urban building blocks: closed, dissolved city block, row, point; place making through assembly and modeling; linear and curved street spaces

Illustrative site plan

Bird's-eye perspective

THE LAYOUT OF DEVELOPMENT SITES, BUILDING LOTS, AND URBAN BUILDING BLOCKS

The heavily frequented
public areas lie on
the pedestrian axis
between the city and
the river.

Bird's-eye perspective

View from the Rachel
Carson Bridge

- **RiverParc Development,** Pittsburgh (US)
- Behnisch Architekten, Stuttgart, with architectsAlliance, Toronto, Gehl Architects, Copenhagen, WTW Architects, Pittsburgh
- www.behnisch.com
- 1st prize
- 2006
- urban redevelopment – commercial conversion – new urban district
- **layout of building lots: axis**
- additive approach; irregular orthogonal grid; representation: perspective

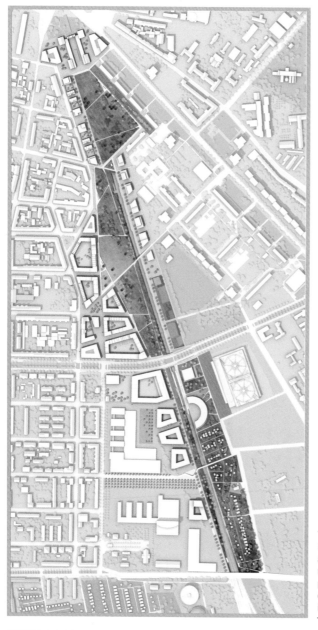

⊕ — **Bayerischer Bahnhof Redevelopment Area,** Leipzig (D)

✎ — Wessendorf Architektur Städtebau with Atelier Loidl Landschaftsarchitekten, Berlin

▭ — www.studio-wessendorf.de, www.atelier-loidl.de

⚲ — 1st prize

📅 — 2011

🗂 — urban redevelopment – railway conversion – realignment of urban districts

◈ — **layout of development sites: axis**

◈ — additive approach; urban building blocks: closed city block, inner-city urban block, Zeile, point; place making through assembly; representation: diagrams

The urban space is threaded along alternate sides of the railway line and the new perimeter development derives from the existing fabric.

Diagrams of the design concept

Symmetry

The origin of the term *symmetry* lies in the ancient Greek word *symmetría* (proportion, from *summetros*, of like measure: "syn-" + "metron" measure).[4] Symmetry thus represents a balanced, equal arrangement of parts within a whole. Two types of symmetry can be distinguished:

• With axial symmetry, also known as bilateral symmetry, objects are mirrored along an axis. The figure and its reflection are congruent, but they are mirror images of one another. In urban design, this organizing principle results in a series of uniformly associated building volumes and/or spaces opening up to the left and right of the axis (e.g., street, public square, etc.).

• Point symmetry, also known as radial symmetry, forms an object by rotating around a central point at a specific angle. If the elements themselves are symmetrical and their axes of symmetry are aligned with the center of rotation, then point reflection yields additional radial axes of symmetry between the elements that also intersect the central point. An example from urban design would be a rond-point, or traffic circle, with evenly distributed radial streets and equally divided city blocks defining the public space.

Purely symmetrical compositions are seldom found in contemporary urban design, especially since for many people they represent a dominating, absolutist, or totalitarian order – due to their history – rather than a pluralistic and open democratic society.

As previously explained, symmetrical figures have a fundamental impact that quickly draws our attention; but this can potentially vanish just as quickly if the form is too simple. The attention-getting effect can be used, however, when partial symmetries are used in an otherwise free composition. Partial symmetries can achieve ordering effects while preserving the freedom of the overall composition. As a result, the composition is on the whole richer and more exciting.[5]

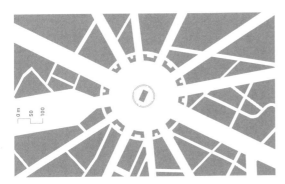

PLACE DE L'ÉTOILE IN PARIS, Georges-Eugène Haussmann, 1860 (F)

Partial symmetries establish order while preserving the freedom of the overall composition

4 http://www.thefreedictionary.com/symmetry (accessed January 7, 2013).
5 Rudolf Wienands, *Grundlagen der Gestaltung zu Bau und Stadtbau* (Basel/Boston/Stuttgart: Birkhäuser, 1985), p. 106.

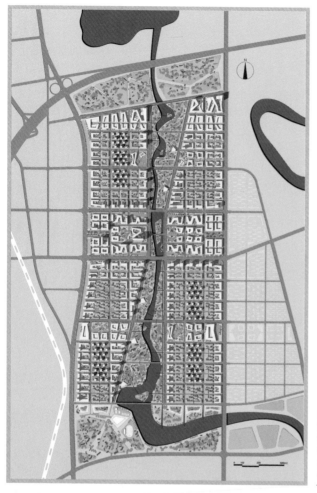

⌗ – **Qingdao Science and Technology City,** Quingdao (PRC)

☑ – KSP Jürgen Engel Architekten, Berlin/Braunschweig/Cologne/Frankfurt/Munich/Peking

⌨ – www.ksp-architekten.de

⌖ – 1st prize

🗓 – 2011

🗂 – urban expansion – new city

◈ – **layout of development sites: symmetry –** point symmetry

🏷 – Prägnanz; orthogonal grid; urban building blocks: closed and dissolved city blocks, inner-city urban block, courtyard, Zeile, point, high-rise tower, spatial structure, meanders, hybrid; district-level green and open space

In compositional terms, the unusual form of the elongated park is based on a 180-degree point reflection of the development sites.

Bird's-eye perspective

The sententious, roughly axisymmetrical subcenters give order to the entire area.

Bird's-eye perspective

 – **Changchun JingYue, Ecological City,** Changchun (PRC)

– AS&P – Albert Speer & Partner, Frankfurt am Main/Shanghai

– www.as-p.de

– 1st prize

– 2007

– urban expansion – new city

– **layout of development sites: symmetry** – partial symmetries

– additive approach and superimposition; layout of development sites: axis, hierarchy, datum, repetition/rhythm

Hierarchy

In an urban design, there are usually areas that are superior to others in the hierarchy. Functional reasons are often decisive: these areas contain major institutions, for example, or they are located on a central square. In addition, formal and symbolic differences can also be a reason for establishing hierarchy. Areas that are higher in the hierarchy set themselves apart from the largely standardized typical areas in terms of location, contour, layout, density, or form.[6]

Size/Density

A district or building lot that is measurably larger in size and density has a dominating effect on the other, smaller or less dense districts or building lots. Conversely, however, even a smaller or less dense district or building lot can assume a prominent position in the overall design.

⌖ — **College Campus Lange Lage,** Bielefeld (D)

✎ — pp als pesch partner architekten stadtplaner, Herdecke/Stuttgart, with Agence Ter, Karlsruhe/Paris

▣ — www.pesch-partner.de

⌗ — honorable mention

📅 — 2007

🗂 — urban expansion — new college campus

◈ — **layout of building lots: hierarchy —** size, density, layout

🏷 — superimposition; green space delimited by buildings

Due to its size and density, the college complex, set on the green corridor as an initial phase, appears dominant in relationship to the remaining building lots.

6 Here and below, see Ching, *Architecture*, p. 350 ff.

Contour/Shape

Areas can even appear dominant when the shape or contour of the development site or the district differs clearly from the other same-sized compositional elements. To avoid arbitrariness, however, the variant shape should be justified in functional or other substantive terms.

⊙ – **Potsdamer Platz/Leipziger Platz,** Berlin (D)

✎ – HILMER & SATTLER und ALBRECHT, Berlin/Munich, with G. and A. Hansjakob, Berlin

▣ – www.h-s-a.de

✪ – 1st prize

▦ – 1991

⬒ – urban repair – reconstruction of districts and squares

◈ – **layout of building lots: hierarchy –** size, density, form

◈ – geometric principle; urban building blocks: inner-city urban block, high-rise tower, hybrid; place making
___ through assembly and modeling

The hierarchically superior areas on both of the squares contrast in size, density, contour, and form from the remaining typical areas.

Model

Layout

Hierarchically superior areas can also be emphasized through their location and layout – for example, at the beginning or end of an axis, at the center of a development site or district, or as an independent adjacent area.

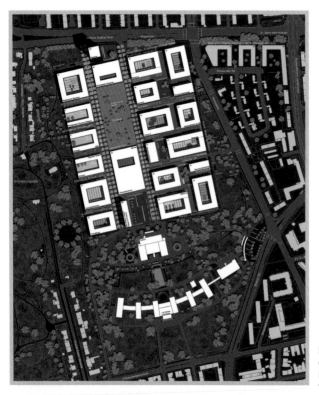

- Goethe University - Westend Campus, Frankfurt am Main (D)
- JSWD Architekten, Cologne, with KLA – Kiparlandschaftsarchitekten, Duisburg
- www.jswd-architekten.de
- merit award
- 2003
- urban redevelopment – military conversion – new college campus
- **layout of building lots: hierarchy –** layout
- Prägnanz; geometric principle; divisional approach; urban building blocks: closed, dissolved city block, high-rise tower; place making through exclusion/omission and assembly; integrated green space delimited by buildings

From the layout, the hierarchy of the buildings is legible.

Nighttime perspective

The hierarchically superior areas are at the start, in the middle, and at the end of the axis.

Illustrations

🎯 — **Residential district in the European Quarter,** Frankfurt am Main (D)

📝 — h4a Gessert + Randecker Architekten with Glück Landschaftsarchitektur, Stuttgart

🖥 — www.h4a-architekten.de

🏆 — 1st prize

📅 — 2002

🗂 — urban redevelopment – railway conversion – new urban district

◆ — **layout of building lots: hierarchy –** layout

🏷 — additive approach; urban building blocks: opened city block, row, Zeile/ high-rise slab, point, high-rise tower; layout of development sites: axis; integrated green space, representation: perspective

Datum

Linear, curved, or planar datums are reference elements suitable for giving order and cohesion to more or less heterogeneous forms, elements, building lots, or districts. A reliable and proven datum for urban design is the linear axis. Highly different elements can be lined up along one or both sides of an axis. It is important that the axis possesses sufficient visual continuity.

If the axis is rigidly defined along one side, that side becomes a spine along which other elements can be lined up. This effect is stronger if the axis emerges from a directional surface that is comprised, for example, of consistently dense building lots. Even public squares, around which building lots or buildings are organized, can be planar reference elements. In general: "If planar ... in form, a datum must have sufficient size, closure, and regularity to be seen as a figure that can embrace or gather together the elements being organized within its field."[7]

A historical example for a datum is the linear city model developed in 1883 by the civil engineer Arturo Soria y Mata, which was to connect the satellite towns around Madrid. In the Ciudad lineal, settlement areas are arranged on both sides of a datum – a broad avenue with an integrated tramline.

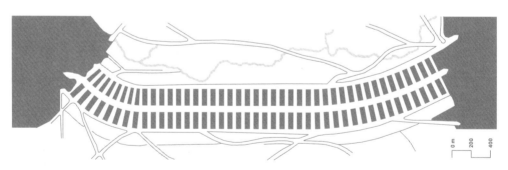

CIUDAD LINEAL, MADRID, Arturo Soria y Mata, 1883 (E)

---

7 Ibid., p. 358.

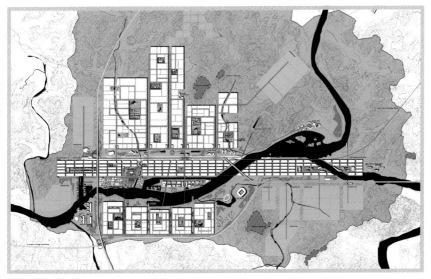

The band-like urban district serves as a datum that gives order to the residential areas to either side.

Perspective

⚙ — **New Multi-Functional Administrative City in the Republic of Korea** (ROK)

✎ — LEHEN drei Architekten Stadtplaner — Feketics, Schenk, Schuster, Stuttgart, C. Flury, F. Müller, S. Witulski, Constance

🖥 — www.lehendrei.de

⚲ — shortlist

📅 — 2005

🗂 — new city — satellite city of Seoul

◈ — **layout of development sites: datum**

🏷 — Prägnanz; additive approach and superimposition; orthogonal grid; layout of development sites: datum, sequence/rhythm; representation: illustrative site plan

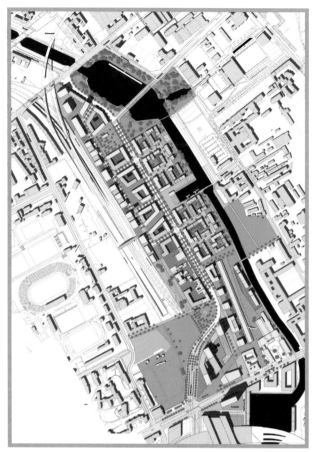

⚙ – **Europacity/Heidestraße,** Berlin (D)

✎ – ASTOC Architects and Planners, Cologne, with KCAP Architects & Planners, Rotterdam/Zurich/Shanghai, and Studio UC, Berlin

💻 – www.astoc.de, www.kcap.eu

🏆 – 1st prize

📅 – 2008

🗂 – urban redevelopment – inner-city development – new urban district for living and working

🔷 – **layout of development sites: datum**

🖐 – additive approach; urban building blocks: closed, dissolved city block, row, Zeile, hybrid; loop street network; place making through assembly and modeling; waterfront living

The rigorously delimited development site along the main arterial road constitutes a backbone for a string of additional development sites.

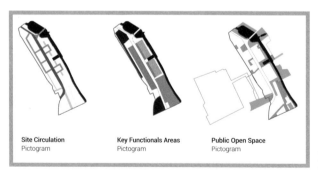

Site Circulation
Pictogram

Key Functionals Areas
Pictogram

Public Open Space
Pictogram

Functional diagrams

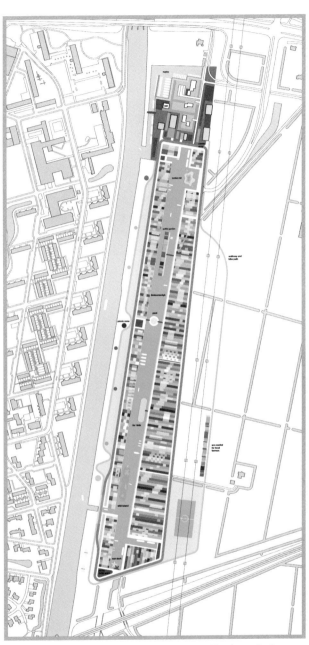

- **Europan 11, Central Lake, Kanaal-zone,** Leeuwarden (NL)
- BudCud, Krakow
- www.budcud.org
- honorable mention
- 2012
- urban expansion – new residential district
- **layout of building lots: datum**
- additive approach; urban building blocks: row, Zeile, point, spatial structure; community/adjacent green and open space, waterfront living; representation: diagrams

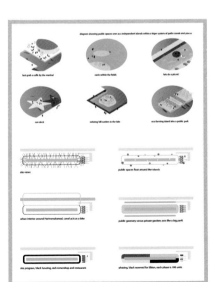

Design diagrams

The datum for the individually developed building lots is the new canal running along-side the existing canal.

Repetition/Rhythm

Urban design can also be described as an art of repetition and variation. In urban design, as in music, a theme first comes alive through repetition. What emerges is a rhythm that organizes the city – without permitting a sense of monotony to develop. Here, the law of similarity takes effect because the same or similarly structured elements are more likely to be experienced as being related to each other than dissimilar elements. The principle of contrast can also be used to strengthen a particular theme, for example by repeating two contrary elements like building fabric (development site/building lot) and open space (parks, squares, expanses of water, etc.). The amount of repetition should be limited, however, or complemented by other elements, superimposed, or disturbed, because the result would otherwise be monotonous.

An odd number of repetitions is desirable: thus a three, five, or seven rhythm has an ordering effect by means of its central axis of symmetry; a two-, four-, or six-part division, by contrast, usually seems imbalanced.[8]

8 Wienands, *Grundlagen der Gestaltung*, p. 116–118.

⊙ — **Innerer Westen,** Regensburg (D)

✎ — Ammann Albers StadtWerke mit Schweingruber Zulauf Landschaftsarchitekten
BSLA, Zurich

▭ — www.stadtwerke.ch

♦ — 1st prize

▦ — 2011

▭ — railway conversion – new residential districts

◈ — **layout of development sites: repetition/variation/rhythm**

◥ — Prägnanz; additive approach; urban building blocks: dissolved city block, Zeile, point;
—— loop street network; integrated green space

Model

Like precisely fitting
molded parts, the
uniformly structured
sectors interlock with
the green interstices.

The rhythm of the development site – green gap – is amplified through the repetition of further design elements like the waterside steps and residential towers.

Site plan

$\circledcirc$ – **New Housing along the Ryck River,** Greifswald (D)

$\boxed{\mathbb{Z}}$ – Machleidt GmbH Office for Urban Design, Berlin

$\boxed{\square}$ – www.machleidt.de

$\boxed{\mathbb{Q}}$ – 2nd prize

$\boxed{\text{▦}}$ – 2006

$\boxed{\square}$ – urban renewal – commercial conversion – new residential districts

$\boxed{\diamondsuit}$ – **layout of development sites: repetition/variation/rhythm**

$\boxed{\diamondsuit}$ – additive approach; urban building blocks: dissolved city block, row, point, freestanding building; place making through assembly; waterfront living

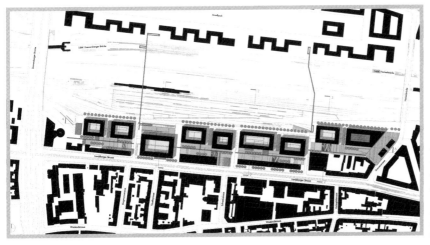

The rhythm emerges through the repetition of the similarly constructed quarters, but also through the slightly shifting individual elements.

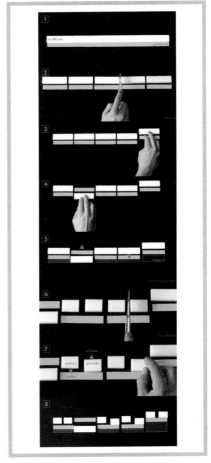

🎯 – **Landsberger Straße – Bahnachse Süd,** Munich (D)

📝 – Rolf-Harald Erz for SIAT GmbH with Bartosch Puszkarczyk, Munich; and EGL GmbH, Landshut

🖥 – www.erz-architekten.de

🏅 – 1st prize

📅 – 2003

🗂 – urban redevelopment – inner-city development – new urban district for living and working

🔖 – **layout of development sites: repetition/variation/rhythm**

🔗 – additive approach; urban building blocks: closed city block, row; place making through assembly; community green and open space; representation: diagrams

(l.) Model

(r.) Design steps

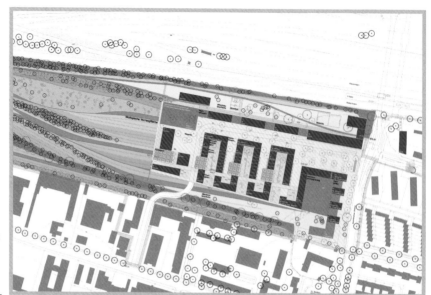

A rhythm emerges through the repetition of a memorable theme: here, it is the spatial sequence of circulation space and garden courtyard.

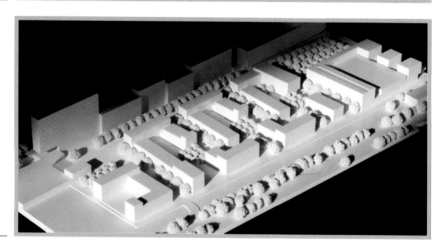

Model

🎯 — **Leben in urbaner Natur (Living in urban nature),** Munich (D)

✏️ — Ammann Albers StadtWerke with Schweingruber Zulauf Landschaftsarchitekten BSLA, Zurich

🖥️ — www.stadtwerke.ch

🔍 — 1st prize

📅 — 2010

📁 — railway conversion — urban development — new urban district

◈ — **layout of building lots: sequencing/repetition**

🏷️ — additive approach; urban building blocks: dissolved city block, courtyard, row, high-rise, meanders; place making through assembly; adjacent green and open space

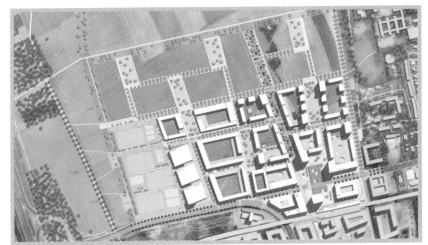

The repetition of neighborhood parks establishes a rhythm on the site.

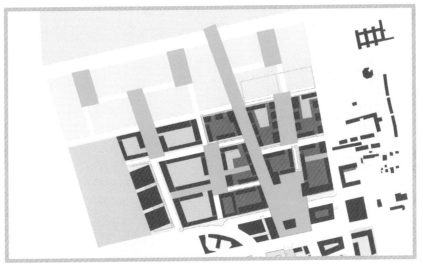

Open spaces diagram

⬡ – **Freiham Nord – District Center,** Munich (D)

✎ – MORPHO-LOGIC Architektur und Stadtplanung with t17 Landschaftsarchitekten, Munich

🖥 – www.morpho-logic.de

🏆 – 3rd prize

📅 – 2011

🗂 – urban expansion – new district center

◈ – **layout of building lots: repetition/rhythm**

🏷 – additive approach; urban building blocks: closed and dissolved city blocks, point/high-rise tower, hybrid; place making through assembly; community green and open space

Grouping

Through proximity and a common reference (e.g., a public square), adjacent elements unite into groups, although similar elements yield more uniform groups than dissimilar elements. Groups can also be viewed as a special case of repetition. The arrangement of the elements within a group as well as the repetition of entire groups creates a distinctive rhythm.

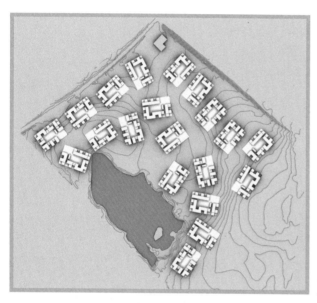

⊙ — **Affordable Housing,** Helsingør-Kvistgård (DK)

✐ — Tegnestuen Vandkunsten, Copenhagen

▣ — www.vandkunsten.com

◉ — 1st prize

▦ — 2004

▭ — urban expansion – new residential district

◈ — **layout of building lots: grouping**

⬚ — additive approach; urban building blocks: courtyard, row, spatial structure; cul-de-sac network; flowing
—— green space

Similar elements result in more uniform groups than dissimilar ones.

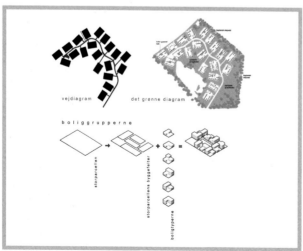

Diagrams

- **Residential districts and landscape park,** Erlangen (D)
- Franke + Messmer, Emskirchen, with Rößner and Waldmann, Erlangen, and E. Tautorat, Fürth
- www.architekten-franke-messmer.de
- 2nd prize
- 2009
- urban expansion – new residential districts
- **layout of building lots: grouping**
- depth (pervasive design idea)

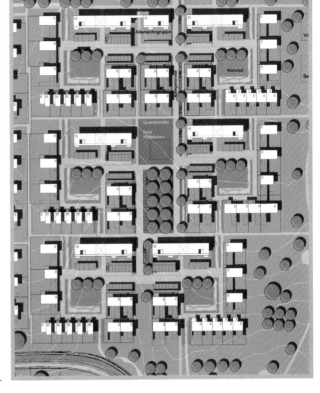

The building lots are grouped around a planar datum, the neighborhood square.

Figure-ground plan

Grouping of urban building blocks on a car-free site with a neighborhood square. On the development sites, the settlement pattern is repeated and varied.

Axonometric

⦿ — **Siemens Site Isar-Süd,** Munich (D)
✐ — JSWD Architekten with Lill + Sparla, Cologne
▣ — www.jswd-architekten.de
♀ — 1st prize
▦ — 2002
🗀 — urban redevelopment – continued development of a commercial site – new urban district
◈ — **layout of the building lot – grouping**
◈ — freestanding building

**⌖ — Schlösserareal und Schlachthofge-
lände,** Düsseldorf (D)

✎ — buddenberg architekten, Düsseldorf,
with FSWLA Landschaftsarchitektur,
Düsseldorf/Cologne

▣ — www.buddenberg-architekten.de

◉ — 3rd place

▦ — 2006

◰ — urban redevelopment − commercial
conversion − new urban district

**◈ — layout of development sites:
grouping**

◆ — additive approach; urban building
blocks: opened city block, row, Zeile;
___ place making through assembly

The space between the
compact development
sites becomes part of
the city.

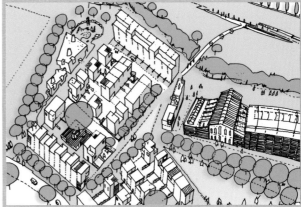

Perspective

7.2 ORGANIZING PRINCIPLES FOR URBAN BUILDING BLOCKS ON THE BUILDING LOT

WHEN laying out urban building blocks on a building lot, questions must first be answered about the significance of the lot within the overall design: What position does it hold in the overall design and how does it relate to the adjoining building lots? Once these conditions have been clarified, the next logical question is: Which urban building blocks are appropriate? In an inner-city context, for example, closed perimeter blocks are a clear option, but in the context of a suburban housing development, by contrast, rows, a Zeile, and points are more likely to be used.

The internal logic of the selected urban building blocks in terms of function, orientation, and access is clearly defined on the one hand, and on the other, the designer also has liberties: For example, the city block per se is self-contained and constitutes an infrastructural entity solely due to the surrounding streets. But here, too, there are contextual possibilities for differentiation − by creating openings in the edge of the perimeter block, for instance, or concentrating the built form at certain places.

The principles by which urban building blocks can be ordered on building lots are closely related to the previously outlined organizing principles: Here again, additive and divisional approaches play a large role, as do axis, symmetry, hierarchy, datum, repetition, sequencing, rhythm, and grouping. Beyond that, mandatory rules governing the spacing between buildings, which may differ from country to country and state to state, must be taken into account.

The following organizing principles are helpful for arranging urban building blocks:

Axis and Symmetry

By arranging urban building blocks along an axis, a clear direction can be given to the building lot. If urban building blocks are arranged symmetrically on the building lot, the site will appear static, whereas an asymmetrical arrangement gives the site a dynamic orientation.

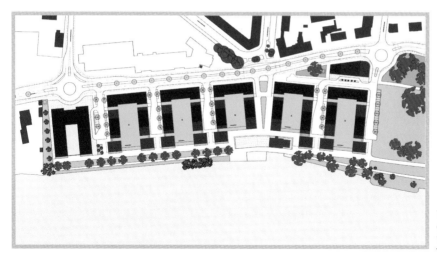

The axisymmetrical city block opens out to the water.

Bird's-eye perspective

⌖ — **Herosé – Stadt am Seerhein,** Constance (D)

✎ — KLAUS THEO BRENNER STADTARCHITEKTUR with Pola Landschaftsarchitekten, Berlin

🖥 — www.klaustheobrenner.de

🏆 — 1st prize

📅 — 2002

🗂 — urban redevelopment – industrial conversion – new urban district

◆ — **layout of urban building blocks on the building lot – axis/symmetry**

🏷 — additive approach; tilted grid; urban building blocks: open city block; layout of development sites: sequence/repetition/rhythm; integrated green space

Hierarchy

Areas with a higher position in the hierarchy stand out from typical areas.[9] In the case of a building lot, this is especially so when different uses or intensities of use come together. Unequal or accentuated distribution of building mass, for example, can make one part of a building hierarchically superior to the other parts, for instance when a building lot is oriented toward a public square. A hierarchy of urban building blocks on the building lot can also result from differences in the traffic loads on adjacent streets or by the location of the building lot in the transition to a green space.

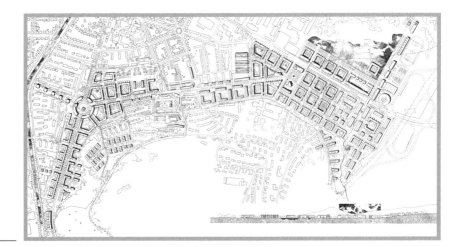

Illustrative site plan

The hierarchically superior and denser areas on the site are located around the square.

🎯 – **Südstadt Tübingen** (D)

📝 – LEHEN drei – Feketics, Kortner, Schenk, Schuster, Wiehl, Stuttgart

🖥 – www.lehendrei.de

🏆 – 1st prize

📅 – 1992

🗂 – urban redevelopment – military conversion – new urban districts

◈ – **layout of urban building blocks on the building lot – hierarchy**

◣ – Prägnanz; additive approach; orthogonal grid; urban building blocks: closed, dissolved city block, row, point; layout of development sites: axis; place making through assembly and modeling

9 See also 7.1.3 Hierarchy

Datum

Only in special cases can a building lot itself become a reference element – at the design level for a development site, for example – but only if it has a sufficient size and is built upon in a prominent manner.

A building lot can, however, readily be a part or edge of a linear or planar datum, namely when the selection and arrangement of urban building blocks substantively, functionally, and formally lend support to the reference element:
- as part of a centrally located area in the district, development site, or city corpus
- as the edge of a centrally located green space or a public square
- as part of an axis rigidly defined by building lots
- as part of a spine in the form of a directional surface comprised of consistently dense building lots.

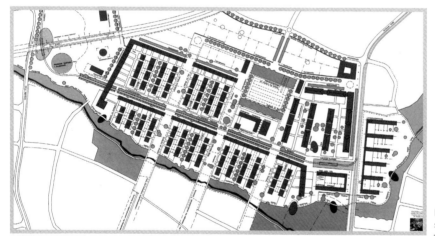

Illustrative site plan and section

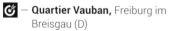 – **Quartier Vauban,** Freiburg im Breisgau (D)

 – Kohlhoff Architekten, Stuttgart

– 1st prize

– 1994

– urban redevelopment – military conversion – new urban district

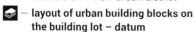 – **layout of urban building blocks on the building lot – datum**

– additive approach; urban building blocks: row, Zeile, point; layout of development sites: axis, sequence/repetition/rhythm; integrated green space

The building lots are part of the single-sided demarcation of an axis; the urban building blocks are correspondingly aligned: parallel to the street along the axis itself and open to the green space.

Repetition, Sequencing, Rhythm

As explained above, every theme requires a certain number of repetitions for it to be recognizable as such. This occurs in urban design through repetition of the same or similar design elements at various levels of scale: repetition of districts in the overall design, of building lots in a district, and of urban building blocks on a building lot. Here, the urban building blocks repeated on the building lot can be of a single type, but they need not be. There are frequently up to three different but repetitive elements that combine on a building lot. Through repetition of the urban building blocks, a rhythm of buildings and open spaces emerges, giving structure to the building lot. The elements are usually placed in rows or face each other at an angle. Of crucial importance for the layout are the planner's design goals, such as strengthening the public realm, optimizing natural lighting and exposure to direct sunlight, and creating a wide diversity of residential options with shared and private areas or a large green space onto which private garden areas are connected.

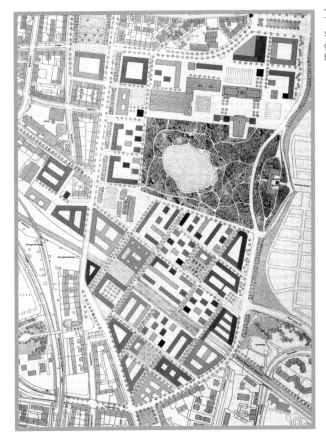

The repetition of open space and built fabric gives rhythm to the building lots.

Ⓖ — **Theresienhöhe,** Munich (D)

✎ — Steidle + Partner Architekten, Munich, with Thomanek + Duquesnoy Landschaftsarchitekten, Berlin

🖥 — www.steidle-architekten.de

🏆 — 1st prize

📅 — 1997

🗂 — urban redevelopment – trade fair conversion – new urban district

◆ — **layout of urban building blocks on the building lot – sequence/repetition/rhythm**

🏷 — Qualitative traits: additive approach; orthogonal grid; urban building blocks: closed city block, dissolved city block, inner-city urban block, row, Zeile, point; hybrid; place making through assembly

The different distances between the rows of the Zeile establish a varied rhythm of buildings, circulation, garden, and squares.

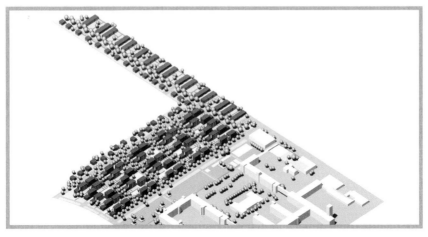

Axonometric

⌖ — **Housing for federal employees,** Berlin-Steglitz (D)
✎ — Geier, Maass, Staab, with Ariane Röntz, Berlin
🖥 — www.geier-maass-architekten.de
🏛 — 5th prize
📅 — 1996
🗂 — urban redevelopment – military conversion – new residential district
◈ — **layout of urban building blocks on the building lot – sequence/repetition/rhythm**
🔖 — additive approach; orthogonal grid; urban building blocks: Zeile, point; place making
— through exclusion/omission and assembly

Grouping

At the level of the building lot, a group is understood as a building composition that is influenced less by external conditions than by internal forces of attraction.[10] With groups, in contrast to sequencing or mere repetition, the idea of community is key: the urban building blocks are, for instance, grouped around a communal area that can simultaneously be an entrance court or garden courtyard.

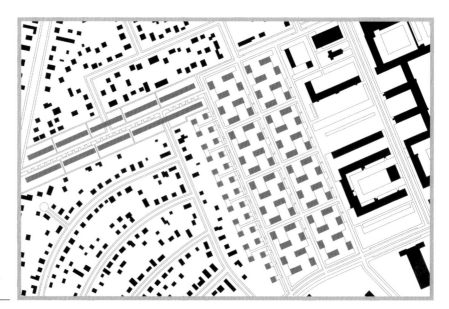

Four point-like urban building blocks are grouped around each shared open space.

Model

Detail of the slightly altered design that was carried out

⌖ — **Housing for Federal Employees,** Berlin-Steglitz (D)

✎ — ENS Architekten with Norbert Müggenburg, Berlin

▭ — www.eckertnegwersuselbeek.de

◉ — 1st prize

▦ — 1996

▭ — urban redevelopment – military conversion – new residential district

◈ — **layout of urban building blocks on the building lot – grouping**

⬦ — additive approach; orthogonal grid; urban building blocks: row, Zeile, point; place making through assembly

10 Thorsten Bürklin and Michael Peterek, *Urban Building Blocks* (Basel/Boston/Berlin: Birkhäuser, 2008), p. 59.

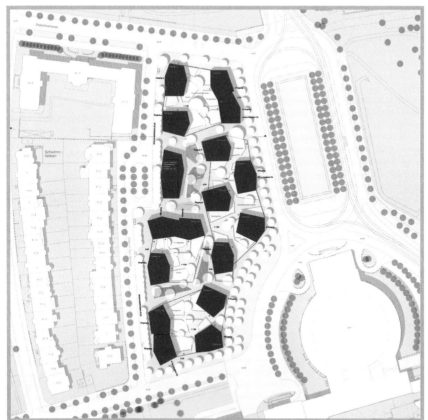

A group of point-like urban building blocks on building lots of different sizes. The continuous base zone strengthens the coherence of the group.

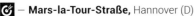 — **Mars-la-Tour-Straße,** Hannover (D)

 — Marazzi + Paul Architekten, Zurich, with Koeber Landschaftsarchitektur, Stuttgart

 — www.marazzi-paul.com

— 1st prize

— 2008

— Inner-city development – residential district on former parking lot

— **layout of urban building blocks on the building lot – grouping**

— additive approach; irregular grid; urban building blocks: dissolved city block, point; amorphous public space

Perspective

8 Road Systems

THE need for mobility is higher today than ever, and never before have so many people wanted individual mobility and also been able to afford it. Whereas in the medieval city it took only ten minutes to go by foot from one city gate to another, today's distances are much longer and the forms of mobility are more diverse. Increasing flows of goods and commuters cause numerous problems that have long since manifested themselves on a global scale in terms of land consumption and the scarcity of energy reserves. On an urban scale, they can be felt in mounting noise and emission pollution and in the decomposition of the spatial structure of our cities.

TRAFFIC flows are bundled into road networks, and the network functions become increasingly specialized as the traffic load grows. Accordingly, road networks can be categorized hierarchically into those that predominantly serve interregional traffic (highways, expressways, overland routes, and local transit routes as well as the main arterial roads) and those that predominantly provide access within districts and also to property lots (local collector roads, secondary access roads, and residential streets, traffic-calmed areas, and separate bicycle and pedestrian connections).

The traffic concept is a substantial part of the urban design. Whereas Modernist planners attempted to divide the city into functional areas – for work, housing, recreation, and transportation, etc. – and to separate the built fabric from the traffic to the greatest extent possible in the process, the tendency today is to bring uses, buildings, and infrastructure together again wherever possible. A consequence of the separation was the dissolution of public urban space and with it came the anonymity of modern cities.

Road systems can only be changed retroactively with great effort. While buildings generally have a limited life span, lots can be divided or combined, and uses can change, street systems are of lasting duration because of the elaborate municipal infrastructure that is integrated into them, such as the water supply lines and sewers.

A distinction can be made between complete and incomplete road networks:

COMPLETE ROAD NETWORKS

THE distinguishing trait of complete road networks is that all the network nodes are connected with one another and each point can be reached via multiple paths within the network without having to use any street more than once. The network itself is not finished, but remains instead open for expansion. Its grid size is dependent on the density and type of building development. As soon as networks have reached a minimum size, it becomes necessary to establish a hierarchy of selected connections, for instance to create main roads.[1]

The complete, uniform, and orthogonal network in the form of a rectangular grid has proven successful in urban design in many respects: Land distribution can be accomplished simply and fairly, with an appropriately chosen grid size, all lots almost automatically lie directly on a street, and additions and extensions can be made as needed. The majority of planned cities – from Miletus to Brasília – are based on an orthogonal street grid for exactly this reason.

Gridded cities are commonly regarded as monotone. Targeted points of emphasis and intentional disruptions in the network pattern are a reliable means to counteract this hazard: Building lots can be consolidated for special uses or omitted for squares and green spaces, and incised diagonals make it possible to connect widely separated subareas with each other across a short distance. Disturbances within a complete network are unproblematic as long as they stay recognizable as a departure from the rule and do not themselves become the norm.

Even irregular, nongeometric networks can be categorized as complete networks if they satisfy the aforementioned criteria. Complete networks can be skewed obliquely, curved to follow the topography, or stretched, and they can be based on more complex geometries, such as triangular or hexagonal grids.[2]

---

1 Here and below, see Gerhard Curdes, *Stadtstruktur und Stadtgestaltung* (Stuttgart/Berlin/Cologne: Kohlhammer, 1997), p. 43 ff.
2 See also Additional Geometric Principles, p. 58 ff.

⊙ — **Rosenstein District,** Stuttgart (D)

✎ — pp a|s pesch partner architekten stadtplaner, Herdecke/Stuttgart, with Agence Ter, Karlsruhe/Paris

▣ — www.pesch-partner.de

⊙ — 1st prize

▦ — 2005

⊡ — urban redevelopment – railway conversion – new district

◈ — **complete road network**

◈ — Prägnanz, regular orthogonal grid urban building blocks: closed city block, point; layout of development sites: sequence/rhythm; place making through assembly; integrated

___ green space

The urban district in the park has a complete road network, meaning that all the network nodes can be in contact with one another.

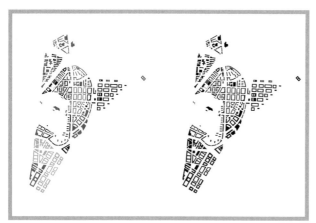

Figure-ground plan with and without differentiation of the existing fabric

INCOMPLETE ROAD NETWORKS

INCOMPLETE road networks only take into account their immediate use and extend only as far into the space as necessary for this purpose. An extension of incomplete networks is possible, but to a very limited degree – and usually only if the extension has already been planned from the beginning, e.g., by keeping lots free for a subsequent access road. Orientation within incomplete networks is often difficult due to the absence of cross connections between the individual isolated areas.

Older incomplete networks can still be found in villages, slowly developed cities or – due to the topography – on hilltops, in valleys, and at the mouths of rivers. Recent planned examples from postwar Modernism through to the present day often have the function of thwarting disruptive through traffic and establishing self-contained, reasonably sized neighborhoods.

Incomplete road networks extend only as far into the area as is required by the uses being served.

— **Tornesch am See,** Tornesch (D)

— Manuel Bäumler Architekt und Stadtplaner, Dresden

— www.schellenberg-baeumler.de

— 1st prize

— 2009

— urban expansion – new residential districts

— **incomplete road network**

— additive approach; urban building blocks: row, Zeile, point; layout of development sites: grouping; bent street space, widened street space; integrated green space

Circulation diagram

Branching Networks and Dead-End Networks

Incomplete networks can be differentiated into branching networks and dead-end networks; both are among the oldest known road systems.

Branching networks are similar in structure to a tree that continually branches out further. They are typical for village settlement patterns, in which more or less distant farmsteads need to be reached.

In dead-end networks, dead-end streets extend irregularly from superordinate access roads, sometimes branching out repeatedly. Dead-end networks are regarded as typical for historical cities in the Oriental and Islamic cultural spheres. Some of the earliest cities, such as Sumerian Ur in Mesopotamia, already covered an area of 100 hectares at the beginning of the third millennium BC and were accessed primarily via networks of dead-end alleys.[3]

Like in a dead-end network, dead ends extend irregularly from superordinate access roads, sometimes branching out repeatedly.

3 See Leonardo Benevolo, *History of the City,* trans. Geoffrey Culverwell (London: Scolar Press, 1991), p. 23 f.

Perspective

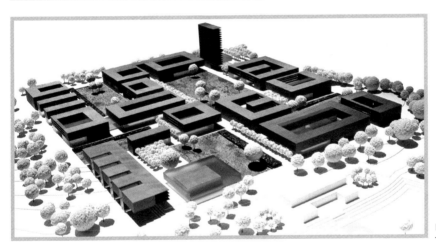

Model

- **Goethe University - Westend Campus,** Frankfurt am Main (D)
- pmp Architekten, Munich, with Atelier Bernburg LandschaftsArchitekten GmbH, Bernburg
- www.pmparchitekten.de
- 3rd prize
- 2003
- urban redevelopment – military conversion – new college campus
- **cul-de-sac network**
- Prägnanz; additive approach; incomplete orthogonal grid; layout of development sites: axis, datum, rhythm; green space delimited by buildings; representation: presentation model

Cul-de-Sac Networks

The modern version of the dead-end network is the cul-de-sac network. The culs-de-sac provide access to lots in a single- or two-sided comb-like pattern of bent, curved, or linear streets at regular intervals along an access road, and terminate as dead ends. The cul-de-sac can be wider at its far end, forming a plaza-like area around which buildings are arranged.

⚙ — **Architektur Olympiade Hamburg, Hinsenfeld Family Housing,** Hamburg (D)

✏ — Wacker Zeiger Architekten, Hamburg

🖥 — www.wackerzeiger.de

🏅 — bronze medal for architecture

📅 — 2006

🗂 — urban expansion – new residential district

◆ — **cul-de-sac network**

◈ — additive approach; urban building blocks: row, point; layout of development sites: repetition/rhythm, grouping; widened, amorphous street space; district-level/adjacent green

___ and open space

The culs-de-sac extend from the access road at regular intervals in a one-sided pattern, terminating as dead ends.

View into one of the culs-de-sac

A variant of the cul-de-sac network is the loop street network, which likewise enables access to the areas to the left and right of an access road. In contrast to the cul-de-sac network with dead ends, the street does not end at the last site for which access must be provided, but makes a loop heading back to the access road. As a result, orientation in a network with loop streets is uncomplicated; in addition, vehicles such as sanitation trucks, for instance, do not need to turn around. Although through traffic can develop, it can nevertheless be prevented with appropriate design measures.

The loop street network is a variant of the cul-de-sac network in which the turnarounds are not needed.

 — **Herrenweg – Meerlach – Schlack,** Kippenheim (D)

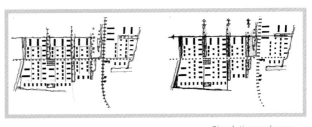

Circulation and open spaces diagrams

- bäuerle lüttin architekten BDA, Constance, with Pit Müller, Freiburg
- www.baeuerle-luettin.de
- 3rd prize
- 2001
- urban expansion – new residential district
- **loop street network**
- additive approach; orthogonal grid; urban building blocks: Zeile, point; layout of development sites: axis, repetition/rhythm; integrated green space

Circulation Loops

Whereas local loop streets merely give access to a small number of lots, circular main roads are suitable for providing access to entire cities, districts, or larger neighborhoods. The circulation loop is located on the periphery or within the building fabric. Appended to the loop or branching off from it, complete networks as well as incomplete networks like culs-de-sac or loop streets are possible. The main traffic load is carried by the loop, and the lots accessed directly via the loop are not affected by through traffic, or if so, just to a slight degree.

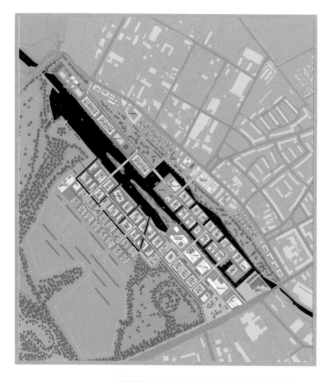

- **Olympic Village,** Leipzig (D)
- ASTOC Architects and Planners, Cologne, with KCAP Architects & Planners, Rotterdam/Zurich/Shanghai and bgmr Becker Giseke Mohren Richard, Landschaftsarchitekten, Leipzig
- www.astoc.de, www.kcap.eu
- 1st prize category
- 2004
- urban redevelopment – harbor conversion – new district
- **circulation loop**
- additive approach; orthogonal grid; layout of development sites: hierarchy, datum; waterfront living; representation: diagrams

(a.) Because the main traffic load is carried by the ring, the subareas accessed via the ring are largely unaffected by through traffic.

(r.) Diagrams: Circulation, relationship to water, and public transport

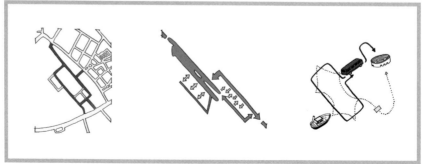

COMBINATIONS

IN practice, it is common to combine different road systems and thereby also to combine their advantages. Especially with larger planning sites, it is necessary to establish a hierarchy for the road system, for instance to direct the traffic flow. It is not imperative that every district be able to be extended, so that if, for instance, a complete network lies adjacent to a green space worthy of preservation, that edge can also be made accessible with a cul-de-sac network.

9 The Intermediate Space as Freestyle Exercise

THE space between buildings is defined as urban space. If functionality is virtually compulsory in urban design, dimensioning and designing the urban space is the freestyle exercise in this discipline: Nothing shapes the image of a city more than the space that emerges through the interplay of built elements, facades, buildings, and intermediate space. If we think about Amsterdam, for example, everyone immediately has in mind the same image of rows of small and large town houses on broad, tree-lined canals. Hardly anyone, however, would mention the large and verdant inner courtyards within the city blocks, like those found along the Herengracht or Keizersgracht canals. These are also urban spaces – private urban spaces that are accessible for only a few residents.

THERE are many types of urban spaces, but we deal here with the ones that are experienced by the public and characterize the city:

The public space is that part of the urban space that is owned by the city or community, is also maintained by the municipality, and is freely accessible to everyone. Public space includes primarily: squares, streets and public thorough-fares, pedestrian zones, and parks and green spaces.

In addition to the public space, there are semipublic urban spaces, which admittedly have a public character but are nonetheless privately owned and whose access can be restricted. These are, for example, farmsteads, shopping arcades, train stations and airport terminals, as well as larger open spaces surrounding private or commercial buildings.

A third category includes nonaccessible and nonpublic open spaces, such as gardens and front yards, which are nonetheless characteristic of the city.

SQUARES

9.1 WHAT is most commonly known in English as a public square can also be called a "plaza" or even a "place." Both words share the same etymology as the German word *Platz*, all of which derive from the ancient Greek word *plateia*, meaning a broad street within the city.[1] But squares are more than just wide streets: they have always been a reflection of a particular urban community. They manifest civic pride as much as economic, religious, or feudal claims to power.

The early Mesopotamian and Egyptian cities did not yet have public squares in the modern sense. These cities were "nothing other than an expanded temple and palace complex with densely built communal facilities."[2] As sites of political activity, squares were feared by the rulers, in Greek Sparta, for instance, the markets and meeting places were left unadorned so the common people would not want to remain there for long. It was in Greece during the sixth century BC that the polis developed, a city-state that was democratically administered and governed by free (male) citizens and, for the first time, needed public buildings and a central gathering place, the agora. The Romans took over the building type of the agora and made the forum into the focal point of political, economic, cultural, and religious life. Vitruvius thereby distinguished between enclosed markets and wooded temple sites.

Many medieval public squares appear to have evolved and are not indebted to any consistently designed form. New or rebuilt cities from medieval times, like the Polish royal city of Krakow were, by contrast, laid out according to specific plans.

---

1 See, for example http://www.thefreedictionary.com/place (accessed on January 15, 2013).
2 Karl-Jürgen Krause, "Plätze: Begriff, Geschichte, Form, Größe und Profil" (Dortmund: Universität Dortmund, 2004), p. 1

Usually, blocks were omitted from the building-lot grid to form public squares. Typical for these public squares is that the squares are accessed tangentially from their corners.[3]

In the cities that were established or restructured during the Baroque by absolutist rulers, on the other hand, axial symmetrical order predominates. The square itself and the demarcating buildings are largely unified, and when passing through, one's view is drawn to the "point de vue," the sovereign ruler's palace, or the statue placed in the middle.

A special case of urban squares is constituted by the English squares that were created beginning at the end of the eighteenth century. These small neighborhood squares were collectively available to the residents from the surrounding apartment buildings and are to this day enclosed with a fence – although they have meanwhile passed into public ownership. According to Stübben, squares are "something halfway between public space and private garden." They not only served "health, comfort, and recreation," but are also the "friendliest means of decoration" for cities.[4] The dynamic urban growth in the nineteenth century brought forth an ambivalent attitude toward squares, leading to a belief among some that squares are unnecessary because people live in houses and not on squares—an attitude reflected by the New York Building Commission in 1811 during the planning of Manhattan's street network. In Europe as well, squares were initially unwanted after the populist revolutions of 1848: Further politically motivated gatherings and demonstrations were feared. It was not until the late nineteenth century

KRAKOW, reconstruction, 1252 (PL)

---

3 Ibid., p. 8.
4 All quotations are from Josef Stübben, *Der Städtebau* (Stuttgart: A. Kröner, 1907), p. 161.

that the emergent middle class again sought fulfillment in creating spacious squares and the newly fashionable urban green spaces that are known from Paris, Berlin, and other large cities of this time.

In the Modernist era, squares delimited by buildings and classical public spaces were regarded as relics of an outdated time. The city was identified as an all-consuming Moloch from which the modern man must be liberated. Under the slogan "light, air, and sun for all," not only should the all-too-obvious ills in the cities be abolished, but the entire spatial structure should also be reorganized. What was not accomplished by the protagonists of Modernism as of 1920 caused little difficulty for the planners of postwar Modernism given the wartime destruction and reconstruction in the era of the economic miracle: "A spatially and architecturally defined public square was unthinkable, squares 'swam' more or less unrecognizably in the flowing open space around large construction projects."[5]

In the course of the increased institutionalization of urban landmark preservation beginning in the mid-1970s, however, a change in thinking had begun, whose lasting impact is still felt today: in numerous cities — not only in large, well-known metropolises like Barcelona or Lyon — the realization grew that squares contribute significantly to people's identification with their city, and that by improving the qualities of public spaces, the entire city can be reactivated as a living environment.

Recommendations on the Layout of Squares

The layout and design of public squares account for a great amount of the literature on urban design. In particular, the ratio of a square's length to width and the ratio of its diameter to the height of the adjacent buildings have been discussed again and again over time. All the authors — with the single exception of those belonging to the Modernist movement — were in agreement that a square must be delimited by buildings: around 50 BC, Vitruvius defines the size of a central urban square as dependent on the number of citizens. The proportion of the square should correspond to 2:3, which approximates the golden section. According to Leon Battista Alberti (ca. 1450) the diameter of a square should be five times the height of the surrounding buildings, and he follows Vitruvius with regard to the square's proportions. In his 1890 essay *Optisches Maass für den Städte-Bau* [Optical measure for city building], Hermann Maertens recommends a proportion of height to width of 1:3–1:6 for the cross section of streets and squares.[6] Camillo Sitte, who criticizes the monotony of nineteenth-century gridded cities in his 1898 book *City Planning According to Artistic Principles*, refers to a balanced ratio of a square's width to length. The appearance of square-shaped plazas is not particularly good and overly long or wide squares prove to be unfavorable if the ratio exceeds 1:3.[7] In his book

5 Krause, "Plätze," p. 16.
6 Ibid., p. 24.
7 George R. Collins and Christiane Crasemann Collins, *Camillo Sitte: The Birth of Modern City Planning*, (New York: Rizzoli, 2006), p. 182. Originally published as *Der Städte-Bau nach seinen künstlerischen Grundsätzen* (Vienna: Gräser, 1889).

Urban Space from the mid-1970s, Rob Krier differentiates public squares according to their basic geometric form: square, rectangle, triangle, ellipse, trapezoid, or a combination of these.[8] In 1994 Hans Aminde proposes evaluating squares in terms of their spatial impact, and he mentions various possibilities, such as closed, pocket-like, or semiopen public squares as well as those interconnected to or grouped with others and ones marked by a dominant building.[9]

Aminde also categorizes the squares according to their "publicness," according to how they function. He lists functions like central market squares, squares in front of train stations or cultural venues, squares in residential, office, and mixed-use districts, and smaller neighborhood squares as well as memorial sites and traffic islands. At the same time, however, he points out that the public square's form and its size are not related: "a sculptural square can just as well be a plaza serving the government or the functional center of a residential district, and a semi-open square can serve a harbor or a marketplace."[10]

Designing Squares

The following section is devoted to the question of how squares are created in the design process. Once the appropriate location for a square is found in the design, the designer essentially has four instruments available that can be used in combination to create a square: through exclusion/omission, assembly, modeling, or definition.

Exclusion or Omission

The simplest method for creating a square is to exclude one or more building lots within a design. This works regardless of the types of urban building blocks used on the site. The more closed the buildings are on the edges of the typical building lots, the greater the spatial impact will be. With an orthogonal grid of city blocks, what results almost automatically is a square demarcated on four sides. With Zeilen arrangements or spatial structures such as courtyard houses, the omission of just a few parcels of land on the building site is sufficient to allow the creation of a small playground or neighborhood square, which would be open or contained depending on the urban building blocks used.

8 Rob Krier, *Urban Space* (New York: Rizzoli, 1979), p. 28 ff. Originally published as *Stadtraum in Theorie und Praxis an Beispielen der Innenstadt Stuttgarts* (Stuttgart: Krämer, 1975).
9 Hans-Joachim Aminde: "Auf die Plätze . . . Zur Gestalt und zur Funktion städtischer Plätze heute," in *Plätze in der Stadt*, ed. Hans-Joachim Aminde (Ostfildern: Hatje Cantz, 1994), p. 44 ff.
10 Hans-Joachim Aminde: "Plätze in der Stadt heute," in *Lehrbausteine Städtebau*, 2nd ed., ed. Johann Jessen (Stuttgart: Städtebau-Institut, 2003), p. 140.

With Zeile structures, the omission of one building is sufficient to allow the creation of a neighborhood square.

Perspective

🎯 — **Residential districts and landscape park,** Erlangen (D)
✏️ — Bathke Geisel Architekten BDA with fischer heumann landschaftsarchitekten, Munich
🖥 — www.bathke-geisel.de
🏅 — 2nd prize
📅 — 2009
🗂 — urban expansion — new residential districts
◈ — **place making through exclusion/omission**
🏷 — additive approach; orthogonal grid; layout of development sites: sequence/repeti-
___ tion/rhythm; combined access network; integrated green space

 **Mobile Regional Airport (MOB),**
Greven (D)

– Fuchs und Rudolph Architekten
Stadtplaner, Munich

– www.fuchsundrudolph.de

– 3rd prize

– 1999

– urban redevelopment – military conversion – new residential district

**place making through exclusion/
omission**

– geometric principle; additive approach; orthogonal grid; urban building blocks: spatial structure; layout
of development sites: axis, datum,
repetition/rhythm

Within a dense spatial
structure, omitting built
fabric to create small,
neighborhood squares
can facilitate people's
orientation.

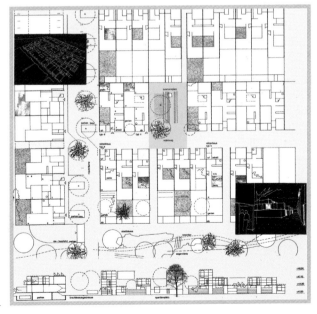

Detail

Assembly

Placemaking through assembly is probably the most elegant method of forming space. The square is thereby created by assembling building lots, and these are joined together or shifted in relation to one another such that the resulting intermediate space generates an open space. To create a greater spatial impact, the building lots should be built upon in a closed manner. By pushing back even one building lot within a grid pattern, for example, a pocket-like widening results, which is then often called a "vest-pocket park" or simply a "pocket park." The depths of the blocks are then adjusted correspondingly.

One of the most common and most beautiful shapes for a public square that results from assembly is the so-called "turbine square," where the building lots are offset like a pinwheel around the square. In this case the streets do not run straight through as they would if the square had been created through omission, but are instead spatially concluded on the opposite side of the square, thereby considerably heightening the spatial experience. Depending on how the building lots are assembled and how they are varied in size and shape, orthogonal or polygonal squares can be formed.

With place making through assembly, building lots are joined together or shifted in relation to one another such that the resulting intermediate space generates an open space.

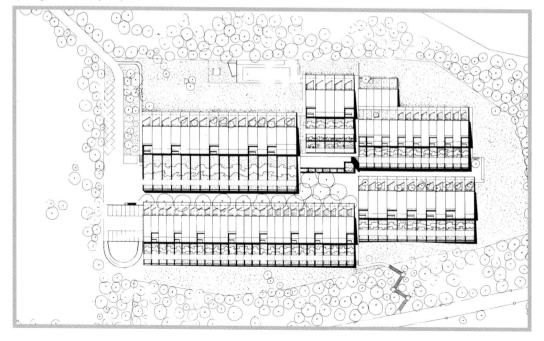

 — **Siedlung Halen,** Bern (CH)

— Atelier 5, Bern

— www.atelier5.ch

— 1956–1961

— urban expansion – new residential district

— **place making through assembly**

— geometric principle; additive approach; urban building blocks: row; layout of development sites: grouping

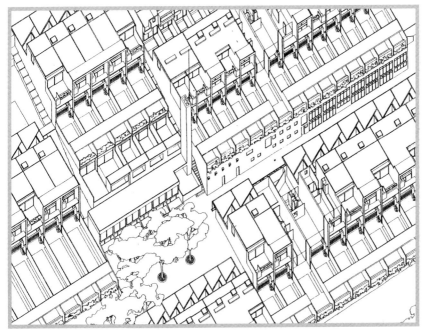

Axonometric of neighborhood square

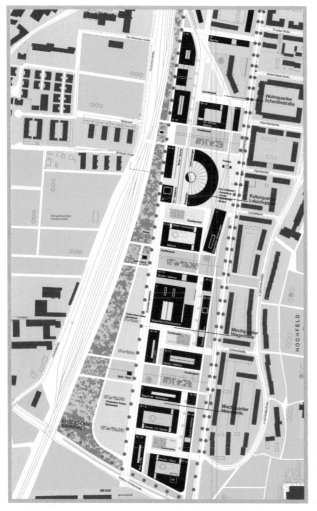

⚙ — **Areal Firnhaberstraße,** Augsburg (D)

✍ — Trojan Trojan + Partner Architekten + Städtebauer, Darmstadt, with Prof. Heinz W. Hallmann, Jüchen

▢ — www.trojan-architekten.de

🏅 — 1st prize

📅 — 2002

🗂 — urban redevelopment — railway conversion — new urban districts

❧ — **place making through assembly**

🏷 — additive approach; orthogonal grid; layout of development sites: axis, sequence/rhythm; green space

___ delimited by buildings

Squares formed through assembly are the common trait of the series of development sites.

Model

- **Bockenheim Redevelopment Plan, Goethe University,** Frankfurt am Main (D)
- K9 Architekten with Andreas Krause, Freiburg im Breisgau
- www.k9architekten.de
- 1st prize
- 2003
- urban redevelopment – new urban district
- **place making through assembly**
- additive approach; urban building blocks: city block, inner-city urban block, high-rise; layout of development sites: axis, datum, sequence/rhythm; representation: presentation model

Existing buildings can also be integrated into an assembled public square, as is the case here in the southern and northern development sites.

Model

The main square is an assembled public square, and the smaller squares are made with combinations of assembly and modeling.

Model

🎯 — **Am Terrassenufer - Urban Redevelopment Ideas for the Pirnaische Vorstadt,** Dresden (D)

📝 — Rohdecan Architekten GmbH with UKL Landschaftsarchitekten, Dresden

🖥 — www.rohdecan.de

🏅 — 1st prize

📅 — 2001

🗂 — urban renewal — new district center and housing

📚 — **place making through assembly**

🏷 — additive approach; urban building blocks: city block, inner-city urban block, row,
— hybrid; complete road network; curved/bent street space

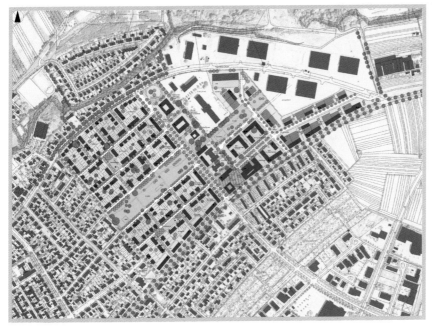

The small, neighborhood open spaces are designed according to the principle of place making through assembly.

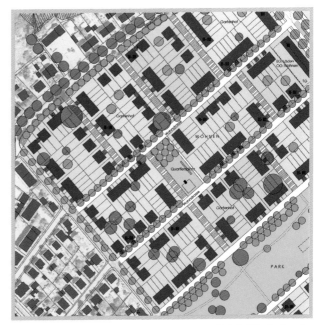

🎯 — **Barracks Site Conversion,**
Karlsruhe-Knielingen (D)

📝 — Architektur und Stadtplanung Rosenstiel, Freiburg im Breisgau, with faktorgrün Landschaftsarchitekten, Denzlingen

🖥 — www.architekt-rosenstiel.de

🏆 — 1st prize

📅 — 2008

🗂 — urban redevelopment – military conversion – new residential district and industrial park

🔷 — **place making through assembly**

🔻 — additive approach; irregular orthogonal grid; urban building blocks: opened city block, row, point, freestanding building; district-level green and open space

Modeling

With modeling, the square is created by shaping and adjusting the surrounding building shapes to match the chosen shape of the public square. This process can also be described as punching out a shape from a homogeneous urban texture.

Modeled squares often have a complex or challenging geometric form, like a circle, ellipse, or octagon. But they can also be rectangular, for instance when the rectangle is cut out from the building lots because it does not inevitably result from their positions. Modeled squares engender an intensive spatial experience that can range from great intimacy and comfort all the way to intimidating monumentality. When designing, still another point should be considered: the smaller the square is, the greater the geometric constraints are for the architectural configuration of the building lots. This can be easily understood by imagining a simple, round plaza: the smaller the radius, the greater the curvature of the wall defining the square, and thus of the building.

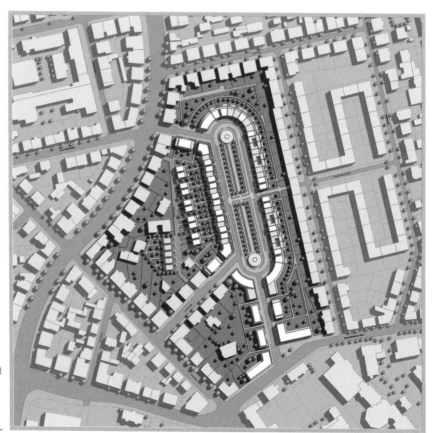

With modeling, the public square is created by shaping and adjusting the building shapes to match the chosen shape.

⊙ — **St. Leonhards Garten,** Braunschweig (D)

✎ — KLAUS THEO BRENNER STADTARCHITEKTUR, Berlin

▣ — www.klaustheobrenner.de

◉ — 2nd prize

▦ — 2007

▭ — urban redevelopment – commercial conversion – new residential district

◈ — **place making through modeling**

◆ — urban building blocks: closed, dissolved city block, row, point; layout of development
—— sites: datum

Axonometric

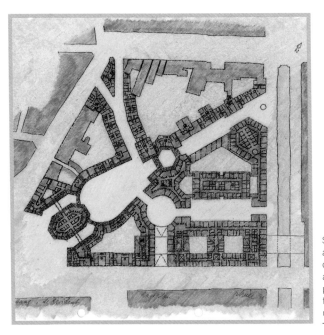

⚙ — **De Resident,** Den Haag (NL)

✎ — Rob Krier + Christoph Kohl, Berlin

▭ — www.archkk.com

▦ — 1990

▭ — urban renewal – inner-city urban district

◈ — **place making through modeling**

🏷 — figure and ground, Prägnanz, additive approach (spaces); urban building blocks: closed city block, inner-city urban block, courtyard, high-rise tower; layout of development sites: axis, symmetry

Squares that are created through modeling can also be described as resulting from punching out a shape from a homogeneous urban texture.

Perspective

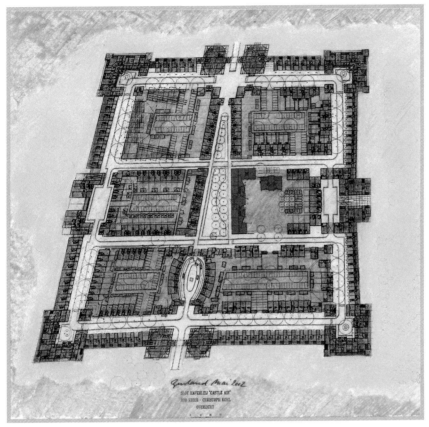

Modeled squares impart an intensive spatial experience.

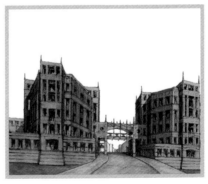

Perspective with view toward oval entry square

 — **Slot Haverleij, Haverleij,** 's-Hertogenbosch (NL)

 — Rob Krier + Christoph Kohl, Berlin

🖥 — www.archkk.com

📅 — 1999

🗂 — urban expansion – part of a new residential district

📑 — **place making through modeling**

🔖 — Ganzheit; figure and ground; Prägnanz; additive approach; urban building blocks: opened city block, row, point; layout of development sites: axis, symmetry; representation: perspective

Define

With a square formed "by definition," the surrounding buildings play a secondary role. The square is defined by its paving surface, a change in height, or as the fore-court and outdoor space of a building standing on the square (or along its edge).

There are impressive squares with freestanding buildings from the postwar Modernist era. The plaza of the Supreme Federal Court in Brasília (from 1955, master plan by Lúcio Costa), for example, and the one in Chandigarh (from 1951, master plan by Le Corbusier) are both laid out as vast, open expanses. The plaza surfaces covered with uniform paving are each flanked to the sides by green spaces and establish a spacious forefield for the expressive, almost sculptural buildings. Mies van der Rohe's Neue Nationalgalerie in Berlin is also exemplary in its staging of vastness: The fully glazed, steel entrance hall stands atop a free-standing plaza-like plinth.

Smaller squares without architectural enclosure – or only to a slight degree – are primarily found in landscape parks or in the green and open spaces of larger residential complexes.

A square is by definition not architecturally delimited, or is so only to a slight degree, and is primarily defined through its surface.

Small neighborhood squares alternate with green spaces.

 — **Mars-la-Tour-Straße,** Hannover (D)

 — pfp architekten, Hamburg

 — www.pfp-architekten.de

 — honorable mention

 — 2008

 — Inner-city development – residential district on former parking lot

 — **place making by definition**

 — divisional approach; orthogonal grid; layout of urban building blocks on
— building lot: repetition/rhythm

The squares interspersed throughout the design are differentiated from the other open spaces through the paving.

Detail of model

🎯 — **Residential district in the European Quarter,** Frankfurt am Main (D)

✏️ — Spengler • Wiescholek Architekten Stadtplaner, Hamburg

🖥️ — www.spengler-wiescholek.de

🏆 — merit award

📅 — 2002

🗂️ — urban redevelopment – railway conversion – new urban district

📖 — **place making by definition**

🏷️ — additive approach; layout of development sites: axis, sequence/repetition/rhythm; circulation loop;

___ representation: illustrative site plan

- ⊙ — **Master Plan for Neckarvorstadt,**
  Heilbronn (D)
- ✐ — MORPHO-LOGIC Architektur und
  Stadtplanung, Munich, Lex Kerfers
  Landschaftsarchitekten, Bockhorn
- ▣ — www.morpho-logic.de
- ◎ — 3rd prize
- ▦ — 2009
- ▭ — urban redevelopment – railway/
  commercial conversion – new waterside district
- ◈ — **place making by definition**
- ◈ — additive approach; urban building
  blocks: opened city block, Zeile;
  layout of development sites: repeti-
  tion/rhythm; place making through
  assembly; community green and
  open space; waterfront living

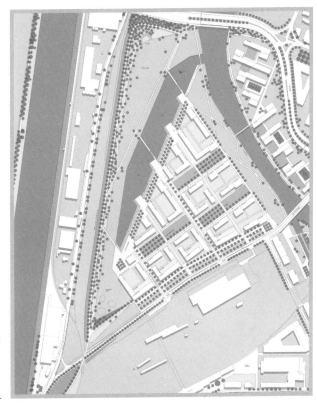

The promenade along
the former harbor basin
is supplemented by
small squares that ex-
tend out into the water
as platforms.

Open space concept

THE INTERMEDIATE SPACE AS FREESTYLE EXERCISE

9.2 **STREET SPACES**

THE street is both urban form and institution,[11] according to Spiro Kostof, who thereby explains that along with having an aesthetic aspect, the street must simultaneously fulfill economic and social functions that are expressed in transport, trade, and communication. Whereas there was no relationship between the street and the introverted buildings of the traditional Chinese city and this was also largely absent in the ancient Greek cities, the prototype of the European city street virtually came into being with the development of the insulae, Rome's multistoried apartment buildings. Shops were accommodated on the ground floor and above them were dwellings that, due to the building's internal density alone, needed to be oriented to the street. Even in the medieval city, people lived in the stories above the places of work and commerce at the ground level – and naturally they put their social status on display in the public realm by individualizing their facades. With the Baroque period and its absolutist rulers, buildings and the street space began to be unified; this effort was later increased with Baron Haussmann's creation of the boulevards in Paris. In reaction to the inhuman conditions in the rear courtyards that hid behind richly decorated facades, in the *Charter of Athens* from 1933 – according to the motto "From then on, the house will never again be fused to the street by a sidewalk"[12] – there was a call to liberate buildings and separate traffic from uses. As a result, a development was initiated that continues to have a noticeable effect to this day, reflected at home and abroad in countless dismal large-scale housing estates. With the renaissance of urban space that began in the mid-1970s, a rethinking came into play that has meanwhile also reached traffic planning. Whereas the street space had predetermined the framework thus far on the basis of requirements for automobile traffic, the spaces to the sides are now derived from what happens along the edges and from the proportions of the street space, and only then is the possible width of the roadway defined.[13]

Recommendations on the Layout of Streets
In the literature on urban design, there are numerous recommendations for laying out streets. Despite his admiration for the old cities, Raymond Unwin, the planner of the first garden city based on Ebenezer Howard's ideas from the *Garden Cities of To-morrow* – Letchworth Garden City near London – attributes a unique purposefulness and beauty to straight streets. In his opinion, these should be used without restrictions in designing modern cities.[14] But Unwin also sees the risk of monotony in straight roads and recommends to introduce breaks in the building alignments, set back individual buildings, and create front yards.

11 Spiro Kostof, *The City Assembled: The Elements of Urban Form Through History* (New York: Little, Brown, 1999; orig. 1992), p. 189.
12 Le Corbusier, *The Athens Charter*, trans. Anthony Eardley (New York: Grossman, 1973), p. 57.
13 Hartmut H. Topp: "Städtische und regionale Mobilität im postfossilen Zeitalter," in *Zukunftsfähige Stadtentwicklung für Stuttgart: Vorträge und Diskussionen* (Stuttgart: Architektenkammer Baden-Württemberg, 2011), p. 42.
14 Raymond Unwin, *Town Planning in Practice: An Introduction to the Art of Designing Cities and Suburbs* (London: T. Fisher Unwin, 1909), p. 259.

Camillo Sitte, on the other hand, criticizes the schematic gridded urban design of his time and denies it every artistic quality. He suggests irregularities, bends, and breaks in the street alignment to make it easier for people to orient themselves.[15]

From Le Corbusier, by contrast, we have the bon mot that the curved street is a donkey track and a straight street is a road for men. In Kevin Lynch's book *The Image of the City*, which is based on empirical research, he writes of identity and the continuity of street space and notes that in addition to spatial aspects, these are also supported by aspects like facade characteristics. According to Lynch, directional qualities are another important trait of streets: Such streets have a directional character that seems different when traveling in one direction as opposed to the other; this is accomplished through gradients, topographic guidance, distinct start and end points, and changes in direction.[16]

Despite highly diverse observations, recommendations, and ideologies that continue having influence to this day, one can use the words of Rob Krier to summarize that streets can yield an "inexhaustible range" of spatial situations.[17]

LETCHWORTH (detail), Barry Parker/Raymond Unwin, 1903 (GB)

Counterproposal by Friedrich Pützer for a villa suburb in Darmstadt based on Sitte's "artistic principles" (l.) and the earlier schematic layout by the Darmstadt city administration (r.), ca. 1900 (D)

15 Collins, *Camillo Sitte*, p. 327.
16 Kevin Lynch, *The Image of the City* (Cambridge, MA: MIT Press, 1960), p. 54 ff.
17 Krier, *Urban Space*, p. 30.

Classification of Street Spaces

Streets and paths within a city are organized hierarchically according to their function, and thereby according to the volume of traffic they carry, into the following: local main roads and collector roads, secondary access roads, residential streets, traffic-calmed areas, and lastly, pedestrian zones and discrete bicycle/footpath connections.

Designing Street Spaces

City streets can be classified not only according to their function, but also according to spatial traits, that is, according to their course and the degree of their built delimitation. The street's course can be straight, curved, bent, interrupted, or widened out to form a square-like area. The street space can be architecturally rigorous, casual, or not at all delimited. Within a street, combinations of the different properties are possible.

For all streets, it is generally the case that if the space is more clearly delimited, the spatial experience will be more intense. With straight roads, what matters is the length: a short, straight street is more likely to be perceived as a space than a long one would.

A special case attributable to topography comprises scenic routes with panoramic views, such as Princes Street in Edinburgh, Scotland: these forgo two-sided development in favor of a scenic vista.

Linear Street Space

A linear street connects two points along the shortest route. The buildings stand along the street as equals, lined up in continuous aggregations that may be tight or loose. A linear street has no destination if it is not spatially delimited where it begins or ends, and it tends to become monotonous over long distances.

With appropriate perimeter development, a visible beginning and end, the tying-in of upscale uses, sufficient width, and suitable greenery — as with the straight thoroughfares Unter den Linden in Berlin and Avenue des Champs-Élysées in Paris — one speaks of a boulevard or avenue.

The linear main access road is spatially captured in two places and cleverly continued with a slight offset.

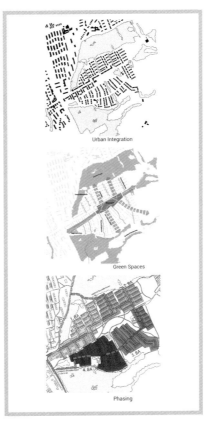

Urban Integration

Green Spaces

Phasing

Figure-ground plan and concept diagrams

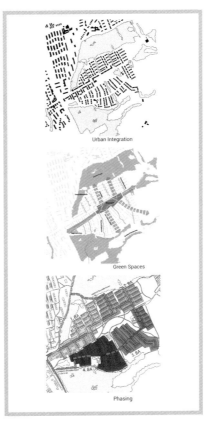 — **Knollstraße Residential Development,** Osnabrück (D)

— STADTRAUM Architektengruppe, Düsseldorf, with Stefan Villena y Scheffler, Langenhagen

— www.stadtraum-architekten.de

— 2nd prize

— 2006

— settlement extension – new urban district

— **linear street space**

— geometric principle, biomorphic/organic principle; layout of development sites: axis, datum, sequence/repetition/rhythm; cul-de-sac network, circulation loop; widened
___ street space

Curved or Bent Street Space

Compared to straight streets, curved streets have the advantage that the viewer's gaze is always directed at the facades of the buildings. Depending on whether one travels along the street in one direction or another, different facades are visible. A similar effect is offered by bent streets – but only near to where the direction changes. Curved streets or perceptibly bent streets have a large spatial impact, since the gaze is always caught by a building and not able to drift off into space.

Compared to straight streets, curved streets have the advantage that the viewer's gaze is always directed at the facades.

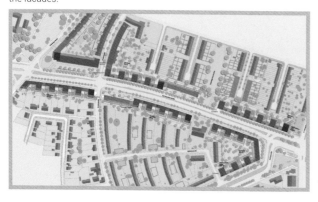

- **Bad-Schachener-Straße Housing Development,** Munich (D)
- florian krieger – architektur und städtebau, Darmstadt, with S. Thron, Ulm, and Irene Burkhardt Landschaftsarchitekten, Stadtplaner, Munich
- www.florian-krieger.de
- 1st prize
- 2009
- urban redevelopment – inner-city development – housing
- **curved street space**
- urban building blocks: dissolved city block, row; representation: perspective

View of the street space

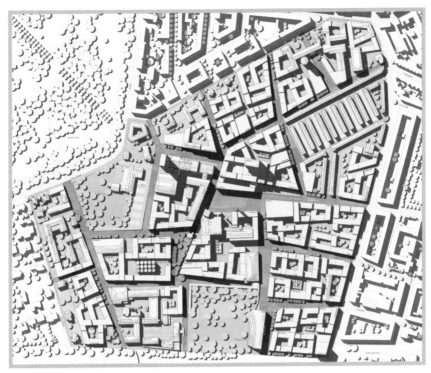

Bent streets, like curved ones, have a large spatial impact, since the gaze is always caught by buildings.

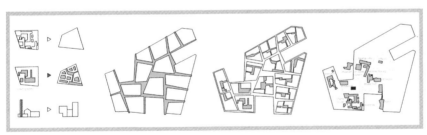

Design diagrams

⌖ – **Development plan for Carlsberg,** Copenhagen (DK)

✎ – Wessendorf Architektur Städtebau with Atelier Loidl and Architect Barbara Engel, Berlin

🖥 – www.studio-wessendorf.de, www.atelier-loidl.de

🏆 – 2nd prize

📅 – 2007

🗂 – commercial conversion – new district

🗁 – **bent street space**

🏷 – additive approach; layout of development sites: grouping; place making through
      assembly and modeling; widened street space

Intermittent Street Space

Long street spaces, whether straight or curved, tend to monotony. They can, however, be organized by architectural and spatial accents, which can also be repeated as a theme. Even small deviations from standard course are helpful: Spatial offsets in the movement sequence create areas of paved open space, small or large, and open up new visual connections. High points at intersections, recessed individual buildings, pocket-like widening of the street space, and transverse green corridors interrupt rigid building frontages.

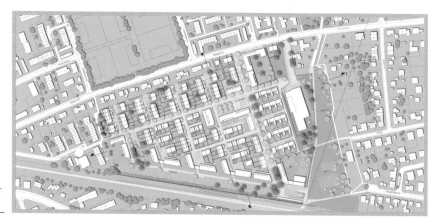

In order to avoid monotony, it is advisable to interrupt long street spaces with squares or green corridors.

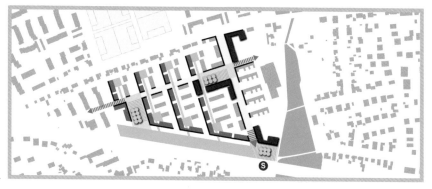

Open spaces diagram

⌖ — **Aubing-Ost,** Munich (D)

✏ — pp a|s pesch partner architekten stadtplaner, Herdecke/Stuttgart, with WGF Land-schaftsarchitekten, Nuremberg

🖥 — www.pesch-partner.de

🏆 — 1st prize

📅 — 2009

🗂 — urban redevelopment — railway conversion — new residential district

◆ — **intermittent street space**

🔖 — additive approach; urban building blocks: row, Zeile, point; layout of development
___ sites: axis; place making through assembly; representation: diagrams

Widened Street Space

Early forms of widened street space can be found in village structures like the so-called Straßenanger, which is somewhat akin to a town commons or village green. The thoroughfare widens out here into an oblong square where the church is often located.

The medieval town was also familiar with such situations. In Freiburg im Breisgau, for example, a widened main road along an old trade route served as a market-place. The German street names Rindermarkt [cattle market] or Fischmarkt [fish market] are still reminiscent of these functions in many cities today. Similar market streets are found in the cities founded by the House of Zähringen: Bern, Rottweil, Villingen, and in the free imperial cities of Augsburg, Nuremberg, and many others.

In contemporary urban design, widening the street spaces is still a proven and effective means, especially if the goal is to provide a common center for one or more districts at low cost – because the street itself already exists. And more building lots can benefit from being on an elongated, commons-like widened street space than on a central, compact square.

TYPICAL STRASSENANGERDORF,
founded ca. 1250

More building lots can benefit from a commons-like widened street space than from a central, compact square.

Illustrative site plan and perspectives of the street space

⌖ — **Herzo Base Residential District,** Herzogenaurach (D)
✎ — studio eu with Stefan Tischer, Berlin
⌨ — www.studioeu.net
🏆 — 4th prize
📅 — 2002
📁 — urban redevelopment — military conversion — new residential district
◈ — **widened street space**
🏷 — additive approach; stretched grid; circulation loop

 — **Senior Living on the English Garden,** Landsberg am Lech (D)

 — Nickel & Partner with mahl-gebhard-konzepte, Munich

🖥 — www.nickl-partner.com

🏅 — 2nd prize

📅 — 2005

🗂 — urban expansion – new residential district

🗂 — **widened street space**

🖐 — urban building blocks: Zeile, point; layout of development sites: datum; curved street space; community green and open space

The commons-like widened street space is likewise a neighborhood square for the adjacent apartments.

Model

Amorphous Street Space

In an amorphous street space, the space formed by the street and buildings does not have a clear and distinct image, but exhibits instead an irregular or fragmented pattern. The close relationship between the buildings is more dominant than the relationship with ones located further away. With the uniform alignment of buildings along a straight street space, on the other hand, this effect can barely be felt. Amorphous street spaces of reasonable lengths offer interesting spatial impressions, but over greater lengths, constant changes in the direction of view can become tiring and disadvantageous to one's sense of orientation.

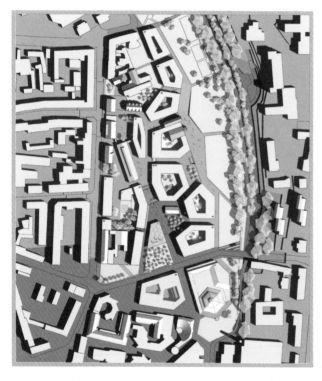

⊙ — **University of Kassel, North Campus** (D)

✎ — raumzeit Gesellschaft von Architekten mbH, Kassel, with K1 Landschaftsarchitekten, Berlin

▣ — www.raumzeit.org

✵ — 1st prize

▦ — 2008

▤ — urban redevelopment — commercial conversion — new college campus

◈ — **amorphous street space**

✎ — additive approach; irregular grid; place making through assembly; green space delimited by buildings; — representation: illustrative site plan

In amorphous street spaces, the close relationship of the buildings dominates

Perspective of the street space

GREEN AND OPEN SPACES

WHEN examining images of cities from the seventeenth century, the contrast between city and nature is immediately apparent. Within the city, there are only solitary
trees – and here and there small gardens squeezed between the closely spaced
buildings – to be recognized, but no larger green spaces. Although beyond the city
walls, there is all the more: not only forests and open landscape, but also fields,
meadows, and gardens as far as the eye can see. City and nature exist here as a
contrasting pair, yet despite all the differences, they are dependent upon one another – as is symbolized, for instance, in the Yin and Yang in Chinese philosophy.
The city has always been dependent on nature and its products, as is nature – at
least the cultural landscape – from the city.

Nature outside of the European city was not only a foundation of life, but was
also a place for relaxation that could always be reached in times of peace within
a few minutes beyond the city gate. The meadows and plots close to the city in
particular accommodated kitchen gardens for city dwellers. In London in 1592,
for example, the fences put up by leaseholders on the open fields outside the city,
the "Commons," had to be pulled down by an act of Parliament to enable military
exercises and for the "recreacion comforte and healthe of her [Majesty's] people."[18]

People have always had the need to relax and recuperate in gardens or nature.
In the days of ancient Rome there were many publicly accessible gardens. In the
seventeenth century, many parks belonging to the English crown were open to
the public, and the royal hunting ground in Berlin, the Tiergarten, was also open
to everyone who wished to take a "pleasurable stroll."

In the Baroque planned cities, the relationship between city and nature was
newly staked out: The city maps of Versailles or Karlsruhe make legible the absolute claim to power of the sovereign leaders over people and nature: Starting from
the palace, axes lead out radially to the residential and administrative center and
also across the palace grounds, far out into nature. In addition, the Baroque city
brought forth a new urban design typology: the perimeter block, which, being only
a few stories high – there was virtually no development pressure – had a large,
open courtyard. In 1648, after the Thirty Years War, Germany's cities were depopu-
lated and the princes needed to lure potential inhabitants to their ideal cities with
benefits like tax exemptions or free building materials.

18 Kostof, *The City Assembled*, p. 167.

0 m   50   100

HUFEISENSIEDLUNG IN BERLIN, Bruno Taut/Martin Wagner, 1925 (D)

Industrialization, new fertilization procedures in agriculture, and population explosion caused cities to grow at the end of the nineteenth century. Within a brief time, tenements emerged in extreme density as speculative property; the deplorable hygienic conditions were unbearable. Politicians attempted to respond by establishing public parks, allotment gardens, zoos, and sports facilities. Camillo Sitte supplemented his book *City Planning According to Artistic Principles* in 1909 with the appendix "Greenery within the City," in which he makes a distinction between the "sanitary green" within city blocks and the "decorative green" in the street space.[19] Ebenezer Howard went even further in the reform approach in his book *Garden Cities of To-morrow.*[20] In the vicinity of major cities, he called for the establishment of small cities with a maximum of 32,000 inhabitants each. The city was to remain cooperative property in order to put a curb on speculation. With the slogan "living and working in the sun,"[21] a life in the countryside was propagated, with subsistence gardens, parks, and places of work. The Garden City movement attracted widespread international attention, even though the number of cities actually founded in accord with these principles remained small. After World War I, social housing stood at the forefront of urban development in Europe. Well-known examples from this period are the Wohnhöfe constructed in Vienna as part of the municipal housing program, with their large communal green spaces, the Dammerstock Siedlung in Karlsruhe, and the housing developments by Bruno Taut in Berlin, with their suffusive greenery.

19 Collins, *Camillo Sitte*, p. 303 f.
20 The title of the book published in 1898 was *To-Morrow: A Peaceful Path to Real Reform.* It was not until the second edition of 1902 that the book bore the well-known title *Garden Cities of To-morrow.*
21 Slogan for the poster advertising Welwyn Garden City, the second garden city initiated by Howard, in Virgilio Vercelloni: *Europäische Stadtutopien: Ein historischer Atlas* (Munich: Diederichs, 1994), p. 149.

The period of reconstruction after World War II was very much under the international influence of the Athens Charter of 1933 and its separation of the city's main functions into dwelling, work, recreation, and transportation. Green spaces were defined less by their usability and more according to their function as a green corridor or "green lung." The traditional urban space should be replaced by a blend of city and landscape to become an urban landscape. The result was a profusion of undefined planted buffer zones and median strips. The rediscovery of the traditional city after the 1973 energy crisis led not only to a reassessment of urban spaces, but also to differentiation of green spaces according to environmental and social aspects. The verdant urbanity imagined by the Modernists did not become a reality; perhaps "the vision of a dual urbanity, in which natural greenery is entwined with the built city,"[22] will yet become reality.

Classification of Green and Open Spaces
Green and open spaces in the city are generally differentiated according to location, function, and user groups in categories reflecting the scope of their user base: citywide, district-level, community/neighborhood, and adjoining green and open spaces.

Citywide Green and Open Spaces
Primary green corridors that link residential areas with the landscape and larger inner-city parks for recreational use by all the city's inhabitants are among the open spaces relevant to the entire city. Aside from their recreational use, these open spaces improve the urban climate and, in the form of biotope networks, help preserve biodiversity.

22 Dittmar Machule and Jens Usadel, "Grün-Natur und Stadt-Struktur: Chancen für eine doppelte Urbanität," in *Grün-Natur und Stadt-Struktur: Entwicklungsstrategien bei der Planung und Gestaltung von städtischen Freiräumen* (Frankfurt am Main: Societäts, 2011), p. 14.

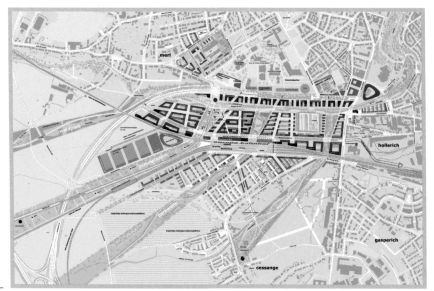

The green corridors extending into the area are part of the citywide green space.

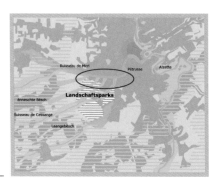

Citywide green space concept

🎯 — **Porte de Hollerich Master Plan,** Luxemburg (L)

✏️ — Teisen – Giesler Architectes with Nicklas Architectes, Luxembourg, BS+ Städtebau und Architektur, Frankfurt am Main, and Landschaftsplaner stadtland, Vienna

🖥️ — www.teisen-giesler.lu

🏆 — 1st prize

📅 — 2004

📁 — urban redevelopment/urban expansion – industrial/commercial conversion – new district

📚 — **citywide green and open space**

🏷️ — additive approach; layout of development sites: datum, sequence/repetition/rhythm; green space delimited by buildings

District-Level Green and Open Spaces

With district-level green and open spaces, residents are within walking distance of recreational, playground, and sporting facilities. The open space can be centrally located or at the edge of the district, axially laid out, self-contained, or part of a city-wide green corridor.

⊘ – **neue bahn stadt:opladen,** Leverkusen (D)

✐ – ASTOC Architects and Planners,
Cologne, with Studio UC, Berlin

▣ – www.astoc.de

◉ – 3rd prize

▦ – 2006

◱ – urban redevelopment – railway
conversion – new district

◈ – **district-level green and open space**

◆ – additive approach; layout of develop-
___ ment sites: datum; circulation loop

The green spaces are primarily associated with the new district, but they are also networked with other districts.

Perspective

Community Green and Open Spaces

Community green and open spaces are small public squares, playgrounds, and parks within a neighborhood that directly serve the residents and employees from the surrounding buildings. This type of open space generally has shade trees, seating, and play equipment. Robust and durable surfaces are desirable to withstand intensive use in a restricted space.

⚙ — **Beckershof,** Henstedt-Ulzburg (D)

✎ — APB Architekten BDA, Hamburg, with JKL Junker + Kollegen Landschafts-architektur, Georgsmarienhütte

▢ — www.apb-architekten.de

◉ — 4th prize

📅 — 2004

🗂 — urban expansion – new district

◆ — **community green and open space**

◈ — layout of development sites: repetition/rhythm, grouping; community green and open space; integrated green space

The new residential neighborhoods are grouped around a district-level green and open space; additionally, they have their own community green and open spaces.

Adjoining Green and Open Spaces

Adjoining open spaces are directly associated with the dwelling and can take the form of private or communal gardens, landscaped street space, front yards, winter gardens, loggias, or balconies.

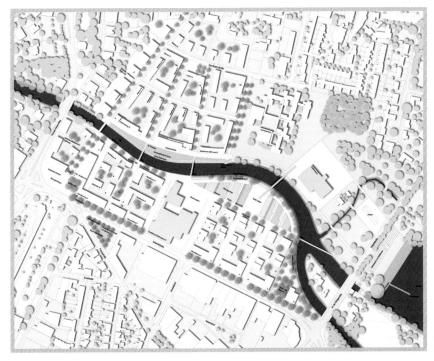

Illustrative site plan

@ — **Industriestraße/Bocholter Aa,**
Bocholt (D)

✎ — pp a|s pesch partner architekten
stadtplaner, Herdecke/Stuttgart,
with scape Landschaftsarchitekten,
Düsseldorf

▣ — www.pesch-partner.de

◎ — 1st prize

▦ — 2009

▤ — urban redevelopment – commercial/
industrial conversion – new urban
district

◈ — **adjacent green and open space**

◥ — urban building blocks: dissolved city
block, row, Zeile, point; layout of development sites: datum (river); green
— space delimited by buildings

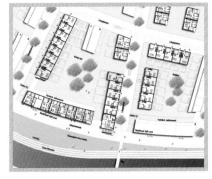

The apartments are directly connected with adjacent open spaces like private or communal gardens.

Designing Green and Open Spaces

When designing green and open spaces, there are three basic options for the relationship between green space and the built fabric of the adjacent building lots and development sites:

- The green space is rigorously delimited architecturally. The built fabric can be partly open to the green space, but the building frontage dominates overall.
- The green space and built fabric are tightly meshed. For larger urban areas, green corridors assume this function. At the scale of the development site, the interconnection can, for instance, be achieved by alternating compact building lots with incised open spaces. At the scale of the building lot, this can be achieved through the positioning of the built elements. The buildings and building lots then logically open up to the green space. Examples of suitable urban building blocks are Zeile structures, points, and U-shaped, open or dissolved perimeter block structures.
- The building lot itself becomes part of the green space due to the type of construction and access. The buildings embedded in the green space can have a freestanding character or they can be grouped.

- **Nordwestbahnhof,** Vienna (A)
- ernst niklaus fausch architekten, Zurich
- www.enf.ch
- 1st prize
- 2008
- urban redevelopment – railway conversion – new urban district and park
- **green and open space delimited by buildings**
- stretched grid; urban building blocks: closed city block; layout of development sites: datum; representation: perspective

The new city park is rigorously architecturally delimited.

Bird's-eye perspective

THE INTERMEDIATE SPACE AS FREESTYLE EXERCISE

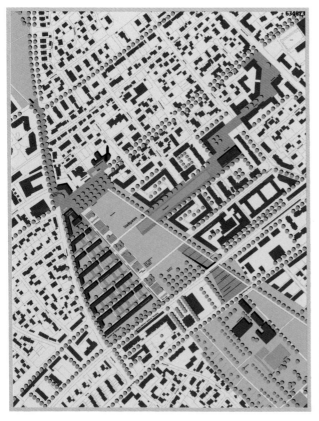

 — **Gilchinger Glatze,** Gilching (D)

— Marcus Rommel Architekten BDA, Stuttgart/Trier, with ernst + partner landschaftsarchitekten, Trier

— www.marcus-rommel-architekten.de

— 1st prize

— 2005

— urban expansion – new residential districts on the park

— **green and open space delimited by buildings – one-sided**

— additive approach; urban building blocks: dissolved city block, row; layout of development sites: datum; integrated green space delimited by buildings

The green and open space is rigorously delimited architectural-ly on one side, whereas on the other side, build-ings are interspersed with open space.

Model

⊙ – **Europan 9, stepscape greenscape waterscape,** Rostock (D)

✎ – florian krieger – architektur und städtebau, Darmstadt

🖥 – www.florian-krieger.de

🏅 – 1st prize

📅 – 2008

🗂 – urban redevelopment – inner-city development – new waterside residential district

◈ – **integrated green and open space**

🏷 – additive approach; urban building blocks: hybrid of spatial structure, row, Zeile, and point; representation:

___ perspective

The interwoven relationship between buildings and open space is a theme of the architectural concept.

Perspective

239

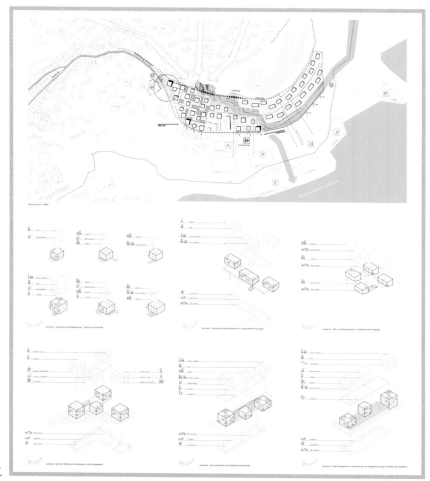

Due to the loosely placed freestanding buildings that are not fixed to any building lines, the building lots themselves become part of the green space.

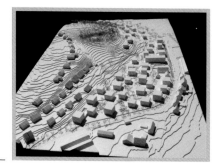

Model

- **Vorderer Kätzleberg,** Stockach (D)
- LS Architektur Städtebau, Stuttgart, with Braun+Müller Architekten BDA, Constance
- www.leonhardschenk.de, www.braun-mueller-architekten.de
- 1st place
- 2011
- urban redevelopment – commercial conversion – new residential district
- **flowing green and open space**
- urban building blocks: point; loop street network; representation: structural concept; presentation model

Design Elements of Green and Open Spaces

Garden design and landscape architecture has a variety of design options: open spaces can be modeled and changed topographically, their impact can be heightened, or water can be integrated into the design in the form of lakes or flowing streams. Depending on the primary function, vegetation elements like trees, shrubs, hedges, and meadows, as well as built elements such as paths, walls, pergolas, and various surfaces can be used in the design.

Two design elements that are routinely used in urban design shall be examined in more detail at this point: trees and water.

Trees as Spatial Design Elements

Trees are an element of nature in the city. They improve the urban climate, reduce CO_2 emissions, and act as a shield against overly intense solar radiation. Beyond that – if only because of their size and volume – they are design elements that, together with the buildings, help define the city. They accentuate and give structure to urban spaces like public squares, streets, and open and green spaces, and they also connect them together visually.[23] The ways in which trees are used for design results from the specific spatial situation. Put simply: In the space of the city, trees are commonly deployed in a geometric system in the form of lines or grids. Within open and green spaces, however, single trees, groups, or gridded arrangements predominate.

Individual Trees. Larger individual trees highlight particular spatial locations in the city, such as small neighborhood squares or the entry points to groups of buildings. In open spaces they are used in a solitary position, for instance to accentuate a distinctive topographic situation.

Rows of Trees. Trees in simple rows or paired in the form of allées underscore the road alignment and direction of streets and elongated urban spaces. In traffic-calmed streets, an irregular row of trees that alternates from side to side can hinder the flow of space and have a positive influence on traffic behavior.

23 Anna-Maria Fischer and Dietmar Reinborn, "Grün und Freiflächen," in *Lehrbausteine Städtebau*, 2nd ed., ed. Johann Jessen (Stuttgart: Städtebau-Institut, 2003), p. 131 ff.

- **Spitalhöhe/Krummer Weg,** Rottweil (D)
- Ackermann+Raff, Stuttgart/Tübingen
- www.ackermann-raff.de
- 1st prize
- 2005
- urban expansion – new district
- **individual trees, trees in rows**
- layout of urban building blocks on building lot: datum, sequence/rhythm, grouping; place making through assembly; curved street space; representation: diagrams

Trees in rows and groups mark the residential streets and neighborhood squares, and individual trees mark the courtyard housing.

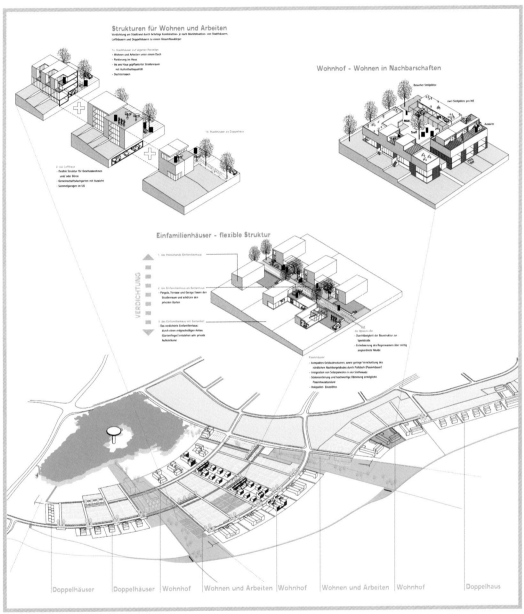

Strukturen für Wohnen und Arbeiten

Verdichtung am Stadtrand durch beliebige Kombination – je nach Marktsituation – von Stadthäusern, Lofthäusern und Doppelhäusern zu einem Gesundbaukörper

1a. Stadthäuser auf eigener Parzelle
- Wohnen und Arbeiten unter einem Dach
- Parkierung im Haus
- bis ans Haus gepflasterter Straßenraum mit Aufenthaltsqualität
- Dachterrassen

1b. Stadthäuser als Doppelhaus

2. das Lofthaus
- flexible Struktur für Geschosswohnen und/oder Büros
- Gemeinschaftsdachgarten mit Aussicht
- Sammelgaragen im UG

Wohnhof - Wohnen in Nachbarschaften

Besucher Stellplätze

zwei Stellplätze pro WE

Einfamilienhäuser - flexible Struktur

VERDICHTUNG

1. das freistehende Einfamilienhaus

2. das Einfamilienhaus als Kettenhaus
- Pergola, Terrasse und Garage fassen den Straßenraum und schützen den privaten Garten

3. das verdichtete Einfamilienhaus mit Gartenhof
Das verdichtete Einfamilienhaus durch einen eingeschossigen Anbau (Gartenflügel) entstehen sehr private Außenräume

- Durchlässigkeit der Baumstruktur zur Spielstraße
- Entwässerung des Regenwassers über mittig angeordnete Mulde

Passivhäuser:
- kompaktes Gebäudevolumen, sowie geringe Verschattung des nördlichen Nachbargebäudes durch Pultdach (Passivhäuser!)
- Integration von Solarpaneelen in der Südfassade
- Südorientierung und hochwertige Dämmung ermöglicht Passivhausstandard
- Holzpellet-Einzelöfen

| Doppelhäuser | Doppelhäuser | Wohnhof | Wohnen und Arbeiten | Wohnhof | Wohnen und Arbeiten | Wohnhof | Doppelhaus |

Locations of trees and house types depicted spatially

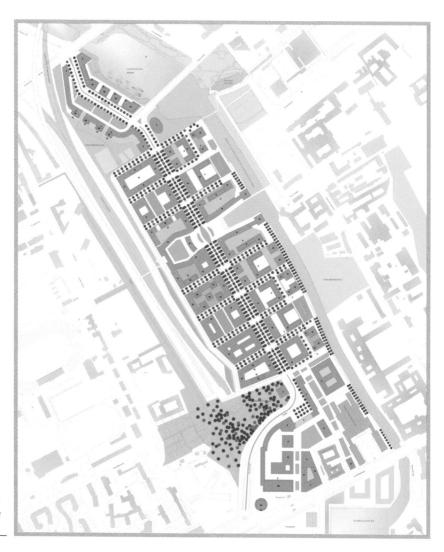

Five rows of trees turn
the main thoroughfare
into a boulevard.

⌖ — **Europacity/Heidestraße,** Berlin (D)

✎ — HILMER & SATTLER und ALBRECHT, Berlin/Munich, with Keller Landschaftsarchitekten, Berlin

🖥 — www.h-s-a.de

🏆 — 3rd prize

📅 — 2008

🗐 — urban redevelopment — inner-city development — new urban district

◈ — **trees in rows**

🔧 — Prägnanz; additive approach; layout of development sites: axis, (partial) symmetry,
___ datum, repetition/rhythm, grouping; place making through modeling

Patterns of Trees. The geometric arrangement of trees as circular or square shapes or in a grid of trees is a common design element in urban spaces. Tree canopies on squares can create intimate protected spaces, and large spaces can be delimited by grids of trees, or subdivided into different sections.

Freely Grouped Trees. In landscape parks, trees are often arranged into freely composed, loose, or tight groups ("clumps") and arranged as groves. The shift between individual trees and clusters of trees results in a shift between open and dense spaces. This arrangement is even used in larger urban green spaces with a park-like character.

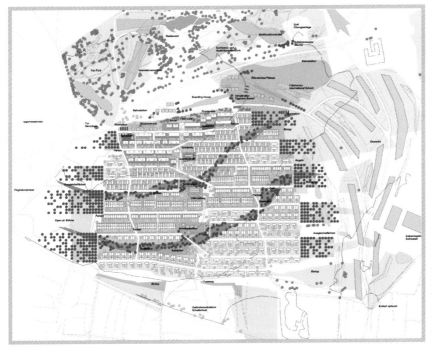

Trees in a tight grid visually extend the building lots out into the landscape, and there are clusters of trees within the green corridors.

🌀 — **Herzo Base Residential District,** Herzogenaurach (D)

✏️ — straub tacke architekten bda, Munich

🖥 — www.straub-arc.de

🏆 — 3rd prize

📅 — 2002

🗂 — urban redevelopment — military conversion — new residential district

🍃 — **tight grid of trees, freely grouped trees**

🔦 — divisional approach; loop street network, circulation loop, place making by definition; representation: diagrams

Water as a Spatial Design Element

Water holds great allure for many people. Living or working with a view of the water is a privilege. For some years now, many old, abandoned industrial sites along rivers or entire harbor areas are being transformed into modern residential and office districts. Well-known examples that are distinguished by innovative urban design and impressive architecture are the Eastern Docklands in Amsterdam – with the new residential districts Java-eiland, KNSM-eiland, Borneo, and Sporenburg; MedienHafen in Dusseldorf; and HafenCity Hamburg. Besides the new use of existing areas along the water, many new urban districts are being built around the world on artificially formed islands, or those in which expanses of water and canals are being laid out. Known from extensive media coverage is the large-scale Palm Islands development on three groups of artificial islands off the coast of Dubai in the shape of a palm tree. The palm-like layout means that nearly all the residents have their own private beach access.

In recent years in the Netherlands, many urban expansion areas – with around 800,000 new dwelling units – have emerged as part of the so-called Vinex program. As part of the same program, the new district of IJburg is currently being built in Amsterdam on several artificial islands in the IJmeer bay. In the Netherlands, for environmental reasons about 10 percent of the settlement area must be reserved for expanses of water – which investors and architects gladly use for new housing opportunities on or along the water.[24] In Ypenburg, the large subarea Waterwijk virtually celebrates waterfront living.

Areas of water can be designed in entirely different ways: The banks of streams can be designed in a natural or architectural manner, and expanses of water can be a pond, lake, or pool. The built fabric along the waterside also offers many design alternatives, ranging from closed city blocks and U-shaped blocks that open up toward the water to point-like building forms that enable the rows of buildings further away, and thus as many people as possible, to also enjoy the attractive views of the water.

THE PALM JUMEIRAH IN DUBAI, HHCP ARCHITECTS, 2001 (UAE)

24 See interview with Jelte Boeijenga and Jeroen Mensink, "Welcome to Vinex Country," in Leonhard Schenk and Rob van Gool, *Neuer Wohnungsbau in den Niederlanden: Konzepte Typologien Projekte* (Munich: Deutsche-Verlags Anstalt, 2010), p. 21.

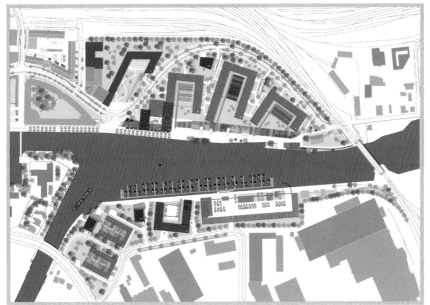

U-shaped open city blocks are particularly suited for waterfront development on deep building lots, since the disadvantages of having buildings in a second or even third row can be avoided.

Perspective

🎯 — **Alter Stadthafen,** Oldenburg (D)

✏️ — BOLLES+WILSON, Münster, with Agence Ter, Karlsruhe/Paris

🖥️ — www.bolles-wilson.com

🏆 — 3rd prize

📅 — 2008

🗂️ — urban redevelopment – harbor conversion – new urban district

📑 — **waterfront living/development**

🏷️ — additive approach; urban building blocks: dissolved, open city block; representation:
    perspective

The design proposes various types of waterfront living: on islands, peninsulas, and on canals.

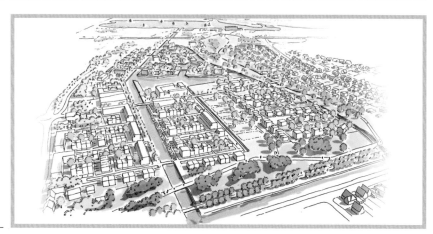

Bird's-eye perspective

⌖ — **Vechtesee – Oorde,** Nordhorn (D)

✐ — pp a|s pesch partner architekten stadtplaner, Herdecke/Stuttgart, with Glück Landschaftsarchitektur, Stuttgart

🖥 — www.pesch-partner.de

🏆 — 2nd prize

📅 — 2009

🗂 — urban expansion – commercial conversion – new residential districts and recreation area

📑 — **waterfront living/development**

🔖 — urban building blocks: dissolved city block, courtyard, row, Zeile, point; layout of
    urban building blocks on building lot: axis/symmetry, grouping

The structure of bent rows and a Zeile acts as a transparent membrane between development following the streets and development along the waterside.

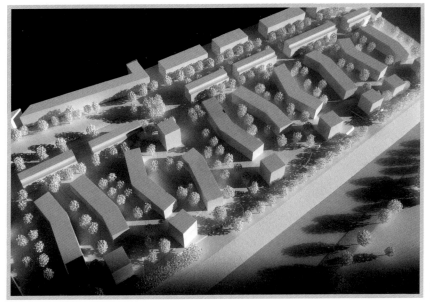

Model

⊚ — **LindeQuartier,** Wiesbaden (D)

✎ — wulf architekten with Möhrle + Partner Landschaftsarchitektur, Stuttgart

🖥 — www.wulfarchitekten.com

🏆 — 1st prize

📅 — 2007

🗂 — urban redevelopment – harbor conversion – new residential district

🌊 — **waterfront living/development**

🏷 — layout of urban building blocks on building lot: datum, sequence/repetition/rhythm;
___ widened street space; integrated green space

Design sketch for the new district in Amsterdam on artificial islands in the IJmeer bay.

Development status, 2010

- **IJburg,** Amsterdam (NL)
- Palmbout-Urban Landscapes, Rotterdam
- www.palmbout.nl
- 1995
- urban expansion – new district
- **waterfront living/development**
- additive approach; layout of development sites: axis, datum, sequence/repetition/ rhythm; linear street; green space delimited by buildings

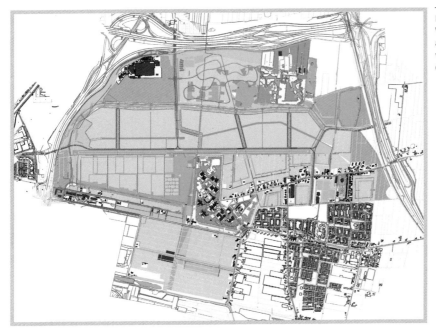

In Ypenburg, the vast Waterwijk subarea was available specifically for waterfront living (middle right in the plan).

Development status, 2010

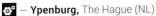 — **Ypenburg,** The Hague (NL)

 — Palmbout – Urban Landscapes, Rotterdam

🖳 — www.palmbout.nl

📅 — 1994

🗂 — urban redevelopment – military conversion – new district

≋ — **waterfront living/development**

🏷 — additive approach; layout of development sites: axis, datum, sequence/repetition/rhythm, grouping; integrated green space delimited by buildings

10 Representation in Urban Design

__ IN contrast to architectural designs, urban designs have a significantly higher degree of abstraction. Buildings are usually represented as simple shapes and volumes; and streets, open spaces, and public squares as more or less articulated areas. Nonetheless, an urban design can also have entirely different levels of abstraction and scale, which are reflected in different types of plans.

10.1 PLANS AND DRAWINGS — LEGAL AND INFORMAL PLANS

A fundamental distinction is made between legally binding regulatory plans (e.g., binding land-use plans) and informal informational plans (e.g., unofficial design plans). Legally binding plans have a legal effect, although the impact can vary depending on the plan type.

Although the specifics of legally-binding plans naturally vary by area of jurisdiction, examples of commonplace regulatory plans in Germany are as follows:

Preparatory Land-Use Plans

The preparatory land-use plan (Flächennutzungsplan, FNP) is a kind of zoning plan in which the municipality defines the types of land use allowed for the intended urban development that can be expected over the next ten to fifteen years. The uses are represented as areas with different colors and patterns. With the adoption of a preparatory land-use plan, the municipality also commits itself to draw up legally binding land-use plans. Third parties, such as the owners of designated development areas, cannot derive any rights from the land-use plan.

In a **PREPARATORY LAND-USE PLAN**, the municipality defines the type of land use; detail of the FNP for the city of Constance (D)

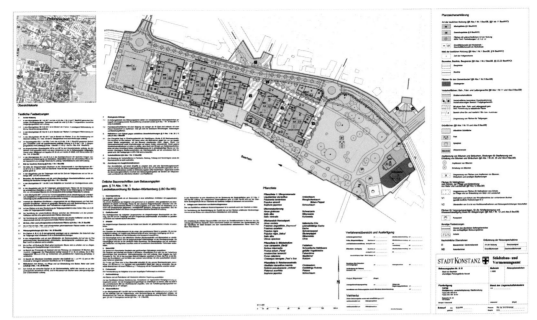

The **BINDING LAND-USE PLAN** defines in legally binding terms how the individual lots may be used and built upon Stadt am Seerhein (City on the Seerhein) – B-Plan for the city of Constance (D)

Binding Land-Use Plans

The binding land-use plan (Bebauungsplan, B-Plan) is a local statute with legal effect for everyone. It covers only a small, specifically defined subarea of the municipality. The stipulations are explained in written form and also graphically illustrated with symbolic line types for aspects like building footprints and mandatory building lines as well as plan notations listing specifics like gross floor area. "The Bebauungsplan is a legally binding urban land-use plan that defines in legally binding terms how the individual lots – also those of private owners – may be used and built upon."[1] Conversely, unlike with a preparatory land-use plan, a property owner can infer rights from a binding land-use plan, meaning that it can be used as the basis to invoke a claim – albeit restricted by provisions – under planning and building law.

---

1 *Mitreden, mitplanen, mitmachen: Ein Leitfaden zur städtebaulichen Planung* (Wiesbaden: Hessisches Ministerium für Wirtschaft, Verkehr und Landesentwicklung, 2001), p. 20.

INFORMAL PLANS INCLUDE:

Municipal Development Plans

Municipal development plans usually formulate a program with statements on economic and demographic development, the environmental situation, and budgetary planning. The focus of a development plan is on the written text, which is usually accompanied by overview maps.

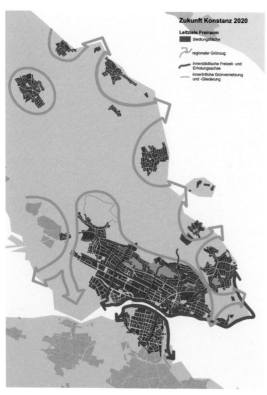

MUNICIPAL DEVELOPMENT PLANS formulate a program with statements about the future development of a city. Leitziel Freiraum (Guiding vision: open space) – detail of the "Constance 2020" urban development concept for the city of Constance (D)

Urban Design Framework Plans / Master Plans

Urban design framework plans, also commonly called master plans, are usually developed for larger parts of a municipal territory. They are generally based on an urban design scheme, such as the result of an urban design competition. Framework plans are used to illustrate binding land-use plans or individual measures in a larger context and to gain support for the planning principles among politicians and in the urban community. The framework plans merely formulate goals; they do not contain legally binding stipulations. Nevertheless, municipal framework plans and the like are adopted by municipal or city councils and thus represent a certain commitment on their part to what is contained therein.

Urban Design Plans

Urban design plans constitute the basis for urban design framework plans and binding land-use plans. They emphasize conceptual, functional, and design aspects. In an illustrative site plan (a so-called Gestaltungsplan), the best possible architectural development is depicted in an exemplary or idealized way.

PLAN TYPES, DRAWINGS, AND MODELS IN URBAN DESIGN

SINCE a detailed description of all the various plan types would exceed the scope of this book, we shall deal here primarily with the urban design plans that are, for instance, demanded by the organizers of urban design competitions.

Illustrative Site Plan

The illustrative site plan is the core of every urban design. In it, all the design statements are included, such as the structure of the building fabric, the distribution of uses, means of access, and green and open spaces. Depending on the size of the area being planned, it is depicted as a site plan at the scale of 1:5000, 1:2000, 1:1000, or for very small areas, at 1:500. The range varies from abstracted but naturalistic to purely graphic plan depictions.

Choosing the appropriate means of representation depends largely on the essence of the design, the target group, and one's personal design and drawing style. Acceptable is whatever supports the legibility of the design. Nonetheless, some means of representation are particularly well-established: the plans are normally oriented with north at the top, and shadows can enhance the sculptural effect of trees, topographical elements, and buildings. Elements like vegetation and bodies of water are usually depicted in green or blue tones approximating their natural colors. Streets and public squares should not be too dark because otherwise they tend to visually shift to the foreground. Using different line thicknesses helps to establish a hierarchy for the elements of the design. The more important the item, the thicker its outline should be. The number of stories is given in Roman numerals, with the notation "+D" for an attic (D = Dachgeschoss) where applicable.

The level of detail also changes with the scale. Although only general structural aspects about traffic, uses, building forms, and open spaces can be recognized in an illustrative site plan at the scale of 1:2000, a scale of 1:1000 already allows aspects such as lot boundaries, roof forms, and basic statements about the design of outdoor spaces and public thoroughfares to be depicted. The scale of 1:500 is suitable for showing even more detail, like building types with circulation cores, the public space, and private outdoor spaces.

A simple trick makes it possible to check the site plan's legibility: the most important structuring elements should still be recognizable when you squint tightly with your eyes. If the light-dark contrast (or color contrast) of these elements is insufficient and they merge together when viewed, the depiction must be revised.

site plan scale 1:5000

In a site plan at 1:5000 scale, only structural assertions about traffic, uses, building forms, open spaces, and integration in the urban fabric can be recognized.

- **Urban Transformation Tempelhof Airport,** Berlin (D)
- Leonov Alexander Alexandrovich with Zalivako Darya Andreevna, Moscow
- www.competitionline.com/de/wettbewerbe/24324
- 2nd prize
- 2009
- urban redevelopment – airport conversion – new district
- **site plan/illustrative site plan**
- superimposition; place making through exclusion/omission, assembly, and modeling

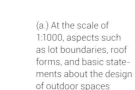

- **Metrozonen, Kaufhauskanal,** Hamburg (D)
- BIG Bjarke Ingels Group, Copenhagen, with TOPOTEK 1, Berlin, and Grontmij, De Bilt
- www.big.dk
- 1st prize
- 2009
- urban redevelopment – harbor conversion – new residential district
- **illustrative site plan**
- stretched grid; layout of urban building blocks on building lot: sequence/repetition/rhythm; waterfront living/development

(a.) At the scale of 1:1000, aspects such as lot boundaries, roof forms, and basic statements about the design of outdoor spaces and public thoroughfares can already be depicted.

(b.) The scale of 1:500 is suitable for showing even more, such as details of the public space and private outdoor spaces.

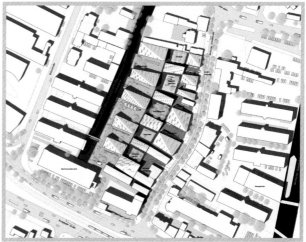

Perspective along Kaufhauskanal

⊙ — **Neufahrn-Ost,** Neufahrn bei Freising (D)

✐ — Ackermann & Raff, Stuttgart/Tübingen, with Planstatt Senner, Überlingen

▣ — www.ackermann-raff.de

▣ — 1st prize

▦ — 2005

▣ — urban expansion — new residential districts

◈ — **illustrative site plan**

◥ — Prägnanz; geometric principle; additive approach; urban building blocks: opened city block, row, Zeile, point, freestanding building; layout of development sites: axis, sequence/ repetition/rhythm, grouping

In bold colors, this illustrative site plan shows the new design and its integration within the city and the landscape. It is clearly recognizable that the design will provide effective protection against noise from the bypass road.

The reserved graphics
of the illustrative site
plan highlight the open,
flowing green space.

🎯 – **Vorderer Kätzleberg,** Stockach (D)

📝 – LS Architektur Städtebau, Stuttgart,
with Braun+Müller Architekten BDA,
Constance

🖥 – www.leonhardschenk.de,
www.braun-mueller-architekten.de

🏅 – 1st place

📅 – 2011

🗂 – urban redevelopment – commercial
conversion – new residential district

📑 – **illustrative site plan**

🏷 – flowing green and open space

Structural Concept

The structural concept shows the most important spatial and functional relationships within a larger urban area. When planning a subarea, for instance, the structural concept is used to show how the design measures support or improve these relationships, or possibly even augment them with new aspects. The base drawing used for explaining the relationships, which are usually shown with symbols, can be a simplified representation of city districts, building lots, and open spaces, or even a figure-ground plan, depending on the size of the area being depicted.

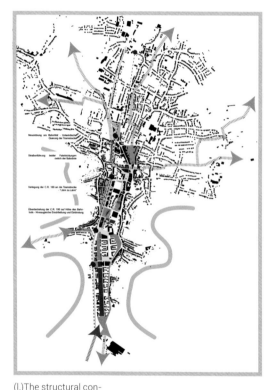
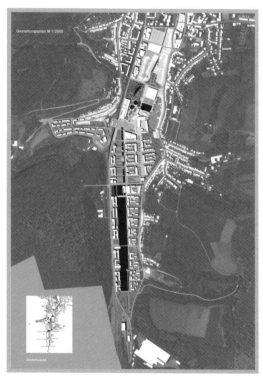

(l.)The structural concept shows the most important spatial and functional relationships within a larger urban area.

(r.) Illustrative site plan

  – **Spatial structure concept for Schmelz Diddeleng** (L)

  – ISA Internationales Stadtbauatelier, Stuttgart/Peking/Seoul/Paris; with Planungs-gruppe Landschaft und Raum, Korntal-Münchingen

  – www.stadtbauatelier.de

  – 3rd prize

  – 2009

  – urban redevelopment – industrial conversion – new district

  – **structural concept**

  – layout of development sites: axis, hierarchy, datum, sequence/repetition/rhythm, grouping

- **Europan 10, Eine urbane Schnittstelle neu denken (Rethinking an urban interface),** Forchheim (D)
- Jörg Radloff, Maximilian Marinus Schauren, Karoline Schauren, Munich
- www.schauren.com
- shortlist
- 2010
- urban redevelopment – industrial/ commercial conversion – new residential district
- **structural concept**
- urban building blocks: row; place making through modeling

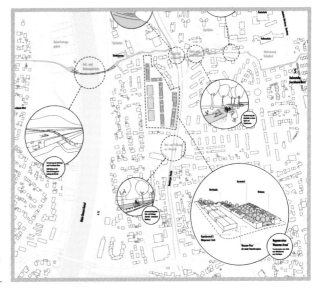

Structural concept with details

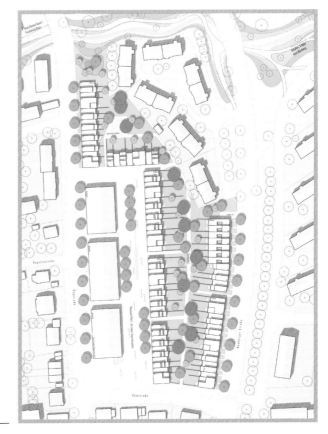

Illustrative site plan

Perspective representation of structural concept

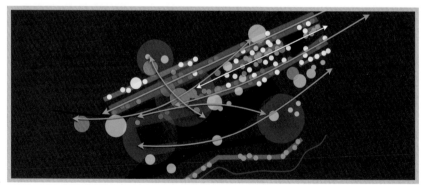

Abstracted structural concept

⊙ — **Europan 9, Empreinte,** Le Locle (CH)

✎ — mwab architectes urbanistes associés, Paris

▣ — www.mwab.eu

◉ — 1st prize

▦ — 2008

🗀 — urban renewal – new residential district, park, and event area

◈ — **structural concept**

🏷 — additive approach and superimposition; urban building blocks: row, point

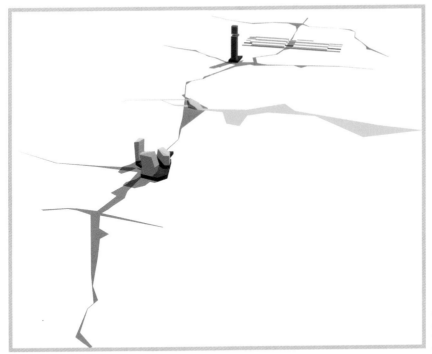

Minimalist structural concept that shows only the most important relationships

Perspective

⚙ — **Partnership Smartinska,** Slovenien (SLO)
✎ — JUUL | FROST ARKITEKTER, Copenhagen
🖥 — www.juulfrost.dk
🏆 — 2nd prize
📅 — 2008
🗂 — urban redevelopment — industrial/commercial conversion — new urban district
◆ — **structural concept**
🏷 — irregular grid; urban building blocks: dissolved city block; bent street space, widened
___ street space

Figure-Ground Plan

The figure-ground plan (Baumassenplan), whose name refers to how the buildings are shown as black figures on a white background, shows whether and how the design fits into an existing building fabric. If inverted to show white buildings on a black background, the perception changes: according to the principle of figure and ground, the urban space moves to the fore as a figure. Both forms of representation are ideally suited for evaluating the design – even repeatedly during the design process.

 – **Innerer Westen,** Regensburg (D)

 – Ammann Albers StadtWerke with Schweingruber Zulauf Landschafts- architekten BSLA, Zurich

– www.stadtwerke.ch

– 1st prize

– 2011

 – railway conversion – new residential districts

– **figure-ground plan (poche plan)**

 – layout of development sites: repetition/ variation/rhythm

(a.) Figure-ground plan highlighting new areas in color

(m.) The figure-ground plan shows how the design fits into the existing building fabric.

(b.) In the reverse figure-ground plan, the urban space is highlighted as a figure.

Section

With urban design, the section is less a technical drawing and more of an informatory and atmospheric one. It is a visual depiction of the structure and quality of the urban space – the space between the buildings – as a function of the topography, proportion, and heights of the buildings.

Longitudinal sections through buildings should be avoided if possible, as this would distort the relationship of built elements to outdoor space. For a pure urban design that is not meant to deal with the specifics of architecture, the elevations of buildings seen in a site section are best depicted in a modest or schematic way, because such facades would otherwise attract too much attention to themselves solely because of the greater density of detail. Enlivening the section with people, trees, and vehicles, on the other hand, has a supportive effect.

In section, the structure and quality of the intermediate space become clear.

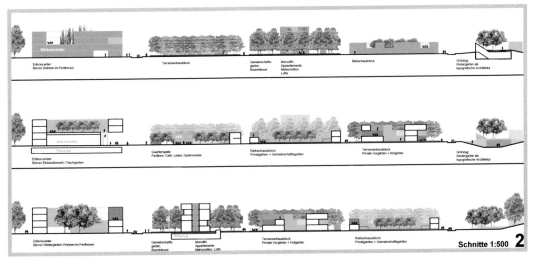

Schnitte 1:500 **2**

⊙ — **Europan 7, Suburban Frames,** Neu-Ulm (D)

✎ — florian krieger – architektur und städtebau, Darmstadt

▣ — www.florian-krieger.de

◉ — 1st prize

▦ — 2004

▭ — urban redevelopment – military conversion – new residential district

◆ — **section**

◈ — additive approach

Perspective

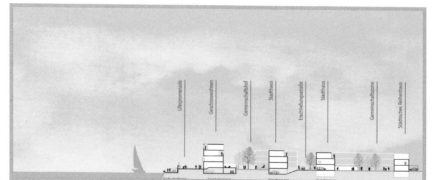

Although the buildings are only depicted schematically, the sections suggest appealing living conditions.

Illustrative site plan

⌖ — **New Housing along the Ryck River,** Greifswald (D)

✐ — pp a|s pesch partner architekten stadtplaner, Herdecke/Stuttgart

▭ — www.pesch-partner.de

◉ — 3rd prize

▦ — 2006

▱ — urban renewal – commercial conversion – new waterside urban district

◈ — **section**

◆ — additive approach; layout of development sites: axis, sequence/repetition/rhythm

Section with detailed
but restrained depiction
of the background
buildings

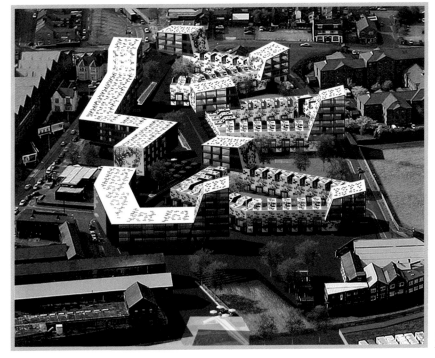

Perspective

🎯 — **Europan 9,** Stoke-on-Trent (GB)

📝 — Duggan Morris Architects, London

🖥 — www.dugganmorrisarchitects.com

🏆 — honorable mention

📅 — 2008

📂 — urban redevelopment – commercial conversion – new residential district

📚 — **section**

🔖 — layout of development sites: datum, repetition/rhythm; place making through
modeling

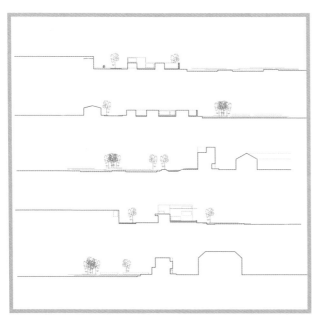

 **Europan 9, Grünkern (Green core),** Babenhausen (D)

 Metris Architekten, Darmstadt/Heidelberg, with 711LAB, Stuttgart

 www.metris-architekten.de, www.711lab.com

— 1st prize

— 2008

— urban redevelopment — military conversion — new urban districts

section

— Prägnanz (external borders), layout of development sites: datum, grouping, layout; district-level green and open space; green space delimited by buildings

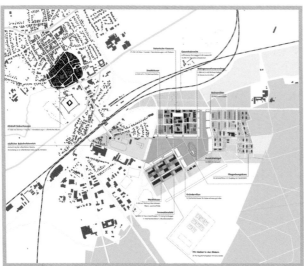

(a.) Abstracted minimalist section

(l.) Structural concept

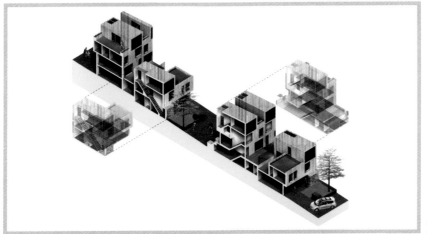

Sectional axonometric

Perspective

⌖ — **Europan 9, city slipway,** Stoke-on-Trent (GB)
✑ — RCKa architects, London
🖥 — www.rcka.co
🏆 — 1st prize
📅 — 2008
🗂 — urban redevelopment – commercial conversion – new residential district
◈ — **section**
🏷 — additive approach; tilted grid; bent street space; waterfront living

Design Sketch

Even in the digital age, a designer can make a striking and personal statement by sketching the basic design concept by hand with a few strokes. To clarify the design intent, the drawing can be colored by hand or with the aid of digital image processing.

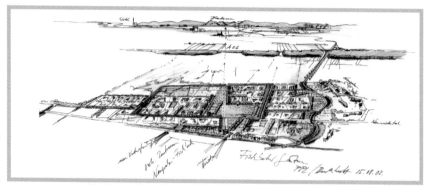

The hand-drawn sketch is still a personal and striking statement by the designer.

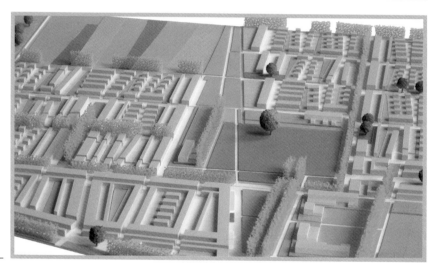

The design idea translated as a model

⊘ — **Neugraben – Fischbek Residential District,** Hamburg (D)

✎ — PPL Architektur und Stadtplanung, Hamburg

☐ — www.ppl-hh.de

◉ — 3rd prize

▦ — 2001

☐ — urban redevelopment – military conversion – new district

◈ — **sketch**

◣ — layout of development sites: axis, datum, repetition/rhythm; green space delimited
—   by buildings

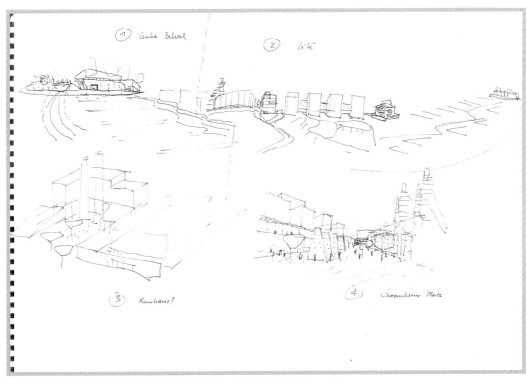

With simple hand-drawn sketches, spatial situations can be developed and reviewed quickly.

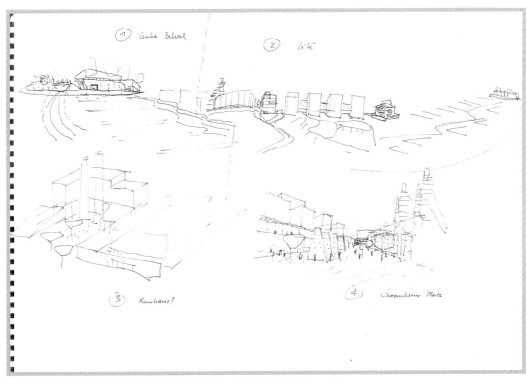 — **Belval-Ouest,** Esch-sur-Alzette (L)

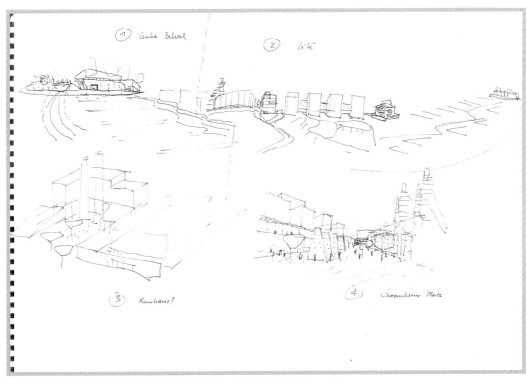 — Jo Coenen Architects & Urbanists, Rolo Fütterer, Maastricht, with Buro Lubbers, 's-Hertogenbosch

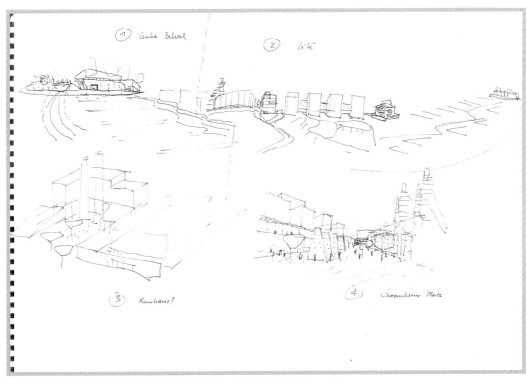 — www.jocoenen.com, www.mars-group.eu

 — 1st prize

 — 2002

 — urban redevelopment – industrial conversion – new district

 — **sketch**

The clearer the con-
cept, the easier it is to
communicate.

⚙ — **Master Plan for Paramount Xeritown,** Dubai (UAE)

✏ — SMAQ architecture urbanism research, Berlin; Sabine Müller and Andreas Quednau
with Joachim Schultz, with X-Architects, Dubai; Johannes Grothaus Landschaftsarchitekten, Potsdam; Reflexion, Zurich; and Buro Happold, London

🖥 — www.smaq.net

📅 — 2008

🗂 — urban expansion – new sustainable urban districts

📑 — **sketch**

🏷 — divisional approach

Diagrams and Pictograms

Diagrams are used in urban design for the graphic representation of data, facts, information, or processes. The spectrum extends from a pictorial depiction to a purely abstract portrayal. Whereas a pictogram is a symbol that only refers to discrete information, diagrams explain complex relationships in a visual and very simple way. Of course pictograms can also be used within a diagram.

Today hardly any architectural or urban design gets by without professional-looking diagrams. That might be because, in the face of today's information overload, quick and targeted communication is more important than ever. Another interpretation is that diagrams are more than just an instrument for conveying ideas; that the diagram itself has already become an element of the design.[2] Both views are probably justified. Well-designed diagrams fulfill their purpose on both sides.

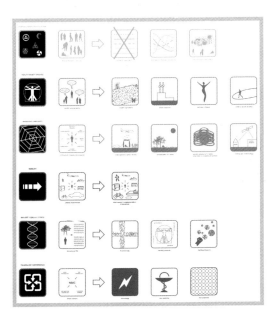

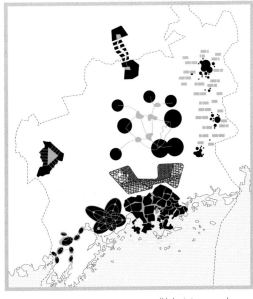

(l.) A pictogram always refers to a single bit of information.

(r.) Diagrams explain complex relationships in the simplest visual way.

— **Holistic Uniqueness Helsinki** (FIN)

— CITYFÖRSTER architecture + urbanism, Berlin/Hannover/London/Oslo/
Rotterdam/Salerno, with Steen Hargus, Hanover

— www.cityfoerster.net

— 2nd prize

— 2008

— development concept for the Helsinki metropolitan area, Finland

— **diagrams and pictograms**

2 Miyoung Pyo, ed., *Construction and Design Manual: Architectural Diagrams* (Berlin: DOM Publishers, 2011), p. 10.

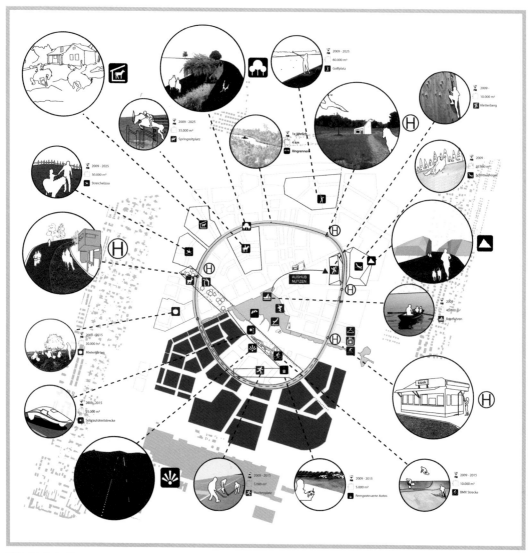

This diagram of temporary use integrates numerous pictograms.

✎ — **Public Space Guidelines for Aspern Airfield,** Vienna (A)

✎ — feld72 architekten, Vienna, with Peter Arlt, urban sociologist, Linz

🖥 — www.feld72.at

📷 — 2nd prize

📅 — 2008

📁 — urban redevelopment – airport conversion – new district

✦ — **diagrams and pictograms**

Functional Diagrams

To create functional diagrams, the design is dissected, as it were, into its layers and the essential aspects are portrayed in the form of a two- or three-dimensional diagram. Typical functional diagrams are:

- the traffic diagram, which describes the road system and modes of transport;
- the open spaces diagram, which shows the provision of private and public green and open spaces and their spatial interconnections;
- the use diagram, which explains the distribution of uses like residential, commercial, mixed use, or public facilities and cultural institutions.

Depending on the design, additional functional diagrams can be useful to clarify aspects like construction phases, visual relationships, differences in building heights, the energy concept, the parking concept, and much more.

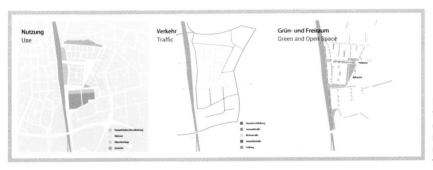

In functional diagrams, the design is broken down into basic statements about traffic, use, and open spaces.

☉ — **neue bahn stadt:opladen,**
   Leverkusen (D)

✎ — pp als pesch partner architekten
   stadtplaner, Herdecke/Stuttgart,
   with brosk landschaftsarchitektur
   und freiraumplanung, Essen

🖥 — www.pesch-partner.de

🏆 — honorable mention

📅 — 2006

🗂 — urban redevelopment – railway
   conversion – new district

◈ — **functional diagrams**

◆ — additive approach; layout of development sites: axis, datum, sequence/
   repetition/rhythm, grouping; green
   space delimited by buildings; representation: illustrative site plan

Illustrative site plan

The topics are each explained in terms of urban design and landscape.

Illustrative site plan

🎯 — **Neckarpark,** Stuttgart (D)

📝 — pp als pesch partner architekten stadtplaner, Herdecke/Stuttgart, with lohrberg stadtlandschaftsarchitektur, Stuttgart

🖥 — www.pesch-partner.de

🏆 — 1st prize

📅 — 2008

🗂 — urban redevelopment – railway conversion – new urban district

📑 — **functional diagrams**

🔖 — additive approach; tilted grid; layout of building lots: axis, datum, sequence/repetition/rhythm; green space delimited by buildings

- **Müllerpier,** Rotterdam (NL)
- KCAP Architects&Planners, Rotterdam/Zurich/Shanghai
- www.kcap.eu
- 1998
- urban redevelopment – harbor conversion – new urban district
- **functional diagrams**
- free composition/collage; additive approach; urban building blocks: opened city block, row, Zeile, highrise; waterfront living/development

Car

Double bottom

Interior

Quay

Ready mades

Strategic intervention

Wideness

Wind

The diagrams explain functional and design aspects of the scheme.

Perspective

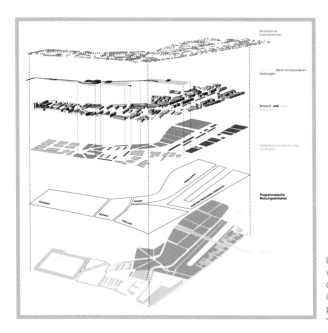

⟨icon⟩ – Magdeburg Science Quarter (D)

⟨icon⟩ – De Zwarte Hond, Groningen, with Studio UC, Berlin

⟨icon⟩ – www.dezwartehond.nl

⟨icon⟩ – honorable mention

⟨icon⟩ – 2010

⟨icon⟩ – urban redevelopment – harbor conversion – new district for science and education

⟨icon⟩ – **functional diagrams** – layering diagram

⟨icon⟩ – representation: pictograms

Like in an exploded view in perspective, the design is broken down into its constituent parts.

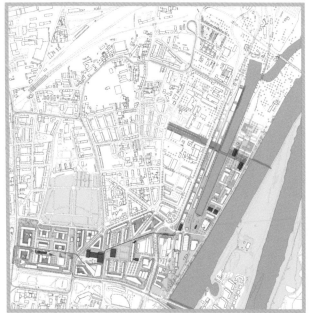

Illustrative site plan

Additional Diagrams

The possibilities for using diagrams to explain complex relationships are as varied as the themes and aspects dealt with in urban design. Diagrams are also suitable for visualizing processes – how, for instance, the individual steps in a design process are derived from the analysis, or how and when certain construction measures need to be initiated during the implementation process.

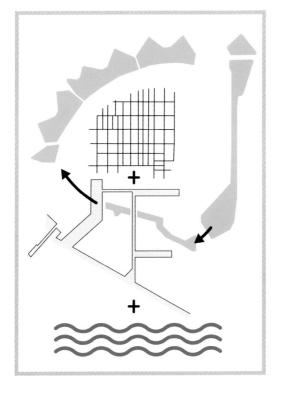

(l.) Diagram of design idea

(r.) Implementation of the idea in the design

⊙ – **FredericiaC,** Fredericia (DK)

▨ – KCAP Architects&Planners, Rotterdam/Zurich/Shanghai

▣ – www.kcap.eu

◉ – 1st prize

▦ – 2011

▤ – urban redevelopment – harbor conversion – new urban district for living and working

◈ – **miscellaneous diagrams**

◈ – superimposition; urban building blocks: closed and dissolved city blocks; waterfront living/development

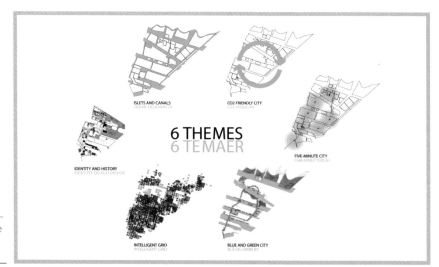

With the aid of six diagrams, the overall concepts of the design are elucidated succinctly and understandably.

Perspective

 — **Copenhagen Northern Harbor:The sustainable city of the future,**
Copenhagen (DK)

 — COBE, Copenhagen/Berlin, with SLETH, Aarhus and Rambøll, Copenhagen

 — www.cobe.dk

 — 1st prize category

 — 2008

 — urban redevelopment/urban expansion – harbor conversion – new district

 — **miscellaneous diagrams**

 — additive approach; orthogonal grid, tilted grid; circulation loop; waterfront living/
development; representation: perspective

 – **Europan 8, Stadtgespräch,**
Leinefelde-Worbis (D)

 – Nicolas Reymond Architecture &
Urbanisme, Paris

 – www.nicolasreymond.com

 – 1st prize

 – 2006

 – urban renewal – upgrade of existing
buildings plus new housing

 – **miscellaneous diagrams**

 – Section

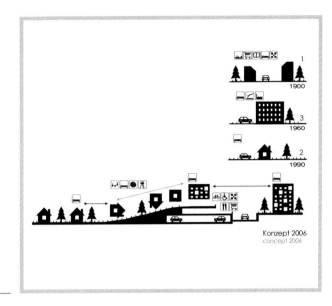

Bold presentation of
the design idea

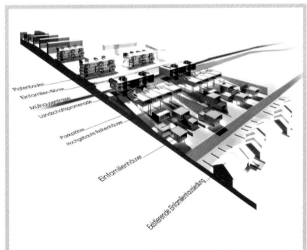

Sectional perspective

⚙ — **Europan 10, garten>Hof,**
Wien-Meidling/Liesing (A)

✎ — Luis Basabe Montalvo, Enrique
Arenas Laorga, Luis Palacios Lab-
rador; Madrid

💻 — www.abparquitectos.com

🏆 — 1st prize

📅 — 2010

🗂 — urban redevelopment — commercial
conversion — new residential district

❧ — **miscellaneous diagrams**

◈ — additive approach; orthogonal grid;
___ complete road network

The diagram demon-
strates the different
building options.

📝 — SMAQ - architecture urbanism research, Berlin

🖥 — www.smaq.net

🏆 — 1st prize

📅 — 2008

🗂 — urban renewal – new center for a
residential district from the 1970s

◆ — **miscellaneous diagrams**

◈ — free composition/collage; layout of
building lots: grouping; representa-
___ tion: perspective

Diagram of rainwater
use

Perspective

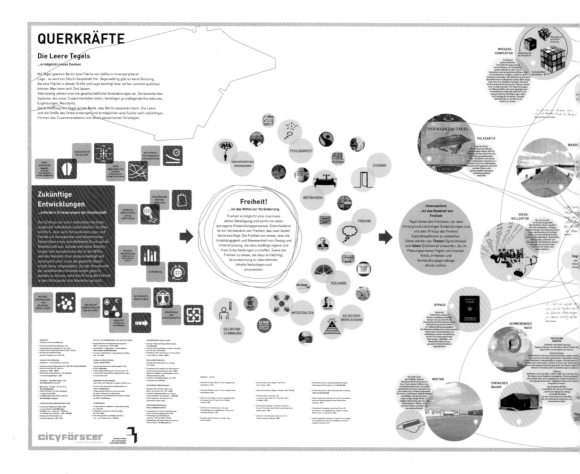

°° – **Querkräfte,** Berlin-Tegel (D)

✎ – CITYFÖRSTER architecture + urbanism, Berlin/Hannover/London/Oslo/Rotterdam/
Salerno, with urbane gestalt, Johannes Böttger, Landschaftsarchitekten, Cologne,
Steen Hargus, Hannover, and Anna-Lisa Brinkmann Design, Berlin

🖥 – www.cityfoerster.net

📅 – 2009

🗂 – development concept for reusing Berlin Tegel Airport

◈ – **miscellaneous diagrams**

🏳 – pictograms

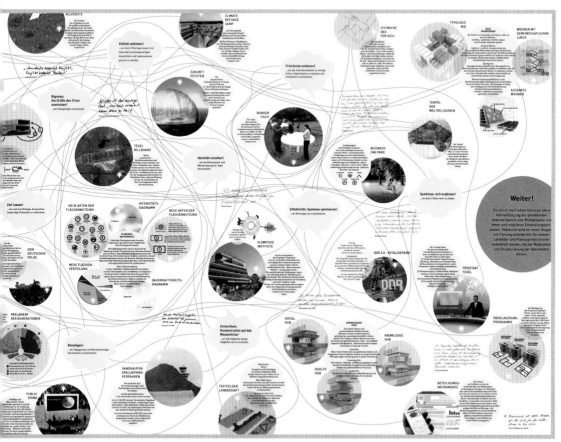

This development concept is presented as a large diagram.

Perspectives

Perspectives and visualizations provide help in reading and understanding the design, especially for laypeople. The bird's-eye view, or aerial perspective, helps illustrate the building fabric and the scheme's integration in its surroundings, whereas a pedestrian's perspective portrays spatial situations in a manner similar to how they will later be perceived in reality. The spectrum extends from simple hand drawings that may have been colored with an image-editing program to photorealistic computer renderings. Recently it can be observed that, after a phase of strong interest in digital methods, the individually crafted, skillful hand drawing has resumed an equal place in the repertoire of presentation methods.

At first glance, this highly detailed perspective can hardly be distinguished from an aerial photo.

⊘ — **FredericiaC,** Fredericia (DK)

☑ — KCAP Architects&Planners, Rotterdam/Zurich/Shanghai

▣ — www.kcap.eu

⚲ — 1st prize

🗓 — 2011

🗁 — urban redevelopment – harbor conversion – new urban district

◈ — **perspective**

◈ — representation: diagrams

In a reserved manner, this perspective illustrates the special waterfront living situation.

Illustrative site plan

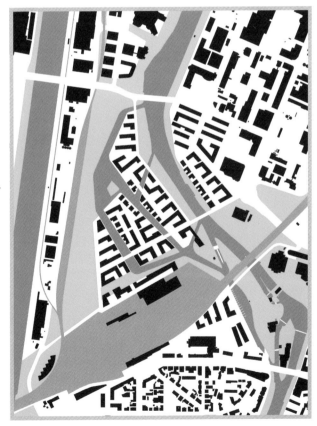

⊚ – **Master Plan for Neckarvorstadt,** Heilbronn (D)

✐ – Christine Edmaier with Büro Kiefer Landschaftsarchitektur, Berlin

▣ – www.christine-edmaier.de

🏆 – 4th prize

📅 – 2009

🗂 – urban redevelopment – harbor/railway conversion – new district

◆ – **perspective**

◈ – waterfront development

 — **Europan 8, L.A.R.S.,** Bergen (N)

 — SMAQ - architecture urbanism research, Berlin

 — www.smaq.net

 — 2nd prize

 — 2006

 — urban renewal – new urban center on the periphery

 — **perspective**

 — urban building blocks: city block, hybrid; placemaking through assembly/modeling

The contrast between the backdrop of a dramatic landscape and the simplified graphic representation of the design draws attention.

Site plan

The perspectives exude great vitality, which results from a skillful combination of hand drawings and digital presentation techniques.

Nighttime perspective

— **Bjørvika Harbor District,** Oslo (N)

— Behnisch Architekten, Stuttgart, with Gehl Architects, Copenhagen, and Transsolar KlimaEngineering, Stuttgart

— www.behnisch.com

— 1st prize

— 2008

— urban redevelopment – harbor conversion – new urban district

— **perspective**

— additive approach; urban building blocks: closed, dissolved city block, freestanding building; waterfront living/development

291

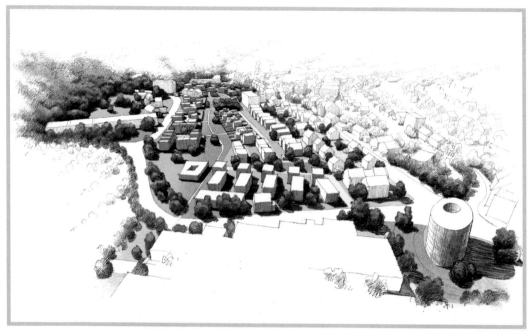

Like in the illustrative site plan, the green spaces and landscape relationships are also given particular emphasis in the perspective.

Illustrative site plan

⌾ — **Ackermann Housing Development,** Gummersbach (D)

✎ — rha reicher haase associierte GmbH, Aachen, with Planergruppe Oberhausen, Oberhausen

▣ — www.rha-architekten.de

☺ — 1st prize

▦ — 2009

▭ — urban redevelopment – commercial conversion – new residential district

◈ — **perspective**

◣ — additive approach; urban building blocks: courtyard, row, Zeile, point; placemaking through assembly;

___ district-level green and open space

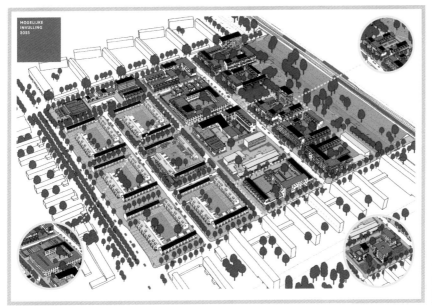

The informative character of the drawing is of primary importance.

The pedestrian's view illustrates the qualities of the open space, while the buildings remain relatively generic.

- **Jacob Geelbuurt, Vernieuwingsplan,** Amsterdam (NL)
- JAM* architecten, Amsterdam
- www.jamarchitecten.nl
- 2012
- urban renewal – housing refurbishment
- **perspective**
- additive approach; orthogonal grid, urban building blocks: dissolved city block

293

⊘ — **Harburger Schlossinsel,** Hamburg (D)

✎ — raumwerk, Frankfurt am Main, with club L94, Cologne

▭ — www.raumwerk.net

⚙ — 1st prize

▦ — 2005

▭ — urban redevelopment — harbor conversion — new urban district

◈ — **perspective**

✎ — depth; additive approach; layout of development sites: repetition/rhythm, grouping; place making through assembly

The hand-drawn and digitally colored perspectives concentrate on depicting the urban space.

Site plan

- **SV Areal,** Wiesbaden-Dotzheim (D)
- Wick + Partner Architekten Stadtplaner, Stuttgart, with lohrer.hochrein landschaftsarchitekten, Munich
- www.wick-partner.de
- 2nd prize
- 2008
- urban redevelopment – industrial conversion – new residential district and industrial park

- **perspective**
- additive approach; urban building blocks: city block, (commercial) courtyard, rows, point; layout of building blocks on the building lot: sequencing/repetition/rhythm

With just a few strokes, the design idea is brought to the point in this perspective.

Illustrative site plan

Urban Design Details

Depending on the planning task, different levels of detail are required. More precise design statements in an urban context are generally possible with scales from 1:500 to 1:50, e.g., for:

- Design principles of public and private open spaces
- Vehicle access and parking
- Landscape elements and vegetation
- Relationships of buildings to public and private open spaces (entrance areas, terraces, communal spaces, etc.)
- Paving for streets and squares, street furniture, and lighting elements

(l.) This plan detail shows the degree of detail that is possible at the scale of 1:500, which can include such aspects as exits from underground garages, design elements for the public realm, and rainwater seepage trenches.

(r.) Illustrative site plan

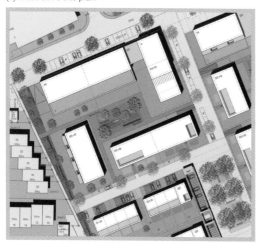

⚙ — **Südlich der Rechbergstraße,** Denkendorf (D)

📝 — LEHEN drei Architekten Stadtplaner – Feketics, Schenk, Schuster, Stuttgart

🖥 — wwwl.lehendrei.de

🔍 — 2nd place

📅 — 2007

🗂 — urban redevelopment – commercial conversion – new residential district

◈ — **urban design details**

◣ — urban building blocks: dissolved city block, row; place making through assembly

Typical section through the main access road at 1:50 scale

Illustrative site plan

⌖ — **Stadtnahes Wohngebiet an der Breiteich,** Schwäbisch Hall (D)

✎ — Wick + Partner Architekten Stadtplaner, Stuttgart, with Gesswein Landschaftsarchitekten, Ostfildern

🖳 — www.wick-partner.de

🏆 — 1st prize

📅 — 2007

🗂 — urban expansion – new residential district

◈ — **urban design details**

❧ — additive approach; layout of development sites: sequence/repetition/rhythm; integrated green space

Plan Layout

The plan layout is in a sense the storyboard for the urban design scheme. The layout should support the legibility of the design, both functionally and graphically. An essential aspect of the layout is a coherent arrangement for the plans. Experience shows that the structural concept, the figure-ground plan, and the functional diagrams should be presented first, then the illustrative site plan and the sections, and lastly the urban design details and supplementary drawings.

Visualizations should be used judiciously. A concise, large-format visualization is suitable as an eye-catcher or as the opening or conclusion of a plan presentation. If supplementary visualizations are really necessary for understanding the design, they can be associated with the individual plans. As is so often the case, less can be more.

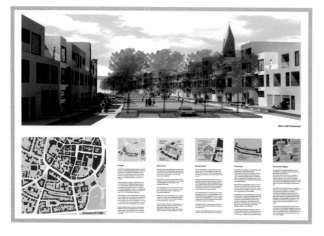

⚙ — **Südliche Innenstadt,** Recklinghausen (D)

✎ — JSWD Architekten with club L94, Cologne

🖥 — www.jswd-architekten.de

🏆 — 1st prize

📅 — 2004

🗂 — urban redevelopment – new inner-city neighborhood

◈ — **layout**

◈ — place making through modeling; representation: diagrams, perspective

A large-format visualization is an eye-catching opening of a plan presentation.

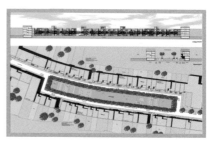

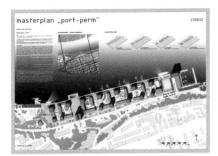

The layout presents the subject matter compactly and in a varied way, so there is something new to discover on every sheet.

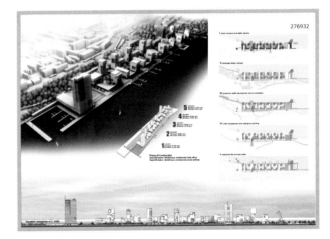

⊙ — **Master Plan for Port Perm,** Russia (RUS)

✐ — Architekt: KSP Jürgen Engel Architekten, Berlin/Braunschweig/Cologne/Frankfurt/Munich/Peking

⊡ — www.ksp-architekten.de

⚲ — 1st prize

▦ — 2008

⊡ — urban redevelopment – harbor conversion – new waterside residential district

◈ — **layout**

◆ — urban building blocks: dissolved city block, point, high-rise, hybrid; representation: diagrams

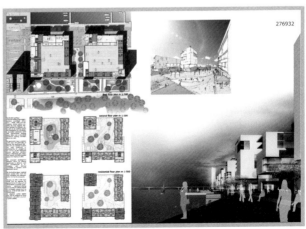

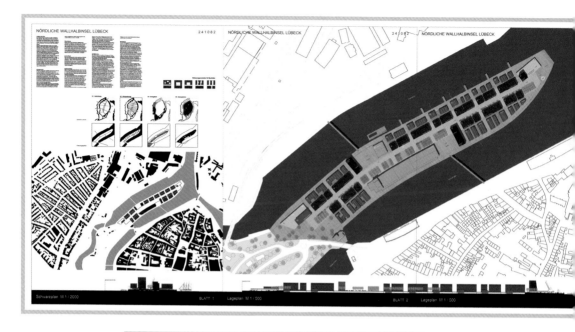

The band with sectional views extends across the bottom edge of all the individual drawings and visually pulls them together.

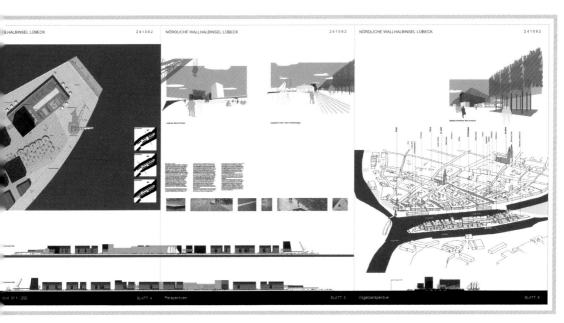

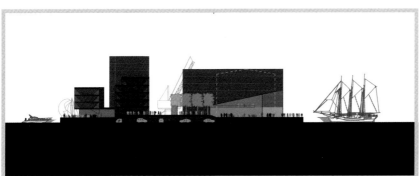

🎯 — **Master Plan for Nördliche Wallhalbinsel Lübeck** (D)

✏️ — raumwerk, Frankfurt am Main, with club L94, Cologne

🖥 — www.raumwerk.net

🏆 — merit award

📅 — 2008

🗂 — urban redevelopment – harbor conversion – new urban district

◈ — **layout**

◈ — representation: urban design details

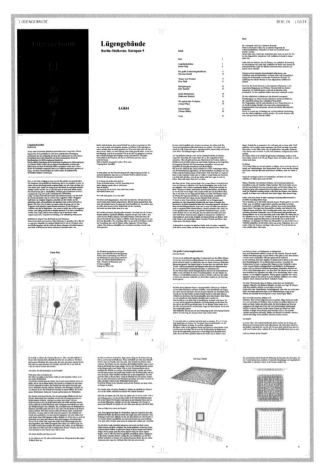

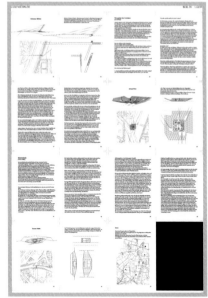

🎯 — **Europan 9, Chancen für den öffentlichen Raum // Walking,** Südkreuz, Berlin (D)

✏️ — Architekten Koelbl Radojkovic, Vienna

🖥️ — www.arch-koelbl-radojkovic.com

⚙️ — prizewinner

📅 — 2008

🗂️ — urban redevelopment – regional pedestrian and bicycle path concept with individual measures along the route

📑 — **layout**

This layout with printer's marks is a fitting way to carry out the idea of presenting the design in literary form.

With a continuous background, the text and design drawings appear to float freely in front of a perspective view of the sky.

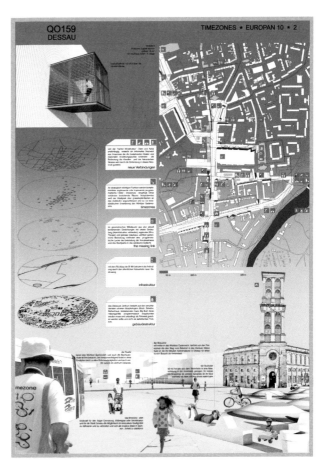

⊙ — **Europan 10, Stärkung urbaner Kerne, Timezones,** Dessau (D)

✎ — Felix Wetzstein, You Young Chin, Paris

💻 — www.wetzstein.cc

◎ — shortlist

📅 — 2010

🗂 — urban redevelopment – transformation of the main arterial road into an urban boulevard

◈ — **layout**

◆ — representation: pictograms, diagrams

Models

Both physical and digital models are suitable for assessing the design concept during the design process, as well as for presenting the final urban design.

A basic distinction is therefore made between simple working models and perfectly crafted presentation models:

The working model should be made of materials that allow for easy revisions, such as cardboard or polystyrene. Nevertheless, working models can have a special charm that is not necessarily found in a presentation model.

For a presentation model, durable, hardwearing materials like modeling plaster, higher-density plastics, and wood are recommended. In some countries, like in Swit-

Working models can can have a special charm that is not necessarily found in a presentation model.

Illustrative site plan

📷 — **geneve 2020 visions urbaines,** Geneva (CH)

✎ — XPACE architecture + urban design, Richmond, Australia

💻 — www.xpace.cc

🏆 — 4th prize

📅 — 2005

🗂 — urban redevelopment – industrial conversion – new urban districts and industrial park

◈ — **model**

◣ — superimposition; representation: pictogram, diagrams

zerland, it is customary that presentation models for competitions are kept mono-chrome white for better comparison. Some firms, such as BIG, OMA, and MVRDV, are known for their colorfully collaged models made of differing, sometimes unus-ual materials.

Whatever the chosen presentation form, the plans and models should always correspond with the design idea they represent.

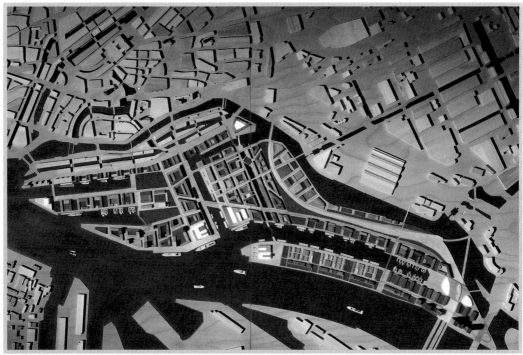

— HafenCity, Hamburg (D)

— ASTOC Architects and Planners, Cologne, with KCAP Architects&Planners, Rotter-dam/Zurich/Shanghai

— www.astoc.de, www.kcap.eu

— 1st prize

— 1999

— urban redevelopment – harbor conversion – new district

— model

— tilted grid

Despite the large scale, the model allows one to surmise the diversity of the future district.

The open spaces within the competition site are colored in the model, reinforcing one's perception of the spatial design.

⌖ — **Neckarpark,** Stuttgart (D)

✎ — pp a|s pesch partner architekten stadtplaner, Herdecke/Stuttgart, with lohrberg stadtlandschaftsarchitektur, Stuttgart

🖳 — www.pesch-partner.de

🛆 — 1st prize

📅 — 2008

🗂 — urban redevelopment – railway conversion – new urban district

🗇 — **model**

🏷 — representation: diagrams

The materials used for a model can also spark associations: valuable, robust, sustainable.

⊙ — **Master Plan for Paramount Xeritown,** Dubai (UAE)

✎ — SMAQ - architecture urbanism research, Berlin: Sabine Müller and Andreas Quednau with Joachim Schultz, with X-Architects, Dubai, Johannes Grothaus Landschaftsarchitekten, Potsdam, Reflexion, Zurich, and Buro Happold, London

▣ — www.smaq.net

▦ — 2008

▤ — urban expansion – new sustainable urban districts

▧ — **model**

▨ — divisional approach; representation: sketch

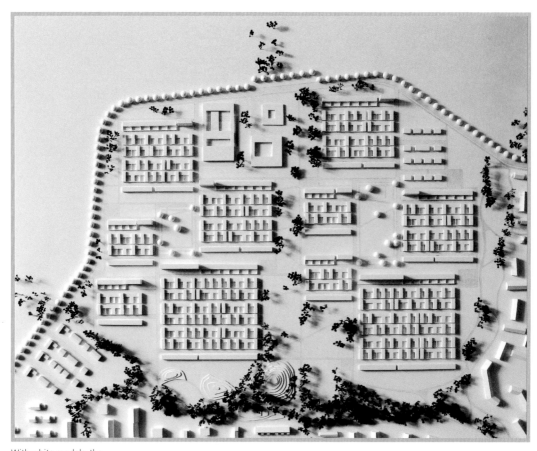

With white models, the
viewer can concentrate
entirely on the design.

 — **Am Bergfeld Residential District,** Poing/Munich (D)

— keiner balda architekten, Fürstenfeldbruck, with Johann Berger, Freising

— www.keiner-balda.de

— 4th prize

— 2007

— urban expansion – new residential districts

— **model**

— urban building blocks: spatial structure/carpet development

A closer look brings a surprise: a model made entirely out of Lego blocks.

Detail of model

– **Watervrijstaat Gaasperdam** (NL)
– HOSPER NL BV landschapsarchitectuur en stedebouw, Haarlem
– www.hosper.nl
– part of the International Architecture Biennale Rotterdam
– 2009
– urban expansion – new residential districts along/in the water
– **model**

The smaller the scale of the model, the more opportunities there are to create an atmosphere.

⊙ — **Werkbundsiedlung Wiesenfeld,** Munich (D)
✎ — Kazunari Sakamoto
🖥 — www.arch.titech.ac.jp/sakamoto_lab
🔍 — prizewinner (urban design), 1st prize after 2nd stage
📅 — 2006
📁 — urban redevelopment – military conversion – new residential district
◈ — **model**
◣ — urban building blocks: point, high-rise tower

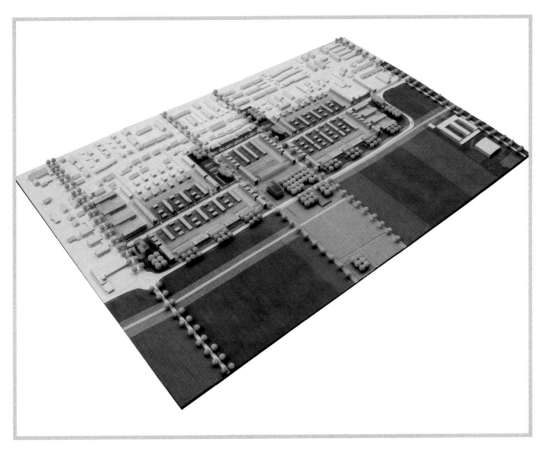

 — **Neufahrn-Ost,** Neufahrn bei Freising
(D)

 — Ackermann & Raff, Stuttgart/Tübin-
gen, with Planstatt Senner, Überlingen

▣ — www.ackermann-raff.de

◉ — 1st prize

▦ — 2005

▭ — urban expansion – new residential
districts

◈ — **modell**

◗ — illustrative site plan

(a.) The model and the
illustrative site plan fit
together perfectly.

(l.) Illustrative site plan

11 Parametric Design

Oliver Fritz

Prof. Dipl.-Ing. Oliver Fritz, Architect

Oliver Fritz, born 1967, has directed the digital media and architectural presentation unit at HTWG Konstanz since 2012, and since 2005 he has been a partner in the office Fritz und Braach, Adaptive Architektur, in Zurich. He is also a founding member of the KAISERSROT research network for architecture, urban design, and computer technology in Kaiserslautern/ Rotterdam/Zurich. From 2008 to 2012 he was a professor for CAD and descriptive geometry at the Cologne University of Applied Sciences. Oliver Fritz is the author of numerous publications on the subject of computer-aided design and construction.

WHAT is parametric design? The word *parameter* derives from Greek and combines two terms: *para* corresponds to "beside," or "near"; and *metron* is the equivalent of "measure." When the variables in a mathematical equation are temporarily replaced with fixed values, one then speaks of parameters. It is similar in computer science: parameters are externally defined variables; they are, as it were, regulating screws that can be used to adjust an object for a while from outside the system, conceivably by the user, and which effect changes according to certain mechanisms. Parameters thereby have a characterizing effect on objects.

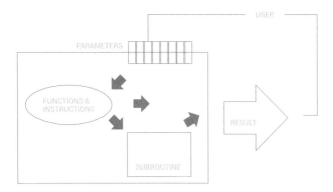

When parameters are applied in a precise relationship, we speak of parameterization. To calculate a repayment plan for a house that will be financed, for example, the following parameters are necessary: loan amount, interest rate, periodic repayment amount, and repayment period.

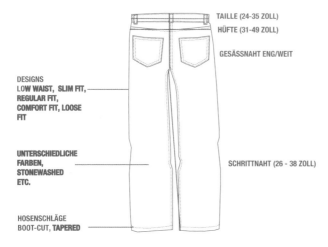

The principle of individualizing mass-market goods is called mass customization: From a large number of parameters, a pair of jeans can be individually configured and manufactured for the customer. This is a parametric object.

IN the attempt to transfer this methodology to architecture or urban design, we determine that essentially every object within the planning process has parameters, such as dimensions, minimum clearances, colors, and materials, for example.

This is of course nothing new, and this kind of consciousness has been around for as long as urban planning itself. All the same, in today's information age the term *parameter* is cast in a new light. They are ubiquitous and can be manipulated by everyone. Every bit of software, every smartphone, has parameters that I can set. I can configure my profile on Facebook using parameters. Or by using parameters defined with the help of configurators on the Internet, I can customize a product to fit my individual needs. And this product is then produced specifically for me.

For the aircraft industry and mechanical engineering, CAD software was developed decades ago to enable full parameterization of the planning and design process. Objects are no longer drawn, but are instead formulated – or, if one prefers to say, programmed – through variables, relationships, and dependencies. Consequently, dimensions or angles must not be specified unnecessarily early and the computer becomes an interactive tool where the interplay of the parameters generates a solution. Variations and versions of the same basic design can be visualized in real time by changing one or more values. Likewise, virtual simulations can be used to verify the real physical applicability of solutions. As part of the DFG research project Media-Experimental Design at the University of Kaiserslautern, the question was posed as to whether similar tools could be developed for architecture or urban planning. After several virtual laboratory experiments in which housing developments were generated with artificial intelligence, the research network KAISERSROT was founded in 2001 in cooperation with the prestigious office of Kees Christiaanse Architects and Planners (KCAP) in Rotterdam. Shortly thereafter, the core team – consisting of architects, urban designers, and programmers – was formed at the CAAD chair at ETH Zurich. Their goal was to develop interactive planning tools for the visualization of solution spaces. Simultaneously there were similar developments by Makoto Sei Watanabe, Procedural Inc./Esri with their CityEngine, and MVRDV, who developed the Region-maker and the Functionmixer. There is no universally accepted definition of what parametric design exactly means in urban design. There are, however, a number of different approaches, of which some KAISERSROT solutions shall be presented in what follows.

The CityEngine software uses parameters and a kind of rule-based grammar to generate artificial cities whose charm resembles known structures. Thus a building block can, for example, be given the parameter for Jugendstil, fin de siècle, or sixteenth-century Venice.

—— POSSIBLE APPLICATIONS IN URBAN DESIGN

Type 1 – Parameters in Urban Design: Legal Constants and Restrictions

Modern urban design has a multitude of rules and stipulations as its legal foundation. Thus zoning plans, binding land-use plans, and design statutes directly and indirectly provide the stipulations for the respective building zone – sometimes much to the distress of the architects or their clients. These rules can specify everything from circulation, visual axes, uses, building typologies, and building heights right up to colors and materials. These parameters regulate the site to be built under aesthetic, socioeconomic, and ecological points of view. That regulated parameters must not necessarily also curtail creativity is demonstrated by the following case in point.

The Stadtraum Hauptbahnhof project, for the area around the main train station in Zurich, was created in collaboration between KCAP and KAISERSROT. Along the edges of the station's tracks in the center of Zurich, a new city district with 320,000 square meters of usable floor area is planned as the home for 1,200 residents. The solution space was determined by two key stakeholders: On the one hand are the investors, who want the development to be as dense and high as possible, in order to optimize the yield per square meter of ground area. On the other hand is the city of Zurich, which stipulates special urban design requirements for dense construction. The so-called two-hour shadow rule, for example, ensures that high-rise buildings are only permitted to cast shadows on residential buildings for two hours each day. Manual verification by means of a prescribed shadow projection is very time-consuming, however, such that ongoing, iterative trial and error is almost impossible in the planning process. The planning team's goal was to develop a dynamic and interactive planning process meant to support consensus building between the different conflicting parties. The project works on two parallel levels: On the one hand, there are the manually defined wireframe grids that describe the respective maximum allowable building volume and the construction heights as an external set of rules. On the other hand, there is an internal, pro-

Limiting what is possible with due regard to the applicable regulations. KCAP and KAISERSROT, Alex Lehnerer

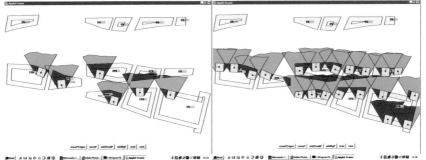

The shadow calculator: In Zurich, a high-rise building is not allowed to cast shadows on a residential building for more than two hours each day. KCAP and KAISERSROT, Markus Braach

grammed set of rules that defines the possible growth of the buildings within this envelope: This includes aspects such as light and shadow conditions, the ratio of housing units to workplaces, sightlines that must be kept free, and the proportional relationships of the buildings. Additionally, the so-called shadow calculator serves as an instrument for distributing the high-rise buildings.

Type 2 – Form-Defining Parameters in Urban Design, Generative Design, and Modeling, Variables for Trials

As soon as parameters are treated in a less regulatory and more design-oriented way, a new solution space opens up. Similar to the classic parametric CAD software for mechanical engineers, a set of rules links lists of basic geometric objects with mathematical or geometric functions, from which a more or less complex form is generated. This can be varied without great effort by making changes to the parameters. These modern tools have been only recently discovered for architecture and are currently drawing much attention. The best known of these are GenerativeComponents from Bentley and the Grasshopper extension to the 3D modeling program Rhino. Free-form architects in particular profit from these tools, with which solutions that previously would have necessitated a very great effort are now modeled in the shortest time. These software products are inexpensive in relation to their capabilities and are easy to use; many colleges and universities integrate such generative tools in the teaching program. Despite the fascination these products induce and certain advantages offered by such modeling, it is already becoming apparent that with the ready-made definitions provided by the applications, only a very limited variety of forms can be developed: the images of twisted high-rise towers may occasionally have their charm, but in their totality they

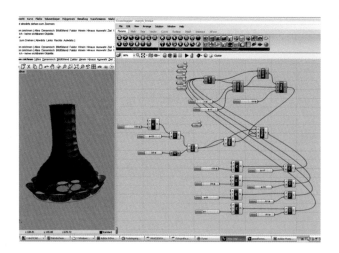

In the software Grasshopper, geometric objects can be linked with operations and variables into complex parametric objects.

seem interchangeable and banal. Thus only time will tell whether the anticipated new style of parametricism develops in this way, as is predicted.

Type 3 – Desires, Probabilities, and Interactions

An entirely different way to systematically employ urban design parameters in the planning process was implemented in some of KAISERSROT's projects as follows: Rather than approaching the design strategy from the large scale to the small, i.e., top-down, the design is developed bottom-up: The parameters of the lots

Comparison of planning procedures: Top-down and bottom-up, finding solutions based on desires.
KAISERSROT

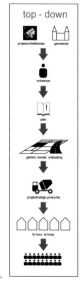

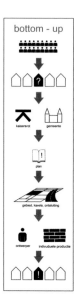

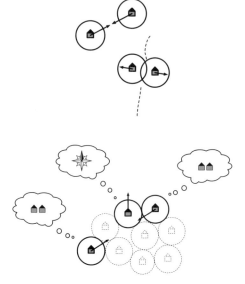

being planned are the desires of their prospective residents: They include the expectations about the size and proportion, the location, the neighbors, and the landscaping of the future plots of land.

The multistep optimizations needed for this purpose can be summarized as follows: At the outset, a purely random solution is generated, quasi by a roll of the dice. Its suitability is evaluated, and another solution is generated. If this new solution is better, it serves as the reference for subsequent alternatives. Using the iterative trial-and-error method, these tasks, which are simple for the computer, can be quickly calculated for thousands of passes so that a good, feasible solution ultimately emerges. Urban attractors, which act like magnets, can be defined for the individual lots.

Thus the software does not generate fixed and final results; what emerges is more of a fluid planning process that adjusts to changing parameters and yields visual feedback, thereby also providing a basis for decision making. In contrast to the relatively slow method of manually producing variants for architectural design, this computer-aided process leads to a new dynamic in planning and design. The impact of a decision – for instance, the definition of a visual axis or the width of a street – can be immediately tested, discussed, and analyzed with the software. This makes it possible to examine the criteria from different parties (planners, clients, authorities, etc.),

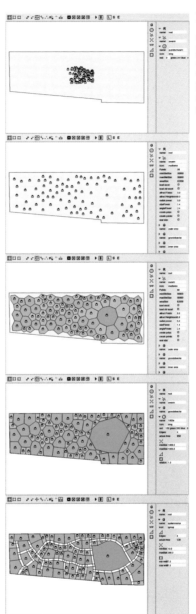

The process of creating a typical KAISERSROT project: The plots of land, initially represented as points, are positioned within the development site based on the buyers' wishes.

compare and evaluate them at an early stage, and thus confirm or dismiss them. The KAISERSROT software is a consensus machine. Using this method, a housing development in the Netherlands was realized together with KCAP as part of the VI-NEX program, studies for the resettlement of flood-prone villages in Upper Austria were developed, and concepts for virtual building site allocation of former agricultural land were developed.

The solution space when designing is always infinitely large. Parametric design is a method to limit the solution space in certain places and to make it more controllable. The methods presented here are not autonomously acting, automated design mechanisms, but are instead finely adjustable search engines that help in the planning process to find a good solution under chosen parameters.

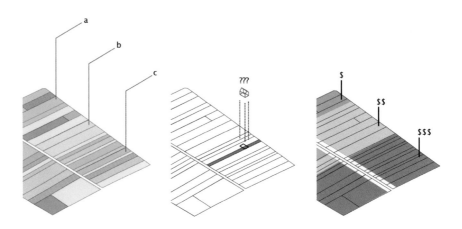

Virtual building site allocation: Former agricultural land meant to be rededicated as buildable property. The proportions are disadvantageous, however, so the land is reevaluated and the ownership structure of longtime neighbors must be reorganized.

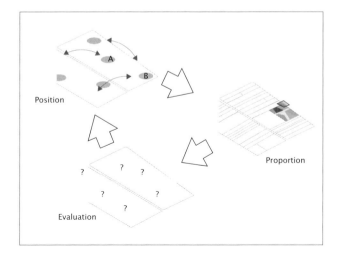

With the KAISERSROT method, the lots are re-arranged in accordance with the desires of their owners, whereby the software also takes the development potential, proportions, and sunlight exposure into account in the process.

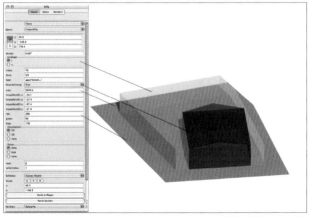

The parameters of each lot can be set individually and have an intelligence of their own, independent of the superordinate planning. The entire process takes only a few minutes, so it would be possible to moderate solutions in meetings with everyone involved.
Development: Fritz and Braach, Adaptive Architektur, Zurich

12 Examples of Best Practice

HafenCity Hamburg,
Competition design
1999

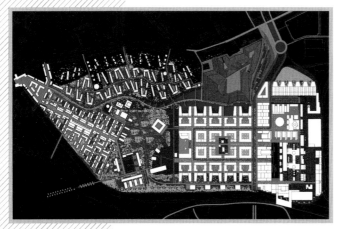

Belval/Esch-sur-Alzette,
Competition design
2002

Südstadt Tübingen,
Competition design
1992

View of the western HafenCity with the city's future symbol, the Elbphil-
harmonie (Elbe Philharmonic Hall), adjoined by the historic Speicherstadt.
Behind that is the downtown area and in the background at the left are the
two Alster lakes

Development of the Master Plan for HafenCity in Hamburg

Markus Neppl

Prof. Dipl.-Ing. **Markus Neppl**, architect, BDA

Markus Neppl, born 1962, has been directing the Chair of Urban Planning and Design at the
Karlsruhe Institute of Technology (KIT) since 2003, from 2008 to 2013 as Dean and since
2013 he has also been serving as Dean of the Department of Architecture. From 1999 to 2003
he was a professor for architectural and urban design at the University of Kaiserslautern. In
1990, together with Kees Christiaanse, Peter Berner, and Oliver Hall, he established the firm
ASTOC Architects and Planners, based in Cologne, where he has remained a partner. He is the
author of numerous publications as well as honored projects and award-winning competition entries, both at home and abroad.

__ INNER CENTER ON THE ELBE

AS we began focusing on Hamburg, an insider told us: "In Hamburg there are 'those from the Alster' and 'those from the Elbe,'" making reference to the city's two main rivers. For long-time residents of the Hanseatic city, the idea of urban development along the bank of the River Elbe was not very appealing. The harbor was considered a place of work and the inner city was a place to see and be seen. The Speicherstadt, Hamburg's historic warehouse district, is located between these two worlds. It served as the main reloading point for goods and, because it was an enclosed free port zone, it was not publicly accessible. The widespread adoption of container shipping fundamentally changed the logistics of the entire port. Today, the harbor is no longer used for storing the goods, but only for the speediest possible transfer from ships to rail or truck.

In the mid-1980s, the city's chief building director at the time, Egbert Kossak, recognized the significance for the urban design of this development. Under his direction, the city began systematically buying up land that became available along the southern bank of the Elbe. In so doing, he pursued different strategies. Whereas the land south of Speicherstadt was acquired in a relatively inconspicuous manner, the "string of pearls" concept for the projects to the west was downright celebrated in several building forums that were open to the public and held in the Deichtorhallen. While the experts were still discussing, the publishing house Gruner + Jahr granted recognition to the attractiveness of the new sites on the Elbe with the construction of its new building. The experiences with these projects in the 1990s furnished an important basis for conceiving the planning process for the HafenCity development. The 1999 master plan competition explicitly called for extending the city center with a small-scale mix of uses. Beyond that, there was the question of how such a master plan should work. People expected a grand vision without anyone having been able to resolve all the basic preconditions. And lastly, the project should also be an economic success.

__ ETIQUETTE GUIDE INSTEAD OF AUTOPILOT

FOR the reasons mentioned above, the master plan by the joint venture comprising the firms ASTOC Architects and Planners, Cologne; KCAP Architects & Planners, Rotterdam; and Hamburgplan AG was conceived from the outset as a tiered set of rules. We did not divide up a finished design into construction phases and then assign rules for development to the scheme. Instead, conceiving in a very early phase individual structural qualities, developed from the very different conditions applying to each of the areas. This means that the first level within the regulatory framework consisted of analytically determined but very rough descriptions of character, which were then refined in three further levels:

- Level 1: Master plan as fundamental planning document
- Level 2: Qualification of the master plan – western and later eastern HafenCity
- Level 3: Plan development of neighborhood quarters, with various trial urban designs
- Assignment of purchase options (Anhandgabe) for lots through joint architect-investor competitions

One of the basic problems in developing former ports, military sites, and railways is that their links with the surrounding urban fabric are totally lacking or at best very poor. Furthermore, the geometric forms of the wharves, which had originally been designed solely to fulfill logistical functions, cannot be easily built upon with the usual urban structures and legal means. So if you were to try to develop these areas according to classic urban design principles, you would quickly come to the conclusion that the site geometry works very poorly and does not allow much contiguous urban fabric.

MASTER PLAN

THE basic principles for the planning therefore had to resolve the two fundamental issues of linkage and metastructure – and had to communicate these in the easiest way possible. The definitions of the individual urban building blocks were determined by pragmatically interpreting the conditions:

- Geometry and size of the buildable area
- Locational qualities and potential for connection to existing structures
- Orientation and visual connection to the water
- Possibilities for links with infrastructural elements
- Special programmatic requirements
- Flood control and efficient, adequate means of access

The main task for the urban design in this phase was, on the one hand, to elicit specific urban qualities from the basic urban structures and, on the other, to guarantee connections to the adjoining neighborhoods.

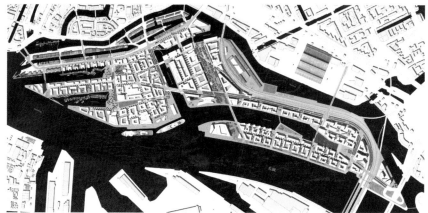

HafenCity will have 6,000 apartments for 12,000 inhabitants, 45,000 jobs, numerous restaurants and bars, cultural and recreational facilities, and retail shops, as well as parks, public squares, and promenades

— QUALIFICATION OF THE MASTER PLAN

SINCE the master plan was adopted by the Hamburg Senate as a formal document, many detail matters could not be taken into account because subsequent changes would only have been possible by obtaining a political resolution. This meant the master plan was first composed in two parts. The plan that was to be formally adopted was rather abstract and universal, and the illustrative plans only served as an informal attachment.

In the subsequent qualification phase, the issues that had initially been set aside were addressed in compact workshops with all the stakeholders. The focus of the considerations was placed on the distribution of uses and their typological implementation. A lot more experimentation could take place in this phase, especially since the real estate company, which is wholly owned by the Hanseatic city, was now interested in specific designs in order to prepare for the marketing campaign.

The GHS (later HafenCity Hamburg GmbH) commissioned all the planning services, while the building authority, under the personal leadership of the chief building director, controlled what was being planned and its implementation according to planning law. Thus the ASTOC/KCAP/Hamburgplan joint venture constantly had to strike a balance between the economic interests of the real estate company, the urban design goals of the building authority, and the public's desire for concrete images. The level of collective qualification was an important instrument in this phase, allowing the visualizations to be relatively tentative at first, while the responses to typological and infrastructural issues could be increasingly defined in a specific way. The working method in this qualification phase was strictly organized according to the various development options. While precise building dimensions were already being discussed at Sandtorkai, at Dalmannkai the question was where to locate the main access route and at Strandkai the issue was possible impairment of the city skyline. The simultaneous work at greatly different scales demanded a high degree of flexibility from all parties.

NEIGHBORHOOD PLAN DEVELOPMENT

THE focus of further planning was quickly placed on the neighborhood quarters on Sandtorkai/Dalmannkai, the former KLG sites and the central part of Magdeburg Harbor. The results of the master plan and the qualification process were again broadly questioned in competitions and workshops, and they were confronted with revised user requirements and laws affecting the infrastructure. At that time it became very clear that all the necessary measures for site development, foundation work, and flood protection would be costly. Since all the land prices were directly coupled to a maximum exploitation of the buildable gross floor area, relatively large contiguous complexes always developed, because it was not possible to accommodate the parked cars in units of a small size. In the first construction phases, a minimum size of approximately 5,000 to 6,000 m² gross floor area crystallized almost automatically. To achieve an even smaller-scale mixture, several building groups were combined on plinths along Dalmannkai in order to comply with the requirements for parking and flood protection.

ASSIGNMENT OF THE LOTS

AFTER the lot sizes and the building volumes had been determined and were specified in binding land-use plans, requests for bids were issued for the individual building lots, which were open to the participation of investors. Accompanying the so-called Anhandgabe process, a fixed-term real estate purchase option, various architectural competitions then took place.

This procedure has its advantages in a very open planning process and relatively high transparency. Friction between the individual developers and investors is avoided by negotiating separately with them, bypassing difficult coordination among the parties. Nevertheless, the first completed projects show that if the ar-

In 2009, the Am Sandtorkai/Dalmannkai quarter became the first neighborhood to be completed in HafenCity. The Magellan Terraces are a popular meeting place from which the entire Sandtorhafen (Sandtor dock) can be seen.

chitectural consultation had been better and more uncompromising along the way, it would have benefited the overall attractiveness of the neighborhoods. The buildings where the requirements were implemented in a very relaxed and confident manner seem on the whole very pleasant and refreshing, whereas the "original" buildings in particular seem rather awkward and disingenuous.

HOLISTIC VISION OR PRAGMATIC PATCHWORK

AT the beginning, the master plan was criticized as being pragmatic and not innovative enough. Critics reproached it for not being a visionary response to the contemporary extension of the European city. Eminent colleagues from Hamburg then presented what they thought of as visions, and did so with great fanfare. Through their size alone, some of the "visions" would have more likely impaired than promoted developments in HafenCity.

The master plan has never tried to pretend it is the be all and end all. It is a plan that stimulates and does not strive to maintain a fixed image that, once designed, must then be implemented with much force and many restrictions. Over the course of its existence (since 2000), it has shown how its contours have been

Urban Flair on the Dal-
mannkai promenade

sharpened rather than diluted through new planning impulses. The philharmonic hall by Herzog & de Meuron on Kaispeicher A or the imaginative outdoor facilities in the western part of HafenCity clearly demonstrate what we mean by stimulating strategic urban planning.

The regulatory framework is neither law nor judicial statute. It is more of a code of conduct for all the parties involved in the planning. In addition to the economic and planning instruments, it is above all the mode of communication that ultimately determines the quality of a plan.

— GREEN CITY OR CO² NEUTRAL?

IN many urban design projects of this size, it is commonplace for political or social objectives to change over the course of the development. If a journalist asks today why HafenCity is a green city, one cannot possibly reply that this term did not even exist when the planning had begun. This means it is vital to continually update any planning. Because of the clearly defined neighborhood developments, new and contemporary issues could always be incorporated without having to challenge the basic decisions.

Hence when the master plan for the eastern HafenCity was updated, completely different issues were on the agenda than a decade ago. At Oberhafen, for instance, the old buildings are supposed to remain, to support the development of a creative milieu at little expense. At Baakenhafen, opportunities for self-build groups are desired and a significantly lower price segment is sought. The need for continuous open spaces and new ideas for using the adjoining areas of water have also changed the planning considerably.

Now as before, however, all new objectives and themes are carefully considered. Every new activity is subject to the highest energy standards and each step that is taken is reviewed according to the evaluation scheme for sustainable urban development. The various protagonists must be shown evidence that they are steadfastly pursuing the goal of a modern and cosmopolitan, yet still traditionally minded extension of the city of Hamburg. That might also be the key to success.

No one today can say with certainty whether this elaborate planning process for HafenCity will really leave behind any visible traces. The success of HafenCity will ultimately depend on how well it is accepted by Hamburg's citizens, and then we will learn whether it will become a vibrant district like Altona or Eppendorf – or whether, like the City Süd project, it fails to be more than a mere expediency.

The Marco Polo Terraces, with their grass islands and wooden platforms, are currently the largest public space in HafenCity

EXAMPLES OF BEST PRACTICE: HAFENCITY HAMBURG

Where Esch-sur-Alzette's newest district is now taking shape, steel was
produced until well into the 1990s

From Steelworks to City,
Belval/Esch-sur-Alzette

Rolo Fütterer

Prof. Dipl.-Ing. **Rolo Fütterer**, architect

Rolo Fütterer, born 1963, has taught as a professor of urban design and open space planning
at the University of Applied Sciences in Kaiserslautern since 2008. He is a founding member
of the office M.A.R.S (Metropolitan Architecture Research Studio) in Luxembourg, which he
has headed since 2010. From 2000 to 2002 he was the director of Jo Coenen & Co Architects
in Maastricht, and through 2009 he subsequently served as their chief executive in Luxembourg. Rolo Fütterer advises numerous cities at home and abroad on matters of urban design
and among other positions, he holds a post as master planner in Belval, Luxembourg. Since
2011 he has served as an auditor for the German Sustainable Building Council (DGNB) on the
subject of urban districts.

THE beginnings of the Belval project in southern Luxembourg can best be explained with a brief analysis of the country of Luxembourg. The south of the country is still heavily influenced by the coal, iron, and steel industries, which began in the 1950s.

On the path of social restructuring, Belval is playing a key role: firstly, educational institutions (universities and research laboratories) are to be established here; and secondly, a counterpart to Luxembourg City will be created to augment the available office space. To achieve a judicious mix, a considerable proportion of living accommodations of diverse categories is also anchored in the spatial program. The mixture is a basic principle of the development, because the past has shown – also in Luxembourg – that a mere accumulation of office space, a monoculture in the city fabric, has no appeal. Stronger still: the percentage of commuters will thereby increase enormously, especially in Luxembourg, which leads to traffic problems because the local public transport system has not yet reached an acceptable level of service and because attractive fuel prices foster private transport. This is in the face of high real estate prices caused by the limited resources of buildable land.

Thus the planning for Belval was predestined to address these topics and to seek problem-solving approaches in a scenario for urban development. Added to this were the complex of problems pertaining to brownfield sites and how to deal with the industrial heritage.

In the case of Belval, both of the blast furnaces were declared industrial landmarks. With their salient presence and heights of over 70 meters, they are predestined to become a historical core element of the area. Unlike with the Völklingen Ironworks, where a straightforward museum concept was pursued, for Belval there was the notion of viewing the historical structure as a unique, iconic feature for a

Parts of the former industrial facility are preserved as landmarked structures and are the symbol of Belval

new city district. At the time the competition was announced in 2000, the program for a mixed urban neighborhood in the direct vicinity of these giants amounted to approximately 1 million square meters gross floor area and the current master plan sets it at roughly 1.3 million square meters.

—— CONCEPT

IF you analyze the site's immediate surroundings, you quickly come to the realization that the area has an inordinate amount of infrastructure. Compactness and development efficiency were therefore essential starting points for the urban design concept. While the buildings in the surrounding area closely follow the street system in a systematic pattern, the new Quartier Belval will have a compact core district around the blast furnaces and, in addition, it shall reestablish a close relationship with the existing small-scale housing along its edges by rounding off and augmenting it with newly developed areas.

These smaller subdistricts are both connected and separated by the centrally located Park Belval. The park was a logical result of the previously mentioned arrangement of the urban quarters and, together with the undulating landfill element (Plateau St. Esprit), it constitutes a sequence of varying types of green spaces. These will ensure the continued existence of a major green corridor through the area.

On the main site itself, the design is based on integrating the highly diverse artifacts from the age of steel production. To do so, the two blast furnaces are not relied upon as the only carriers of meaning; additional elements are also assembled to create an "architectural promenade." This is first and foremost the artificial topography of the steelworks site. The steel yard shall be preserved at the original level of the existing grade and, together with the existing concrete piers from the railroad, it will remain as a kind of showcase displaying the history of the site. Together with the giant smokestacks, the sinter pools, and the gas flare, the "found elements of history" were complete.

Belval has four districts: in the foreground is the Hochofenterrasse (blast furnace terrace) with its colorful mix of culture, education, housing, and work-places; then comes the Square Mile, Belval's mixed residential and business district; and in the background are the two residential districts pervaded by greenery – Quartier Belval and Parc Belval.

BUILDING ON THE MOON

CONVERTING such a large and inhospitable area to make it fit for a city's population demanded a special growth and phasing strategy: Individual clusters will always receive a redefined open space, which will serve as an attractor and constitute a strong symbol in the public sphere, thus uniting the construction measures undertaken by the pioneer investors in an interesting new environment. These preliminary and guiding investments were also necessary to give earnest support to the principle of public-private partnership.

With the elements of industrial culture and the array of exciting urban spaces, the most important parameters of the design and the cluster-like growth strategy were defined. The layout of the public access ways is made with constant regard to visually upgrading the prominent and characteristic industrial elements. Thus directed views and axes are established to integrate blast furnaces, basins, and smokestacks as significant elements in the new space of the city. This owes to the basic need for orientation – which is even stronger in an area that is only first being gradually discovered by a population and endowed with life.

FROM PLAN TO REALITY

THE main idea of linking the industrial elements with new urban spaces was easy to communicate and was respected by all the decision makers, as was the use of the topography and the built surroundings to establish differences between the residential districts. Thus the DNA of the site was quickly defined to a large extent without depriving the next planning steps of any latitude. Since the area had previously been completely closed off to the outside world, there was great curiosity among the local population about what was still there. In general, the approach of preserving the traces of history while developing the workplaces of their forefathers into a vibrant neighborhood met with broad support.

The issues of landscape and traffic had already been integrated into the competition, so no significant changes to the basic road system were necessary. As a result, the matrix from the competition could simply be refined further.

The crucial step was obtaining building rights. At the same time, initial inquiries from investors were discussed in a form of constructive dialogue, so as not to impose any temporal restrictions on their willingness to invest.

For my part, I received the role of supervisor. My experiences with several European planning systems were an asset here for developing optimal planning, both formal (laws) and informal (dialogue, recommendations).

This was done using a catalog of recommendations, underpinned with reference images and summarized in an urban design manual *(Manuel Urbanisme)* and a landscape manual *(Manuel Paysage)*. It was meant to establish a code pertaining to visual appearance and the use of materials, which was used in striving for the development a neighborhood guarantee. This is of great interest to the real estate industry, because real estate is only worth as much as the environment in which it stands. In this respect, the discussions about integration within a well-balanced sociocultural environment, or generating the same, are of great importance for giving direction to the opportune rate-of-return thinking of the real estate funds that often supply the financing. The close cooperation and coordination with the sanctioning authorities is of particular importance because the various requirements and recommendations complement one another and are reflected in a building permit granted on a statutory basis.

QUALITY ASSURANCE PROCESS

ASCRIBED to the concept of strong open spaces for the formation of clusters, a competition was held for the central square (steel yard). A range of designs can better illustrate the developmental and residential qualities that can be attained in the future. The designs for the buildings being planned by the government will also be selected through competitions.

The recommendation to hold competitions was also made to private investors, and they have complied in part. Such a procedure is not necessary for buildings of every size and relevance. In this connection it is significant to note that in the absence of a competition from the side of the overall site developer (AGORA), a stronger dialogue with the master planner is required.

CURRENT STATUS

Significant themes have been addressed to date in the overall configuration of the site. The stacking of uses in the blocks around the steel yard could be brought into being. Condominium apartments were created on the topmost level. In the Belval Nord area, the first V-shaped blocks, initially viewed with suspicion, have been completed and are now occupied. The concept for jointly managing and maintaining the overall Belval Nord site has also been implemented. Boundary fences and demarcations of the border between individual lots have been ruled out in favor of a spacious, fluid landscape. Furthermore, the junction between the bases of buildings and privately used outdoor spaces has been regulated in terms of design.

Additional competitions and reconfigurations within the central Hochofenterrasse district can be easily integrated into the existing basic structure of the master plan.

The relatively highly regulated basic geometry has proven successful – having started from the premise that over the course of the project, deregulation is more likely than the creation of new regulations. The adaptability of the basic urban geometry has thereby been confirmed.

The Place de l'Académie (steel yard) is the center of the Hochofenterrasse district and connects the university to the train station.

Urban diversity in the Loretto District

Citizens Build a City: The Südstadt District in Tübingen

Leonhard Schenk

"LA bataillon de la garde n'existe plus!" The withdrawal of the French military at the beginning of the 1990s came unexpectedly for the city of roughly 88,000 inhabitants in southwestern Germany, but it was not unprepared. Shortly after the fall of the inner-German border, a roundtable of political and administrative figures met at city hall to discuss future urban development. With the abandonment of the French garrison and coinciding deliberations by the department of transportation about relocating a federal highway out of the Südstadt district and into a tunnel, there were suddenly entirely new opportunities for urban development.

A QUESTION OF POLITICAL WILL

ANDREAS Feldtkeller, then director of the city's urban redevelopment office, looked to the successfully completed restoration of Tübingen's old town and proposed developing new urban fabric on the recently vacated barracks sites. Shortly thereafter, Feldtkeller, supported by the city's first female mayor, Gabriele Steffen, and the deputy mayor for building and construction, Klaus Blanke, succeeded in establishing broad political support for the paradigm shift away from the housing estate and toward the city.

The sites were not initially at the free disposal of the city, because they were owned by the German federal government. An instrument that had just been reintroduced into planning law a few months earlier, the urban development measure, offered a means to resolve this problem. (The 1987 revision to the federal building code had dispensed with this instrument, but it was reintroduced in 1990 during the process of German reunification.) The implementation of an urban development measure by a municipality enables it, in the case of great public interest and "particularly to meet an increased need for residences and places of work" to acquire property for a purchase equivalent to the value of the undeveloped land; in the event that the property owner does not wish to cooperate, he or she can be expropriated if necessary upon payment of compensation.

In March 1991 the municipal council passed a resolution that was used as the basis to initiate an urban design competition in June of the same year. It required:
- a dense, mixed-use urban area with small-scale parceling of lots and inner-city character
- a mixture of uses that includes both housing and work spaces as well as social and cultural institutions
- a diversity of housing forms to accommodate highly varied target groups
- an attractive mixture of old and new buildings

- street space that is usable in everyday life
- a district in which environmentally friendly means of transport have priority and central parking areas take pressure off the public space.

— THE COMPETITION

WE — a group of young architects from whose midst the firm LEHEN drei Architekten Stadtplanung developed — were driven by the task that had been formulated: The program corresponded with our own life experiences and beliefs, with how we preferred to live and work — and did so not in a historical district but in a contemporary one. It was not only the objective that fascinated us, however, but also the fact that the competition documents included an abundance of articles on urban development. We were particularly impressed by the Berlin urban planner Dieter Hoffmann-Axthelm, who in his essay described why future urban planning must take place in parcels or individual lots.[1] For Hoffmann-Axthelm, the parcel is a unit of distribution, a functional unit (also for mixed use), and a foundation for urban ecology. Moreover, the building on the plot of land functions as a social unit, a unit of historical memory, and a unit of perception. Even the absence or failure of individual cells does not cause the overall system to collapse. Hoffmann-Axthelm speaks of the "capacity of the city," of a stable grid that enables individuals to maintain and assert places of their own, and concludes that neither the Modernist housing estate nor the machine for living could achieve all of this.

Equipped in this way, we got to work. We found that the Südstadt, separated from the old town by train tracks and the Neckar River, was a patchwork of various urban fragments and uses. There was admittedly a small and attractive, late-nineteenth-century Gründerzeit neighborhood surrounding Sternenplatz, but also everything that could not be accommodated in the city center — or was not wanted there: both of the barracks complexes used after World War II by the French military forces, municipal public utilities, numerous private business establishments, the Wennfelder Garten housing estate, which was built after World War II for displaced persons — and the Bundesstraße B27, a federal highway that bisected all of this. For our competition entry, we worked with clearly defined subdivided and mixed-used blocks that were each derived from their particular situation. The Hindenburg Barracks from the 1930s offered the opportunity to integrate blocks of buildings into the roughly 100-meter-wide parade grounds and to introduce a central axis, the French Allée, through the site. In the Loretto Barracks, an elongated square was inserted, which was intended to serve as a major rendezvous point in

---

1 Dieter Hoffmann-Axthelm, "Warum Stadtplanung in Parzellen vor sich gehen muss," *Bauwelt*, no. 48 (1990), pp. 2488–91.

the middle of the Südstadt district. In order to connect the two barracks sites to one another, we proposed upgrading Stuttgarter Straße to a boulevard between the square-shaped square in the east and the rond-point, a circular square, in the west. In their statement explaining the decision to award first place to our entry, the jury praised the "high level of urban significance," the "distinct spatial borders," and the "multifaceted squares and street spaces." Furthermore, they accentuated that the bold urban design "reacts sensitively to the existing condition," the public urban and green spaces are well distributed, and there is a mix of private and shared open spaces within the city blocks.

FROM PLAN TO REALITY

TO successfully implement the urban design concept, the urban design master plan was developed in the next step in collaboration with LEHEN drei and the municipal redevelopment office. It consisted of the urban design itself, which was developed further, and the written goals and basic planning principles. The competition objectives were further differentiated, and procedural steps, financing, and the nature of public participation were concretized. Numerous modifications to the urban design were needed: Additional existing buildings were to be preserved for social, cultural, and commercial uses on limited budgets, the public space was refined, and the

The former tank shed in the French Quarter is today a covered area for sports and events.

city blocks, which had only been shown abstractly as in the competition model, were now portrayed as a colorful assemblage of individual buildings. In light of the large number of modifications, the stringent spatial concept from the competition turned out to be extremely resilient.

The legally binding land-use plans derived from the master plan were developed in collaboration with LEHEN drei in a learning process, accompanied by events pertaining to the public participation on public space. In particular parking caused

The master plan already displays the urban structure of small-scale lot division. *Left*, the Loretto Quarter; *right*, the French Quarter.

great difficulties. The small-scale parceling of lots should not be encumbered by having to verify sufficient parking spaces, but in light of the urban density and the sought-after treatment of the public space, on-grade parking was out of the question. The idea was that the distance to private cars should be approximately the same as the distance to reach local public transport. Parking was therefore located in decentralized parking garages that were built by private as well as municipal owner-operated enterprises. Great hopes were aroused by space-saving mechanical parking equipment. This technical solution proved to be too complex and prone to breakdown, however, so that in the final development stages, a change was made to use shared, conventional "low-tech" underground garages in the inner courtyards of the subdivided blocks. To do so, the municipal property office broke new legal ground and supplied the necessary know-how.

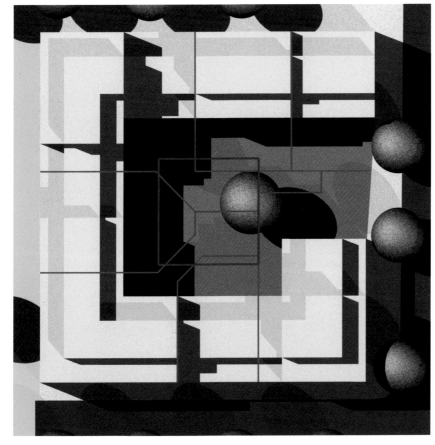

A typical city block in the French Quarter: red lines show the division of land and blue indicates the communal garden; private gardens are possible directly adjacent to the buildings.

New, mixed-used urban districts can be successfully realized with Baugruppen (self-build cooperative groups).

— CITIZENS BUILD A CITY

THE municipal redevelopment office recognized early on that the desired small-scale mixed use could hardly be realized with real estate developers. According to the master plan, the lots should preferably be given to Tübingen citizens. So the city relied on what was then still a relatively new principle, the Baugruppe – a self-build cooperative in which several private clients work together with an architect to build a jointly owned, individualized town house. A prerequisite for purchasing the property was that the building owners not only build apartments for their own use, but also create rented or owner-occupied commercial units on the ground floor – and in so doing, they would contribute to the revitalization of the district. In the search for a suitable lot, prospective co-owners, and prospective commercial tenants, the Baugruppen received extensive support from the municipal redevelopment office.

Initially the building cooperatives were viewed critically by Tübingen's residents, but once the first buildings were completed in 1997, a dynamic process began, and in the end, there were many more groups of applicants than available lots.

The great diversity of building forms within a very small area was often faulted by the architectural critics – with absolute justification – as being too colorful, loud, or chaotic. Nevertheless, Tübingen's Südstadt district became a great success, especially thanks to the Baugruppen. The experiment worked: New sections of urban fabric can be successfully realized with Baugruppen. But one should add: A small-scale structure might only be possible with Baugruppen. Maybe the most important factor of success, however, was that – despite changes in departmental leadership, jurisdictions, political majorities, and clerks, as well as a new mayor – the Tübingen precept "away from the housing estate, toward the city" has proven to be exceptionally stable for more than twenty years. Even more, the city of Tübingen has meanwhile successfully developed a new precinct with building cooperatives on a postindustrial brownfield site according to the principles developed in Südstadt, and another is currently under way.

___ SÜDSTADT AS A MODEL

THE national and international interest in the Tübingen model remains unusually high. The project has been distinguished with many awards, including the Deutsche Städtebaupreis (German urban design award) and the European Urban and Regional Planning Award. As a delegation from the Dutch city of Almere visited the Südstadt a few years ago, expecting to gain inspiration from the project for the development of a new district of their own, they were interested in beginning with the way in which Baugruppen can be initiated and implemented. In a shared dialogue, it became clear to the guests that Baugruppen can be a resilient instrument for development, but that the fundamental issue is to create new sections of urban fabric. Thus, the exhibition in Almere's cASLa architecture center in late 2009 was called: *Tübingen – Model for Almere: It's About the City.*

Bibliography

Albers, Gerd. *Stadtplanung: Eine praxisorientierte Einführung.* Darmstadt: Wissenschaftliche Buchgesellschaft, 1988.

Aminde, Hans-Joachim. "Auf die Plätze . . . Zur Gestalt und zur Funktion städtischer Plätze heute," in *Plätze in der Stadt.* Edited by Hans-Joachim Aminde. Ostfildern: Hatje Cantz, 1994, pp. 44–69.

Aminde, Hans-Joachim. "Plätze in der Stadt heute," in *Lehrbausteine Städtebau,* 2nd ed. Edited by Johann Jessen. Stuttgart: Städtebau Institut, 2003, pp. 139–49.

Benevolo, Leonardo. *History of the City.* Translated by Geoffrey Culverwell. London: Scolar Press, 1991. Originally published as *Storia della città* (Rome: Laterza, 1975).

Bott, Helmut. "Stadtraum und Gebäudetypologie im Entwurf," in *Lehrbausteine Städtebau: Basiswissen für Entwurf und Planung,* 6th ed. Edited by Hans-Joachim Aminde, Johann Jessen, and Franz Pesch. Stuttgart: Städtebau Institut, 2010, pp. 145–54.

Bürklin, Thorsten, and Michael Peterek. *Urban Building Blocks.* Basel: Birkhäuser, 2008

Ching, Francis D. K. *Architecture: Form, Space, & Order.* New York: Wiley, 1979.

Curdes, Gerhard. *Stadtstruktur und Stadtgestalt.* Stuttgart: Kohlhammer, 1997.

Fehl, Gerhard. "Stadt im 'National Grid': Zu einigen historischen Grundlagen US-amerikanischer Stadtproduktion," in *Going West? Stadtplanung in den USA—gestern und heute.* Edited by Ursula von Petz. Dortmund: Institut für Raumplanung, 2004, pp. 42–68.

Fischer, Anna-Maria, and Dietmar Reinborn. "Grün und Freiflächen," in *Lehrbausteine Städtebau,* 2nd. ed. Edited by Johann Jessen. Stuttgart: Städtebau Institut, 2003, pp. 119–38.

Herrmann, Thomas, and Klaus Humpert. "Typologie der Stadtbausteine," in *Lehrbausteine Städtebau,* 2nd. ed. Edited by Johann Jessen. Stuttgart: Städtebau Institut, 2003, pp. 233–47.

Hoffmann-Axthelm, Dieter. "Warum Stadtplanung in Parzellen vor sich gehen muss," *Bauwelt* no. 48 (1990): 2488–91.

Howard, Ebenezer. *Garden Cities of To-morrow.* Cambridge, MA: MIT Press, 1965 (orig. publ. 1898).

Humpert, Klaus, and Martin Schenk. *Entdeckung der mittelalterlichen Stadtplanung: Das Ende vom Mythos der gewachsenen Stadt.* Stuttgart: Konrad Theiss, 2001.

Knauer, Roland. *Entwerfen und Darstellen: Die Zeichnung als Mittel des architektonischen Entwurfs,* 2nd. ed. Berlin: Ernst & Sohn, 2002.

Kostof, Spiro. *The City Shaped: Urban Patterns and Meanings Through History.* New York: Little, Brown, 1991.

Kostof, Spiro. *The City Assembled: The Elements of Urban Form Through History.* New York: Little, Brown, 1992.

Krause, Karl-Jürgen. "Plätze: Begriff, Geschichte, Form, Größe und Profil." Dortmund: Universität Dortmund, 2004.

Krier, Rob. *Urban Space.* New York: Rizzoli, 1979. Originally published as *Stadtraum in Theorie und Praxis an Beispielen der Innenstadt Stuttgarts* (Stuttgart: Krämer, 1975).

Le Corbusier. *The Athens Charter.* Translated by Anthony Eardley. New York: Grossman, 1973.

Lynch, Kevin. *The Image of the City.* Cambridge, MA: MIT Press, 1960.

Machule, Dittmar, and Jens Usadel. "Grün-Natur und Stadt-Struktur: Chancen für eine doppelte Urbanität," in *Grün-Natur und Stadt-Struktur: Entwicklungsstrategien bei der Planung und Gestaltung von städtischen Freiräumen.* Edited by Dittmar Machule and Jens Usadel. Frankfurt am Main: Societäts, 2011, pp. 7–17.

Metzger, Wolfgang. *Laws of Seeing.* Translated by Lothar Spillmann. Cambridge, MA: MIT Press, 2006. Originally published as *Gesetze des Sehens* (Frankfurt am Main: Kramer, 1936).

Mitreden, mitplanen, mitmachen: Ein Leitfaden zur städtebaulichen Planung. Wiesbaden: Hessisches Ministerium für Wirtschaft, Verkehr und Landesentwicklung, 2001.

Pyo, Miyoung, ed. *Construction and Design Manual: Architectural Diagrams.* Berlin: DOM Publishers, 2011.

Reinborn, Dietmar. *Städtebau im 19. und 20. Jahrhundert.* Stuttgart: Kohlhammer, 1996.

Richter, Jean Paul, ed. *The Notebooks of Leonardo Da Vinci: Compiled and Edited from the Original Manuscripts,* vol. 1. Mineola, NY: Dover Publications, 1970.

Rubin, Edgar. *Visuell wahrgenommene Figuren.* Copenhagen: Gyldendal, 1921.

Schumacher, Fritz. *Das bauliche Gestalten.* Basel: Birkhäuser, 1991 (orig. publ. 1926).

Sitte, Camillo. "City Planning According to Artistic Principles," in *Camillo Sitte: The Birth of Modern City Planning.* Translated and edited by George R. Collins and Christiane Crasemann Collins. New York: Rizzoli, 2006, p. 182f. Originally published as *Der Städte-Bau nach seinen künstlerischen Grundsätzen* (Vienna: Gräser, 1889).

Sitte, Camillo. "Greenery within the City," in *Camillo Sitte: The Birth of Modern City Planning.* Translated and edited by George R. Collins and Christiane Crasemann Collins. New York: Rizzoli, 2006, p. 299f. Originally published as *Der Städte-Bau nach seinen künstlerischen Grundsätzen, vermehrt um "Großstadtgrün"* (Vienna: Gräser, 1909).

Stübben, Josef. *Der Städtebau.* Stuttgart: A. Kröner, 1907.

Topp, Hartmut H. "Städtische und regionale Mobilität im postfossilen Zeitalter," in *Zukunftsfähige Stadtentwicklung für Stuttgart: Vorträge und Diskussionen.* Stuttgart: Architektenkammer Baden-Württemberg, 2011, pp. 38–45.

Unwin, Raymond. *Town Planning in Practice: An Introduction to the Art of Designing Cities and Suburbs.* London: T. Fisher Unwin, 1909.

Vercelloni, Virgilio. *Europäische Stadtutopien: Ein historischer Atlas.* Munich: Diederichs, 1994.

Vitruvius. *The Ten Books on Architecture.* Translated by M. H. Morgan. New York: Dover Publications, 1960.

von Ehrenfels, Christian. "On 'Gestalt Qualities,'" in *Foundations of Gestalt Theory.* Translated and edited by Barry Smith. Munich: Philosophia Verlag, 1988, p. 106. Essay available online: ontology.buffalo.edu/smith/book/FoGT/Ehrenfels_Gestalt.pdf

von Ehrenfels, Christian. "On Gestalt Qualities (1932)" in *Foundations of Gestalt Theory.* Translated by Barry Smith and Mildred Focht. Edited by Barry Smith. Munich: Philosophia, 1988, p. 121. Essay available online: ontology.buffalo.edu/smith/book/FoGT/Ehrenfels_Gestalt_1932.pdf

von Naredi-Rainer, Paul. *Architektur und Harmonie: Zahl, Maß und Proportion in der abendländischen Baukunst,* 5th ed. Cologne: DuMont, 1995.

Wienands, Rudolf. *Grundlagen der Gestaltung zu Bau und Stadtbau.* Basel: Birkhäuser, 1985.

FURTHER READING

Urban Planning

Albers, Gerd, and Julian Wékel. *Stadtplanung: Eine illustrierte Einführung.* Darmstadt: Wissenschaftliche Buchgesellschaft, 2008.

Brenner, Klaus Theo. *Die schöne Stadt: Handbuch zum Entwurf einer nachhaltigen Stadtarchitektur.* Berlin: Jovis, 2010.

Feldtkeller, Andreas, ed. *Städtebau: Vielfalt und Integration.* Munich: Deutsche Verlags-Anstalt, 2001.

Hassenpflug, Dieter. *The Urban Code of China.* Basel: Birkhäuser, 2010.

Jessen, Johann, Ute Margarete Meyer, and Jochem Schneider. *Stadtmachen.eu. Urbanität und Planungskultur in Europa.* Stuttgart: Krämer, 2008.

Koch, Michael. *Ökologische Stadtentwicklung: Innovative Konzepte für Städtebau, Verkehr und Infrastruktur.* Stuttgart: Kohlhammer, 2001.

Kraft, Sabine, Nikolaus Kuhnert, and Günther Uhlig, eds. *Post-Oil City, die Stadt nach dem Öl:*

Die Geschichte der Zukunft der Stadt. Arch+ 196/197. Aachen: Arch+, 2010.

Streich, Bernd. *Stadtplanung in der Wissensgesellschaft: Ein Handbuch.* Wiesbaden: Verlag für Sozialwissenschaften, 2005.

City Design

Alexander, Christopher, Sara Ishikawa, and Murray Silverstein. *A Pattern Language: Towns, Buildings, Construction.* New York: Oxford University Press, 1977.

Curdes, Gerhard. *Stadtstrukturelles Entwerfen.* Stuttgart: Kohlhammer, 1995.

Heeling, Jan, Han Meyer, and John Westrik. *Het ontwerp van de stadsplattegrond.* Amsterdam: SUN, 2002.

Kasprisin, Ron. *Urban Design: The Composition of Complexity.* London: Routledge, 2011.

Meyer, Han, John Westrik, and Maarten Jan Hoekstra, eds. *Stedenbouwkundige regels voor het bouwen.* Amsterdam: SUN, 2008.

Prinz, Dieter. *Städtebau.* Vol. 1, *Städtebauliches Entwerfen,* 7th ed. Stuttgart: Kohlhammer, 1999.

Prinz, Dieter. *Städtebau.* Vol. 2, *Städtebauliches Gestalten,* 6th ed. Stuttgart: Kohlhammer, 1997.

Reicher, Christa. *Städtebauliches Entwerfen.* Wiesbaden: Vieweg + Teubner, 2012.

Reinborn, Dietmar, and Michael Koch. *Entwurfstraining Städtebau.* Stuttgart: Kohlhammer, 1992.

Urban Building Blocks

Firley, Eric, and Caroline Stahl. *The Urban Housing Handbook.* Chichester: Wiley, 2009.

Firley, Eric, and Julie Gimbal. *The Urban Towers Handbook.* Chichester: Wiley, 2011.

Hafner, Thomas, Barbara Wohn, and Karin Rebholz-Chaves. *Wohnsiedlungen: Entwürfe, Typen, Erfahrungen aus Deutschland, Österreich und der Schweiz.* Basel: Birkhäuser, 1998.

Knirsch, Jürgen. *Stadtplätze: Architektur und Freiraumplanung.* Leinfelden-Echterdingen: Alexander Koch, 2004.

Mozas, Javier, and Aurora Fernández Per. *Densidad: Density.* Vitoria-Gasteiz: a + t ed., 2004.

Panerai, Philippe, Jean Castex, and Jean-Charles Depaule. *Vom Block zur Zeile: Wandlungen der Stadtstruktur.* Bauwelt-Fundamente 66. Braunschweig: Vieweg, 1985.

Schenk, Leonhard, and Rob van Gool. *Neuer Wohnungsbau in den Niederlanden: Konzepte – Typologien – Projekte.* Munich: Deutsche Verlags-Anstalt, 2010.

van Gool, Rob, Lars Hertelt, Frank-Bertolt Raith, and Leonhard Schenk. *Das niederländische Reihenhaus: Serie und Vielfalt.* Munich: Deutsche Verlags-Anstalt, 2000.

Urban Greenery

Becker, Annette, and Peter Cachola Schmal, eds. *Stadtgrün. Europäische Landschaftsarchitektur für das 21. Jahrhundert / Urban Green: European Landscape Design for the 21st Century.* Basel: Birkhäuser, 2010.

Gälzer, Ralph. *Grünplanung für Städte.* Stuttgart: Ulmer, 2001.

Hennebo, Dieter, and Erika Schmidt. *Geschichte des Stadtgrüns in England von den frühen Volkswiesen bis zu den öffentlichen Parks im 18. Jahrhundert.* Geschichte des Stadtgrüns 3. Hanover/Berlin: Patzer, 1977.

Mader, Günter. *Freiraumplanung.* Munich: Deutsche Verlags-Anstalt, 2004.

Richter, Gerhard. *Handbuch Stadtgrün. Landschaftsarchitektur im städtischen Freiraum.* Munich: BLV-Verlagsgesellschaft, 1981.

Urban History

Benevolo, Leonardo. *The European City.* Translated by Carl Ipsen. Oxford: Blackwell, 1993.

Eaton, Ruth. *Ideal Cities: Utopianism and the (Un)Built Environment.* London: Thames & Hudson, 2002.

Gruber, Karl. *Die Gestalt der deutschen Stadt: Ihr Wandel aus der geistigen Ordnung der Zeiten.* Munich: Callwey, 1952.

Gutschow, Niels, and Jörn Düwel. *Städtebau in Deutschland im 20. Jahrhundert: Ideen–Projekte–Akteure.* Stuttgart: Teubner, 2001.

Harlander, Tilman, ed. *Stadtwohnen: Geschichte, Städtebau, Perspektiven.* Munich: Deutsche Verlags-Anstalt, 2007.

Heigl, Franz. *Die Geschichte der Stadt. Von der Antike bis ins 20. Jahrhundert*. Graz: Akademische Druck- u. Verlags-Anstalt, 2008.

Hotzan, Jürgen. *dtv-Atlas zur Stadt: Von den ersten Gründungen bis zur modernen Stadtplanung*. Munich: Deutscher Taschenbuch Verlag, 1997.

Irion, Ilse, and Thomas Sieverts, eds. *Neue Städte: Experimentierfelder der Moderne*. Munich: Deutsche Verlags-Anstalt, 1991.

Lampugnani, Vittorio Magnago. *Die Stadt im 20. Jahrhundert: Visionen, Entwürfe, Gebautes*. 2 vols. Berlin: Wagenbach, 2010.

Lange, Ralf. *Architektur und Städtebau der sechziger Jahre*. Schriftenreihe des Deutschen Nationalkomitees für Denkmalschutz 65. Bonn: Deutsches Nationalkomitee für Denkmalschutz, 2003.

Lichtenberger, Elisabeth. *Die Stadt: Von der Polis zur Metropolis*. Darmstadt: Primus, 2002.

Mumford, Lewis. *The City in History: Its Origins, Its Transformations, and Its Prospects*. New York: Harcourt, Brace, 1961.

Wolfrum, Sophie, and Winfried Nerdinger, eds. *Multiple City: Stadtkonzepte 1908/2008*. Berlin: Jovis, 2008.

Urban Theory

Cuthbert, Alexander. *Understanding Cities: Method in Urban Design*. New York: Routledge, 2011.

de Bruyn, Gerd. *Die Diktatur der Philanthropen: Entwicklung der Stadtplanung aus dem utopischen Denken*. Bauwelt-Fundamente 110. Braunschweig: Vieweg, 1996.

Dell, Christopher. *Replaycity: Improvisation als urbane Praxis*. Berlin: Jovis, 2011.

Frick, Dieter. *Theorie des Städtebaus: Zur baulich-räumlichen Organisation von Stadt*. Tübingen: Wasmuth, 2006.

Hilpert, Thilo. "Stadtvisionen der sechziger Jahre." Arch+ nos. 139/140 (1997): 50–57.

Koolhaas, Rem. *Delirious New York: A Retroactive Manifesto for Manhattan*. New York: Oxford University Press, 1978.

Müller-Raemisch, Hans Rainer. *Leitbilder und Mythen in der Stadtplanung 1945–1985*. Frankfurt am Main: Kramer, 1990.

Rowe, Colin, and Fred Koetter. *Collage City*. Cambridge, MA: MIT Press, 1978.

Venturi, Robert, Steven Izenour, and Denise Scott Brown. *Learning from Las Vegas: The Forgotten Symbolism of Architectural Form*. Cambridge, MA: MIT Press, 1977.

PICTURE CREDIT

Own illustrations: p. 10 to 13, 18 (t.), 19 to 23, 33, 34, 38, 51, 57, 59, 63, 67, 68, 73, 78, 120, 123, 134, 155, 162, 199, 219, 225, 230, 246

Own illustrations, after Rubin: p. 18 (b.)

Own illustrations, after Gruber: p. 107

Luc Viatour, Brüssel (B): p. 32

OMA AMO: p. 50 © 2013 ProLitteris, Zurich

MVRDV: p. 74 © ProLitteris, Zurich

Plans: Jelte Boeijenga, Jeroen Mensink: Vinex Atlas, Rotterdam 2008.

Reprint by the kind permission of nai010 publishers, Rotterdam (NL): p. 250 (b.), 251 (b.)

City of Konstanz (D) p. 254 to 256

adaptive Architektur | Fritz and Braach, Zurich (CH): p. 314, 318 (t.), 321 (b.)

Esri Deutschland GmbH, Kranzberg (D), © Esri 2012: p. 315

KAISERSROT, Zürich (CH): p. 316, 317, 318 (b.), 319, 320, 321 (t.)

ELBE&FLUT, Thomas Hampel, Hamburg (D): p. 324, 329, 330

AGORA s.à r.l. & Cie, Esch-sur-Alzette (LU): p. 332 to 334, 337

Manfred Grohe, Kirchentellinsfurt (D): p. 338

Leonhard Schenk, Stuttgart (D): p. 331, 341, 344

All other pictures were kindly provided by the respective offices to the author, the images of the Werkbundsiedlung Wiesenfeld by Deutscher Werkbund Bayern e.V.

The cover design by Rainer Gärtner, Brigade Eins Markenmanufaktur is based on a drawing by jan foerster teamwerk-architekten, Munich (D)

Project list

1956

Siedlung Halen, Bern (CH); Atelier 5, Bern; p. 205

1990

De Resident, Den Haag (NL); Rob Krier + Christoph Kohl, Berlin; p. 212

1991

Conversion of Airport Grounds, Munich-Riem, Munich (D); Andreas Brandt, Rudolf Böttcher, Berlin; p. 25

Conversion of Airport Grounds, Munich-Riem, Munich (D); Frauenfeld Architekten, Frankfurt a. M., mit Baer + Müller Landschaftsarchitekten, Dortmund; p. 101

Potsdamer Platz/Leipziger Platz, Berlin (D); Studio Daniel Libeskind, New York; p. 48

Potsdamer Platz/Leipziger Platz, Berlin (D); HILMER & SATTLER and ALBRECHT, Berlin/Munich, mit G. and A. Hansjakob, Berlin; p. 159

1992

Gartenstadt Falkenberg, Berlin (D); Architekten BDA Quick Bäckmann Quick & Partner, Berlin; p. 125

Südstadt Tübingen (D); LEHEN drei – Feketics, Kortner, Schenk, Schuster, Wiehl, Stuttgart; p. 178, 338 ff

1994

Quartier Vauban, Freiburg i. Br. (D); Kohlhoff Architekten, Stuttgart; p. 179

Ypenburg, Den Haag (NL); Palmbout - Urban Landscapes, Rotterdam; p. 251

1995

Ørestad Masterplan, Copenhagen (DK); ARKKI App. (KHR arkitekter, Copenhagen, mit APRT, Helsinki); p. 94

IJburg, Amsterdam (NL); Palmbout-Urban Landscapes, Rotterdam; p. 250

1996

Masterplan Chassé Terrein, Breda (NL); OMA, Rotterdam/Beijing/Hong Kong/New York, with West 8 Urban Design & Landscape Architecture, Rotterdam/New York; p. 50

Layenhof/Münchwald District, Mainz (D); Ackermann+Raff with Alexander Lange, Tübingen; p. 64

Master Plan for Wasserstadt Berlin-Oberhavel, Berlin (D); Arbeitsgemeinschaft Kollhoff, Timmermann, Langhof, Nottmeyer, Zillich, Berlin; p. 90

Westufer Hauptbahnhof, Darmstadt (D); Atelier COOPERATION Architekten & Ingenieure, Frankfurt a. M.; p. 145

Housing for federal employees, Berlin-Steglitz (D); Geier, Maass, Staab with Ariane Röntz, Berlin; p. 181

Housing for federal employees, Berlin-Steglitz (D); ENS Architekten with Norbert Müggenburg, Berlin; p. 182

1997

Das bezahlbare eigene Haus (The affordable single-family house), Bamberg (D); Melchior, Eckey, Rommel, Stuttgart; p. 124

Theresienhöhe, Munich (D); Steidle + Partner Architekten, Munich, with Thomanek + Duquesnoy Landschaftsarchitekten, Berlin; p. 180

1998

Müllerpier, Rotterdam (NL); KCAP Architects &Planners, Rotterdam/Zurich/Shanghai; p. 279

1999

Mobile Regional Airport (MOB), Greven (D); LK | Architekten, Cologne; p. 56

Mobile Regional Airport (MOB), Greven (D); Fuchs und Rudolph Architekten Stadtplaner, Munich; p. 203

HafenCity Hamburg, Hamburg (D); ASTOC Architects and Planners, Cologne, with KCAP Architects&Planners, Rotterdam/Zurich/ Shanghai; p. 92, 305, 324 ff

Grauenhofer Weg, Aachen-Forst (D); Baufrösche Architekten und Stadtplaner with Planungsgemeinschaft Landschaft + Freiraum, Kassel; p. 122

Slot Haverleij, Haverleij, 's-Hertogenbosch (NL); Rob Krier + Christoph Kohl, Berlin; p. 213

2000

Former Airport Grounds, Böblingen/Sindelfingen (D); ap'plan . mory osterwalder vielmo architekten und ingenieurgesellschaft mbh with Kienle Planungsgesellschaft Freiraum und Städtebau mbH, Stuttgart; p. 139

2001

Am Terrassenufer - Urban Redevelopment Ideas for the Pirnaische Vorstadt, Dresden (D); Prof. Günter Telian, Karlsruhe; p. 109

Am Terrassenufer - Urban Redevelopment Ideas for the Pirnaische Vorstadt, Dresden (D); Rohdecan Architekten GmbH with UKL Landschaftsarchitekten, Dresden; p. 208

Olympic Village, Leipzig (D); ASTOC Architects and Planners, Cologne, with KCAP Architects&Planners, Rotterdam/Zurich/Shanghai and bgmr Becker Giseke Mohren Richard, Landschaftsarchitekten, Leipzig; p. 194

Technology park for automotive supply sector with residential town, Beijing (PRC); GABRYSCH+PARTNER Architekten Stadtplaner Ingenieure, Bielefeld, with Landschafts-ArchitekturEhrig, Sennestadt and Büro Liren, Beijing; p. 99

Affordable Housing, Helsingør-Kvistgård (DK); Tegnestuen Vandkunsten, Copenhagen; p. 172

Masterplan Porte de Hollerich, Luxemburg (L); Teisen - Giesler Architectes with Nicklas Architectes, Luxemburg, BS+ Städtebau und Architektur, Frankfurt a. M., and Landschaftsplaner stadtland, Vienna; p. 232

Südliche Innenstadt, Recklinghausen (D); JSWD Architekten with club L94, Cologne; p. 298

2005

Rosensteinviertel, Stuttgart (D); Prof. Dr. Helmut Bott, Darmstadt, and Dr. Michael Hecker, Cologne, with Dr. Frank Roser Landschaftsarchitekt, Stuttgart; p. 69

Rosensteinviertel, Stuttgart (D); KSV Krüger Schuberth Vandreike, Berlin; p. 98

Rosensteinviertel, Stuttgart (D); pp a|s pesch partner architekten stadtplaner, Herdecke/Stuttgart, with Agence Ter, Karlsruhe/Paris; p. 188

Marchtaler Straße, Ulm (D); studioinges Architektur und Städtebau with H. J. Lankes, Berlin; p. 142

New Multi-functional Administrative City in the Republic of Corea, Sejong (ROC); LEHEN drei Architekten und Stadtplaner – Feketics, Schenk, Schuster, Stuttgart, with C. Flury, F. Müller, p. Witulski, Constance; p. 163

Senior Living on the English Garden, Landsberg am Lech (D); Nickel & Partner with mahl-gebhard-konzepte, Munich; p. 227

Gilchinger Glatze, Gilching (D); Marcus Rommel Architekten BDA, Stuttgart/Trier, with ernst + partner landschaftsarchitekten, Trier; p. 238

Spitalhöhe/Krummer Weg, Rottweil (D); Ackermann+Raff, Stuttgart/Tübingen; p. 242

Neufahrn-Ost, Neufahrn bei Freising (D); Ackermann+Raff, Stuttgart/Tübingen, with Planstatt Senner, Überlingen; p. 260, 311

Harburger Schlossinsel, Hamburg (D); raumwerk, Frankfurt a. M., with club L94, Cologne; p. 294

geneve 2020 visions urbaines, Genf (CH); XPACE architecture + urban design, Richmond, Australia; p. 304

2006

Europan 8, Kalakukko, Kupio (FIN); CITYFÖRSTER architecture + urbanism, Berlin/Hannover/London/Oslo/Rotterdam/Salerno; p. 39

Europan 8, Stadtgespräch, Leinefelde-Worbis (D); Nicolas Reymond Architecture & Urbanisme, Paris; p. 283

Europan 8, L.A.R.p., Bergen (N); SMAQ - architecture urbanism research, Berlin; p. 290

Kartal Pendik Masterplan, Istanbul (TR); Zaha Hadid Architects, London; p. 44

ThyssenKrupp Quartier, Essen (D); Zaha Hadid Architects, London, with ST raum a. Landschaftsarchitekten, Berlin/Munich/Stuttgart; p. 49

Werkbundsiedlung Wiesenfeld, Munich (D); Meck Architekten with Burger Landschaftsarchitekten, Munich; p. 28

Werkbundsiedlung Wiesenfeld, Munich (D); Allmann Sattler Wappner Architekten GmbH, Munich, with Valentien + Valentien & Partner Landschaftsarchitekten und Stadtplaner, Weßling; p. 79

Werkbundsiedlung Wiesenfeld, Munich (D); Kazunari Sakamoto with Ove Arup; p. 128, 310

Architektur-Olympiade Hamburg, Röttiger-Barracks, Hamburg (D); MVRDV, Rotterdam p. 74

Architektur-Olympiade Hamburg, Family Housing Hinsenfeld, Hamburg (D); Wacker Zeiger Architekten, Hamburg; p. 192

Auf der Freiheit, Schleswig (D); studioinges Architektur und Städtebau, Berlin; p. 93

Knollstraße Residential Development, Osnabrück (D); ASTOC Architects and Planners, Cologne, with Lützow 7, Berlin; p. 127

Knollstraße Residential Development, Osnabrück (D); STADTRAUM Architektengruppe, Düsseldorf, with Stefan Villena y Scheffler, Langenhagen; p. 221

RiverParc Development, Pittsburgh (USA); Behnisch Architekten, Stuttgart, with architectsAlliance, Toronto, Gehl Architects, Copenhagen, WTW architects, Pittsburgh; p. 153

New Housing along the Ryck River, Greifswald (D); Machleidt GmbH Büro für Städtebau, Berlin; p. 168

New Housing along the Ryck River, Greifswald (D); pp a|s pesch partner architekten stadtplaner, Herdecke/Stuttgart; p. 268

Schlösserareal and Schlachthofgelände, Düsseldorf (D); buddenberg architekten, Düsseldorf, with FSWLA Landschaftsarchitektur, Düsseldorf/Cologne; p. 175

neue bahn stadt:opladen, Leverkusen (D); ASTOC Architects and Planners, Cologne, with Studio UC, Berlin; p. 233

neue bahn stadt:opladen, Leverkusen (D); pp a|s pesch partner architekten stadtplaner, Herdecke/Stuttgart, with brosk landschaftsarchitektur und freiraumplanung, Essen; p. 277

2007

Masdar Development, Abu Dhabi (UAE); Foster + Partners, London, with Cyril Sweett Limited, W.p.P Transsolar, ETA, Gustafson Porter, E.T.A., Energy, Ernst and Young, Flack + Kurtz, Systematica, Transsolar; p. 11, 75

Designing Cities
Basics, Principles, Projects
Leonhard Schenk

With the kind support of

STIFTUNG
LEBENDIGE STADT

Translation from German into English: David Koralek
Copy editing: Keonaona Peterson
Project management: Annette Gref, Katharina Kulke
Layout, cover design and typography: Rainer Gärtner, Brigade Eins Markenmanufaktur

A CIP catalogue record for this book is available from the Library of Congress,
Washington D.C., USA.
Bibliographic information published by the German National Library
The German National Library lists this publication in the Deutsche Nationalbibliografie;
detailed bibliographic data are available on the Internet at http://dnb.d-nb.de.

This book is also available in a German language edition (ISBN 978-3-0346-1320-0).

© 2013 Birkhäuser Verlag GmbH, Basel
P.O. Box 44, 4009 Basel, Switzerland
Part of De Gruyter

Printed on acid-free paper produced from chlorine-free pulp. TCF ∞

Printed in Germany

ISBN 978-3-0346-1325-5

9 8 7 6 5 4 3 2 1

www.birkhauser.com